OUR MAN IN... HEAVEN AND HELL

CLIVE ANDERSON

BBC BOOKS

For the last few years Clive Anderson has appeared on Channel 4 presenting *Clive Anderson Talks Back*, *Whose Line Is It Anyway?* and other television programmes.

Before that he was a barrister whose hobby was comedy. Now he tries to be funny for a living and reads Law Reports in his spare time.

For the BBC he has travelled to Outer Mongolia, studied the Bayeux Tapestry and stood in for Jeremy Paxman, Ned Sherrin and Terry Wogan.

In his private life he lives in London with seven and a half million other people.

This book is published to accompany
the two television series entitled *Our Man In...* which were
broadcast in 1995 and 1996.
Both series were produced by Tiger Aspect for the BBC.

Published by BBC Books,
an imprint of BBC Worldwide Publishing.
BBC Worldwide Limited, Woodlands,
80 Wood Lane, London W12 0TT

Chapters 1–6 first published as Our Man In... in 1995
Chapters 7–10 and this edition first published 1996

ISBN 0 563 37196 X

Maps by Line and Line

Set in Times Ten and Futura
Printed in Great Britain by Martins the Printers Ltd, Berwick-upon-Tweed
Bound in Great Britain by Hunter & Foulis Ltd, Edinburgh
Cover printed by Clays Ltd, St Ives plc

CONTENTS

INTRODUCTION, EXPLANATION AND UPDATE

THIS book is written to accompany two television series called *Our Man In ...*, for the purposes of which a film crew and I were dispatched by the BBC to a variety of places around the world. In the first we went to six famously beautiful locations to report on their problems. We were going to call that series *Trouble In Paradise* until it occurred to us that it might be difficult getting permission to film in some countries using a name which so obviously suggested things were not quite as wonderful as they seemed. Governments can be so sensitive. So *Trouble In Paradise* was reduced to a sub-heading and *Our Man In...*, aptly enough, became our more diplomatic title. It was not chosen just so our film about Cuba could be called *Our Man In ... Havana*.

In the first series we went to Goa (India), the Maasai Mara (East Africa), the Timberlands of Oregon (North West America), Cuba and Dominica (the Caribbean) and Hawaii (the Pacific).

Such is the way of the modern world, in beautiful places it soon became clear that the effects of international tourism were going to crop up nearly everywhere we looked. In Goa, it was the corrosive effect of tourism itself which was the subject of our film. On the other hand, in the Maasai Mara, tourism, and the proper distribution of income derived from it, emerged as a possible solution to the threat posed to Kenya's wilderness and wildlife by the expansion of economic activity.

In the small island of Dominica, the absence of a substantial tourist industry contributed to a dangerous dependence on the banana trade.

Hawaii is, of course, very well known as a tourist destination and we touched upon tourism there too, although our film concentrated upon calls for Hawaiian independence from America.

In Cuba we looked at the problems facing Castro's bankrupt island paradise, still Communist after all these years. But even there, the rich tourist raises his sunburned head as Cuba desperately seeks hard currency from luxury hotel development to sustain its egalitarian society.

Only in the Timberlands of Oregon, where we considered the fate of the ancient forests, was there no real tourist dimension to be explored.

Somewhere along the way we reckoned we should do another series, but this time take the opposite approach. Instead of going to the world's famous beauty spots, we should go to its famous black spots. Instead of *Trouble In Paradise*, this would be *A Hope In Hell*. We would go to places (cities, as it turned out this time) whose very names each conjured up the worst the world had to offer, and see if things really were as bad as everyone claimed. (We were clearly suffering from a puritan need to punish ourselves for getting to go to such fabulous locations on the first time round.)

There was only time to make four films in this series, in the course of which we went to Calcutta, famous for its Black Hole and its slums; Beirut, familiar to television viewers everywhere for the damage done in its seemingly interminable civil war; the Bronx, notorious for its arson, drugs, violence and crime; and Lagos, infamous for its climate, its climate of corruption and its military government.

Although all the films involved going to faraway places, they were not intended to be simply travelogues. We were supposed to examine serious issues, in more or less exotic locations, while having some fun along the way. We spent about two weeks in each country, most of which was spent interviewing key players in the situations we were looking at, or travelling to and from places relevant to our story. It is an unusual way to see a foreign country. Filming allows you to meet a lot of interesting and important people and those with strong opinions. But the work involved also prevents you from visiting many of the sights and scenes that most casual visitors regard as essential.

The genesis of the TV series was a slow one. I first started talking to a small production company called Aspect Film and Television about making some documentaries for the BBC several years ago. In fact I am not sure if the original idea was to do documentaries at all; things changed such a lot as we went along that it may all have started off as quiz shows. Anyway, my training as a lawyer does not help in these matters. I always want time to consider the next step forward, and I can always think of reasons to delay, to postpone, to adjourn *sine die*.

Probably I would still be holding things up, but the project fell on to whichever BBC desk Janet Street-Porter was occupying at the time. She suggested that I found out how I got on with documentaries in general and the distinguished director Mark Chapman in particular, by sending us off to Outer Mongolia by way of a railway journey from Hong Kong. This resulted in a *Great Railway Journey* on BBC television and a chapter in a BBC book of the same name.

I found the whole thing enjoyable enough to start making *Our Man In ....* Mark found the whole thing enjoyable enough to start making commercials instead.

The project was taken up by Mark's business partner, the equally distinguished Paul Sommers, and finally we set off to make the films. By now Aspect Film and Television had, by a process of merger and amalgamation, become part of the multimedia conglomerate Tiger Aspect Productions and Janet Street-Porter had been promoted to an even grander BBC desk. (When we finished the first series of films she left the BBC altogether. I hope it was nothing I said.)

The first series (*Trouble In Paradise*) was filmed in 1994 and broadcast in 1995. The second series (*A Hope In Hell*) was filmed in 1995 and broadcast in 1996.

My written account of filming the six places in the first series, which constitutes the first six chapters of this book, appeared in a glossy hardback in 1995. The four chapters covering the second series appear here for the first time.

Inevitably, things have moved on in the various locations since we filmed there. Indeed, as I noted in the hardback edition, the visit of our camera seemed to act as a catalyst for change, ensuring that our film was out of date before it got back from the processors.

And, of course, in the case of the first series, things have had time to move on even further. For example, in Dominica, after fifteen years in office, Dame Eugenia Charles is no longer Prime Minister. She did not stand in the 1995 election, and her party, the Dominican Freedom Party, only secured five of the parliament's twenty-one seats. She has been replaced by Eddison James of the United Workers' Party. Even more significant than these political changes has been damage by tropical storms, the latest of which, in September 1995, destroyed 90 per cent of its banana crop. Of the greatest significance to our story, at the end of 1995, Geest sold its banana business to a consortium fifty per cent owned by Fyffes and and fifty per cent owned by the Windward banana producers themselves. So the battle to control their own banana trade is half won. But the battle to preserve the trade against American competition is still to be fought..

In Cuba, crises continue to come and go. Since I was there, a huge increase in people leaving in rafts provoked a reaction from the Clinton administration. That issue has faded a little and the Cubans are now making it easier for exiles to pay a visit, and some American dollars, to the island. This once again puts the United States' embargo to the test. Whatever else may or may nor change in Cuba, Castro's ability to run rings around American policy-makers is unaltered through his many years in power.

In the Timberlands of America itself, the battle still rages over Warner Creek, the area of burnt out woodland I visited in Oregon. Politically and legally, things seem to have swung in the favour of the logging companies. Some of the force has been taken out of the Endangered Species Act and the Forest Service is now allowed to permit the logging of timber susceptible to fire and pests. The last I heard, Earth Firsters were camping out at Warner Creek trying to save trees, already killed by fire, from being chopped down for timber: a grotesque parody of the battle to save an environment already damaged beyond repair.

In Hawaii, a plebiscite of native Hawaiians to test their views on the sovereignty issue has been postponed, ostensibly on grounds of cost. Windy Lorenzo (King Kamehameha VI) is nearing the end of his prison sentence but Bumpy Kanahele has now been sent to gaol, having been caught in the company of a criminal on the run and for not paying some parking tickets (he does not recognize US traffic laws). The former state-owned land where I interviewed Bumpy has been developed to provide good homes for previously homeless Hawaiians, but independence seems as far off as ever.

In the Mara, the clash between conservationists and developers continues. More Maasai are getting interested in the group ranch scheme at the centre of the film; but the power and influence of William Ntimama, the Minister for Local Government in the Kenyan government, is unabated. The government has increasingly vocal critics abroad and at home, and Richard Leakey, the deposed head of the Kenya Wildlife Service, has now formed his own political party to challenge for power.

The film about Goa was almost more controversial than all the others. A number of journalists, most of whom seemed to have enjoyed pleasant holidays there, complained I was guilty of scaremongering about the problems caused by hotel development. It seems you can expose any sort of problem in a Third World country but you must not blame the First World's travel industry without hitting a raw nerve. On the other hand, I have been contacted by a great many Goa organizations and Goans living in Britain expressing their gratitude that someone has paid some attention to the damage done to their beautiful country. I understand the suggestion that hippies in Goa might be a dying breed may be somewhat inaccurate as there has been a recent resurgence of travellers' parties, raves and gatherings.

Since we went to the cities of the second series more recently, and we were covering more far-reaching problems, fewer things will have changed. Having said that, Nigeria seems scarcely ever to be out of the headlines at the moment. Given the arrests, detentions and death sentences handed out in that former Commonwealth country, my problems in Lagos seem very small beer indeed.

The Prime Minister of Lebanon has resigned and been reappointed at least once since I visited but the plans to rebuild Beirut continue. Prospects for peace in the Middle East appeared to be growing, but the assassination in Israel of Yitzhak Rabin has obviously put that in doubt.

In contrast to making the documentaries, which is very much a group effort, writing the book has been a solitary activity. In the book I have tried to give my impression of the countries and cities we visited, the issues which we were there to discuss, plus something of the process of filming as well. Although a book like this is conventionally described as 'accompanying' the television series, in this case, the better word would probably be 'amplifying'. There is only so much you can put in a forty-minute film. So much more you can put in a book.

The words and opinions in the book are all mine, but I have obviously drawn upon the research, planning and thought which went into the making of the two TV series. Thus the book could not have been written without the tremendous work of the series producer, and director of five of the films, Paul Sommers.

Also heavily involved were Sam Anthony and Jeremy Lovering. They had different job descriptions on the various films of the first series but between them they were responsible for producing the best ideas and the most interesting stories with a great deal of enthusiasm. Jeremy Lovering directed the Beirut film with an artistic style which he will no doubt employ eventually in Hollywood, and Sam Anthony has been kind enough to help me update events for the purposes of this introduction.

Many thanks also to Russell England, who directed two of the films in the first series, and to Emma Cahusak and Clive Maltby, the producer and director with me on the particularly eventful trip to Lagos.

Toby Follett and Arlen Harris were towers of strength throughout the second series so thanks, too, to them and to the several other excellent researchers, informers and fixers who accompanied and assisted me in the different parts of the world: they include Alison Aylen, Susmita Gupta, Stephen McLaren, Lis Perry, Ken Richards, Carolyn Roumeguerre and Sudeshna Roy. And to Charles Brand for the lunches.

I am particularly grateful to Emma Pierce who has acted well beyond the call of her duties at Tiger Aspect to help me with the fact-checking for many of the more complicated parts of the text.

Since this is already reading like the first draft of an Oscar winner's speech I will refrain from thanking the marvellous camera crews and everyone else who worked on the series. But I must say how grateful I am to Sheila Ableman, Linda Blakemore, Nicky Copeland, Susannah Playfair, Jane Struthers and Doug Young at BBC Books for encouraging me to get this book written, almost on time, and for doing their best to make my prose readable.

OUR
MAN
IN... GOA

GOA is the smallest of the states which make up the Republic of India. It occupies a mere 1429 square miles (3701 square kilometres, if you want it in the metric system; one-fifth of the size of Wales, if you want it in Welsh). It is on India's west coast which, on a map, is on the left-hand side, an inch or two below Bombay. It is different from the rest of India largely because of its history.

The area was conquered by the Portuguese in about 1510 and it remained a Portuguese possession for more than four hundred years. Thus the Portuguese were in Goa a couple of centuries before the British began to establish their Empire in the rest of the subcontinent. And they were still there after India gained its independence from Britain in 1947. The languorous Portuguese rule continued until the Government of India 'reclaimed' Goa in 1961: impatient for a solution to the demands for decolonization, the Indian Army moved in and took over. The Portuguese had lacked the will to leave, but when it came to it they also lacked the determination to stay. But they certainly left their mark on Goa, chiefly by introducing Christianity.

India has never been exactly short of religions: firmly established within its borders are Hinduism, Muhammadanism, Sikhism, Buddhism and a variety of other isms and schisms. To the modern eye, it looks as though India has always had quite enough creeds to be getting on with. But in the sixteenth century the Portuguese felt there ought to be Christianity as well. With the high-mindedness and high-handedness of all European colonizers of the time, they set about converting the natives. And preaching the gospel of brotherly love was not then done in the milk-sop, clap-hands-come-to-Jesus style of today, but with a more red-blooded call to the faith, backed up with threats, violence, punishment and torture. It must have come as a shock: nobody expects the Portuguese Inquisition. Harsh methods, perhaps, but they worked. And today Goa still has a population of devout Roman Catholics.

For some time now they have been outnumbered within Goa by the Hindus who have migrated to this comparatively wealthy state, but it is the Christian tradition which sets this section of India apart. This is

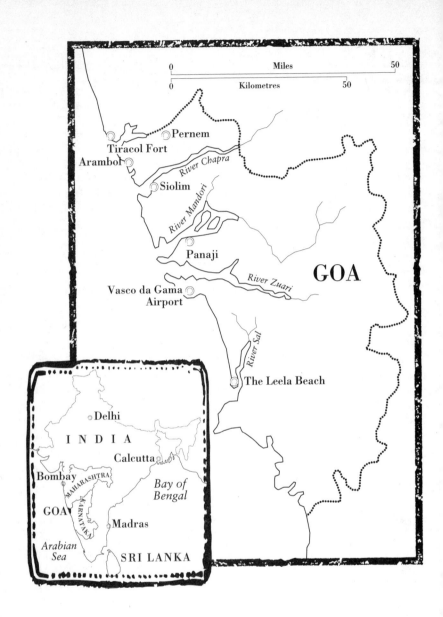

apparent not only in the white-walled baroque churches which are to be discovered in pretty well all the coastal towns and villages, but also in the lifestyle of the Goan people and their legal system.

I suppose that, in Europe, Roman Catholicism is not particularly associated with hedonism, nor with the emancipation of women. But in the context of Hindu and Muslim India, Catholic Goa has a more relaxed attitude to the pleasures of life – especially with regards to the availability and consumption of alcohol. And Catholic women have always been accorded greater property rights and are altogether less deferential to their menfolk than their Hindu and Muslim sisters.

So with its attractive beaches, available drink and free-thinking women, Goa has long been famous within India and without as the place to go for a good time. Some Goans profit from this, others rather resent it. Especially the women, who are naturally unhappy with the notion that because they look a man in the eye they must be making themselves sexually available to him. A notion which certainly seems to occur to lorry-loads of drunken young men who on holidays arrive from out of state.

In recent times, the first foreigners to put Goa on the map as a travel destination were what are still referred to in this part of the world as hippies. In the 60s and 70s, Goa was one of the great destinations at the end of the overland trail from Europe. Perhaps I should have come here then, hair down to my shoulders, beard down to my chest, drugged up to my eyeballs. Instead I went to law school. But I made it at last in 1994, even if most of my hair did not make it with me.

The hippies came from Europe to get away from it all, to discover Oriental religions, to live cheaply and to take drugs. Their arrival was not entirely problem-free. The introduction of a drug culture was resented by many local people, nude bathing by even more. But for the most part the hippies received a warm welcome from the people and the weather. They slept on the beach, survived on as little as possible and lived out the message of free love. For them Goa must really have seemed a paradise, which only had to be abandoned when their savings ran out, or the University term was about to start. All you needed was love. Plus, in the monsoon season, an umbrella.

But in the wake of the 'Beautiful People' of the 60s and 70s has come the mass tourism of the 80s and 90s. This involves building hotels, roads and restaurants and everything else the modern traveller requires to make him feel at home. In this there is far greater potential for making money, but also a greater potential for the destruction of the very paradise that people are seeking.

The growth of tourism is not a problem unique to Goa, but in many ways Goa is itself unique. I visited it to see how it was coping with the problems created by tourism. Was the way of life of the Goan people being destroyed by the arrival of foreigners looking for two weeks in the sun? Or did that represent a path to economic improvement? Did a few people staying in luxury 5-star hotels do more or less damage than larger groups of cut-price tourists? And was there any room left for the hippies?

To find out, I had to visit the beaches, go to the luxury hotels, seek out the beautiful and the exotic. It was a tough assignment, but somebody had to do it.

• Advance to Goa •

Since tourism was the subject of my visit, it was appropriate that I arrived in Goa by tourist charter flight direct from Gatwick. So much more convenient than a scheduled flight via Bombay, the producers assured me. Oh, and cheaper too.

The airport is not really an airport at all but an aerodrome operated by the Indian Navy. They allow package tourists to land there, but not scheduled passengers. Scheduled flights are presumably too much of a security risk. There is no photography or filming allowed in the terminal, for the same reason. So I had to be filmed later on, arriving in Goa by train.

Getting through the various airport entry procedures is not much fun anywhere, but in Goa the delicate balance between bureaucracy and chaos is a particular delight. Reaching the head of a queue to have a piece of paper stamped by an official affords you no special relief as you immediately have to join another queue for a second official to check that the stamping has been done correctly by the first one. A system of checks and balances which keeps half the population employed and the other half waiting. This is, I think, typical of all India.

The hot and shabby arrivals hall gently simmers travellers' tempers, never quite bringing them to boiling point, as officials and clerks go about their business of stamping and docketing like nobody's business.

It is my special pleasure to arrive with a film crew, together with dozens of tin crates of film stock, cameras and other equipment. Who knows what amount of inspection and delay this might warrant? Earlier travellers to a foreign land would have employed a scout or guide to lead them across rivers and over mountain ranges. We modern-day television folk employed a man who came from Bombay simply to help us negotiate our way through the thickets of Indian officialdom.

Once past Passport Control, Customs and Excise, Baggage Reclaim and Visa Inspection, Goa was to be my introduction to India. And it was bound to be a pretty gentle one according to every Indian expert I spoke to in advance. Hardly any human misery or suffering to write home about. Oddly enough, this always sounded more of an apology than a reassurance. It was as though they were worried I might feel short-changed by the lack of typical experiences in the subcontinent, much as a visitor to England could be annoyed by the present-day absence of smog. Or a traveller touring the peaceful districts of America might be disappointed not to come across a genuine New York mugging or a real Los Angeles race riot.

Goa did turn out to be pretty, and mostly gentle, but there was quite enough human misery and poverty, thank you very much, for me to get the general idea.

• Paradise found and lost •

At first sight, Goa is certainly very beautiful. And at second and third, come to that. Washed by the warm waters of the Arabian Sea, its palm-fringed beaches look and sound for all the world like a holiday brochure. Inland, the countryside is more like an illustration from the *Jungle Book*. Forests and scrub land look wild and yet they are really quite densely populated. In amongst the trees are simple houses and shacks which are home to rather dusty, scruffy-looking men, whose wiry legs emerge from shorts or dhotis. All of them the living image of Spike Milligan in the Desert Campaign. In addition there are beautiful, dignified women, their slim bodies elegantly wrapped in spotless saris, patiently going about their tasks of washing clothes in the open air and cooking on pots over wood fires.

The roads are a hoot. For many years India has protected its car industry from outside competition. Its car makers have not, therefore, had to keep up with the advances made in Japan, or even Britain. So whatever was the rage on the road in 1947 is more or less still the rage now. Car parks look like a Morris Oxford Owners' Club Rally on a very sunny day in England. On closer inspection, the larger cars are called Ambassadors, an extremely good name for expensive, out of date, old warhorses which are only put on the road to maintain national prestige. Even more evocative of a bygone British era are the Indian-produced Enfield motorbikes, which continue to be made to an ancient Royal Enfield design. And how weird to see the cows walking in and out of the traffic (a very Hindu side of Goa). Even weirder that it will only take a couple of days for this to seem completely normal.

In fact, for the first couple of days' filming I spent quite a long time on the roads, being driven around in a taxi by an extremely cheery driver called Ellias. He had five different horns which he used according to whether he was passing a lorry, warning a pedestrian, reversing or doing two other things not covered by the above. I think it is only in Britain that hooting at someone is unequivocally aggressive, its meaning ranging from 'Get out of my way' through to 'You are a complete idiot'. In most other countries it is usually no ruder than clearing one's throat to attract someone's attention. Here in Goa most of the lorries carry big signs which actually invite you to hoot when you come up behind them.

Driving conditions here generally feature that scary Third World combination of narrow roads, fast cars, overloaded lorries, bullock carts and people trying to stay alive while walking or cycling along the highway. Living a subsistence existence miles away from the big city grants you no immunity nowadays from the tyranny of the internal combustion engine.

More than once we came across someone lying in the road just out of the range of the passing traffic. It would be utter folly for us to stop and try to assist, Ellias insisted as he skirted round the body. It was probably a con man and not the victim of a traffic accident at all. Either way, to stop would be to invite a financial claim or being taken in for questioning by the police. Well, would we have stopped if we had knocked him down? Absolutely not, said Ellias, that would invite a financial claim, arrest by the police and being beaten to death by passers-by.

• Where have all the hippies gone? •

Calangute is my first port of call. Twenty years ago this was a little fishing village which became a famous hang-out for hippies. Now, the hippies are gone and most of the fishermen too. Today it is a lively seaside town with a collection of modestly priced hotels and boarding houses. The main street is lined with traders selling jewellery, blankets, souvenirs and knick-knacks. Is this the way the residents of Calangute make their money nowadays? Not quite. Most of the traders are from either Kashmir or Tibet. (There is political upheaval or war in both regions which has played havoc with the tourist trade at home.) Kashmiris are very insistent salesmen. Each one is offering a special bargain on the highest quality goods. Everyone has a brother round the corner who has even better stuff to sell. All are astonished if you pass by without looking, or look without buying, or buy something without buying something else. The Tibetans are more placid, sitting quietly behind their trays of jewels, much less inclined to haggle.

Calangute has a pleasant, rather than a spectacular beach, and an agreeable array of cafés and restaurants in which its visitors may refresh themselves. It is no longer a hippie paradise; it is not really a paradise at all, but it is perfectly congenial. It is neither cordoned off for the rich, nor trampled down by the masses. In many ways it is like a small English seaside resort, in the days when people went to small English sea-side resorts for their annual holiday. I even bumped into a couple from Birmingham who explained they had been coming back to the same boarding house here each year, for several years. They hoped Goa would not get too popular and so get spoiled. I went off to the Planters restaurant for a lunch of kingfish and chips.

Ellias said that the hippies had moved further north, so I made my way up the coast to Anjuna market. This market was established years ago by the hippies themselves and it was sufficiently underground to be suppressed by the local authorities for a while. It is now back in full swing.

The market is by a beach, more or less in the middle of nowhere. The road to it takes you past little villages, corner shops and houses and empty fields, and past some signs to a German bakery which I never managed to visit. The market attracts large crowds who arrive on foot, on scooters, in large Ambassador taxis, smaller taxis of some other make (possibly Cultural Attachés?), or in mini-vans. The best way to arrive is on an Enfield. With your long hair, deep suntan, no helmet and a large bike thrumming between your legs you are forever in a real-life *Easy Rider* movie.

At the market we are all travellers, wanderers, beautiful people. Well, we are for the afternoon. Most of us are really tourists who are here to look at the beautiful people. Tourists may be driving the hippies away from here, but in the market the hippies are a tourist attraction.

Most of the stalls are the same as the ones you can find in Calangute or Panaji (Goa's capital). But there are enough spaced-out people in tie-dye shirts, girls with Janis Joplin hairstyles, shell-shocked victims of years on the road selling the contents of their backpacks to survive, to make the experience of underground culture seem real enough.

Alongside a highly organized leather goods salesman is a chancer selling half-empty bottles of sun cream gathered who-knows-how from sunbathers. A Scotsman in a kilt offers haircuts. All in all it is a fantastic ragbag of a place, a near-Bombay-mix of peasant market, Indian craft fair and Camden Lock, with a car-boot sale thrown in for good measure. It certainly takes me back to my youth because the Indian style of clothes and music was dead fashionable in England then. But I suppose it has always been fashionable here in India.

Most mysterious to me, although I am assured they are fairly common in India, are the ear-cleaners. Or, to be precise, certified ear-cleaners. One happened to approach while I was standing around – well, all right, posing – for a photograph to be taken for this book. In one hand he had a piece of paper on which somebody, possibly himself, had typed out that he was authorized to clean ears. He grabbed me by my right ear and, for the sake of a good photograph, I let him look into it … No obligation to buy, he assured me. Just checking to see if I needed any remedial ear-cleaning work. But while I was getting instructions from the photographer, the cleaner scurried round behind me and, before I knew what he was doing, thrust what appeared to be a large rusty nail into my left ear. It was like having your windscreen washed at a traffic light, only painful.

Removing the nail from my ear, the ear-cleaner triumphantly displayed a large dollop of brown wax impaled on its point. Had that come from my ear, or was it on the nail from a previous client? Or was the whole thing a trick? Having a nail inserted into the ear struck me as a rather dangerous procedure, especially if the patient does not know that it is happening. Hey, there are even warnings on packets of cotton buds saying that on no account should they be inserted into the ear. Surely they put the same warning on packets of nails in India? I began to speculate what nasty diseases I might have caught. Burst ear drum? Tetanus? Hearing Aids? Anyway, when he asked for payment, I turned a deaf ear.

Still clutching the side of my head, I bumped into two young English computer programmers who were travelling the world, on the proceeds of money earned from a few months' work in Hong Kong. Their earnings from programming computers meant they were able to spend many more months on the move. (Later in the year they were planning to go to a huge gathering at Machu Picchu in South America.) Goa was great … The only drawback came from riding around on locally hired scooters. There was no way of getting the right licence and insurance, so any policeman hoping to augment his meagre salary could always stop you when you were riding around and demand a bribe. He could ask for an even bigger one if you happened to be carrying hashish.

The computer programmers confirmed that the real centre of hippie activity, the way it used to be in Calangute, was further north, in Arambol.

• The answer, my friend •

The coast road winds its way north past Catholic churches and Hindu temples. Some of the houses are guarded by little model figures of soldiers, which is a Portuguese tradition.

The Portuguese language does not seem to have survived nearly as well as the models or the church. In fact, to my untutored ear, there was no Portuguese to be heard on the streets and none to be seen either: no signposts, no posters, no newspapers … I did try out one or two words of Portuguese of my own in Goa. Admittedly I remembered them from a couple of holidays in Portugal, but to say this produced nothing but blank looks would exaggerate the size of response I managed to achieve, even in people who had told me they still remembered Portuguese from their schooldays. Maybe it only comes back to them when they are doing quadratic equations.

And maybe it has not survived because the Goans have their own language to protect. It has been a struggle but the Goans have managed to retain Konkani, despite opposition to its use from Indian bureaucracy after independence, and centuries of severe suppression by the Portuguese before. It is still under pressure from the more widely spoken Marathi and, indeed, English. But there still exist Konkani books, Konkani schools and, for all I know, Konkani rhyming slang.

There is a river to cross, the Chapura, at a small town called Siolim. There is no bridge but an efficient ferry service carries about ten cars, plus as many motorbikes and foot passengers as can be crammed on. I chewed the fat with a couple of German motorcyclists. One of them had been bumming round the world for fifteen years. No wonder he looked like a disaffected youth of the 70s: he had been one.

Goa has several rivers like this and several ferries, but they are gradually being replaced by bridges. Bridges are grand things, things of beauty even. But a short ferry trip is a joy. Even for ten minutes it literally puts everybody in the same boat. Once a bridge is built, to the motorist it becomes just another stretch of road. The gain in time is minimal for the sacrifice in pleasure and interest. I dare say people said the same thing when bridges were being built across the Thames but, for an economy based on agriculture and tourism, speed is not everything. Anyway, we chugged across the muddy waters of the Chapura, waving to villagers splashing around doing their washing at the water's edge. It was absolute bliss. Another half-hour on the road on the other side and I was in absolute heaven.

Arambol village is a scattering of houses in the trees alongside Harmal beach. The beach is a huge stretch of sand, empty except for three or four fishing boats, basking in the sun and four or five refreshment shacks – *chai* shops, as they call them – stationed at the high-water line but not doing a roaring trade. In fact, not doing any trade at all.

So this was a beautiful, remote, uncommercialized stretch of coast. All the elements necessary for a hippie beach. But where were the hippies? Perhaps we had to wait for hippie hour.

Actually, the hippies were round the bend. A path round a headland leads to what is arguably an even more beautiful stretch of beach. It is certainly more remote. Out of sight of the village the New Age travellers, lotus eaters and sun seekers can strip off and dive naked either into the sea or the sweet water lake which is on the other side of the beach and fed by a freshwater stream which flows down a shady valley. It is not entirely a nudist beach, but drop out can become droop out and nobody will turn a hair.

Like a threatened, exotic species of life on earth, *Homo hippius* has been pushed to this northern end of his Goan range. Would I at last make contact with this fantastic breed, here in its natural habitat? Would I be able to talk to them? How could I break it to the hippies that the term 'hippie' has not been used seriously in Europe for about twenty years?

Actually I did make contact with Mike, who was originally from Switzerland. His lifestyle goes way beyond what anyone would usually call hippie. He lives in the trees next to the stream. His domain is a small platform of beaten cow dung. His worldly possessions are a hammock, a cooking pot, a flute and a catapult. The catapult serves no useful purpose, he only has it to aim stones at cans or tree trunks. He certainly does not use it to kill animals as he is strictly vegetarian. He has no books and no music except what he plays for himself on the flute. He does not appear to have any clothes; he certainly was not wearing any when I came with the camera crew to interview him. He sits naked in the woods, occasionally cooking himself a pot of beans. Back to basics, indeed.

His only vice, or indeed activity, was to smoke the occasional joint. Well, it might have been a frequent joint, come to think of it. The air in his clearing was quite intoxicating. I did not smoke, but I did inhale.

Mike has rejected the consumer society, Switzerland, Europe, the modern world and all its works. All of these he said were 'fucked'. I was not really able to establish anything much more specific than that. When I called on him he had a friend who was visiting from Germany. He was even quieter than Mike but was wearing clothes.

Mike's body was slim and healthy looking – perhaps we are supposed to live in the wild. His face looked quite old for his twenty-five years: perhaps smoking has an ageing effect, or Mike was troubled by his life back in civilization.

Strictly speaking, Mike was not getting away from it all. He, along with more or less everybody who comes to Goa to hang out in the great outdoors, goes back to Europe during the monsoon season which comes in the rainy months of June to September. Mike goes home to Switzerland to work for three months or so each year. He has very few outgoings (nothing on dry cleaning, for example). So he makes enough in three months in Switzerland to stay for nine months in India. In that sense he is really working for three months to take a very cheap nine-month-long holiday and is perhaps not so different from someone who works for eleven-and-a-half months so they can take an expensive fort-night's holiday.

At any rate, Mike has found the lifestyle to suit him. In a remote corner of a forest in the back of beyond. Even so, it is not that easy to get away from it all. For the benefit of hermits like himself, hippies and unconventional travellers generally, boys from the village wander up and down this isolated valley with baskets of water melons and sand-wiches, which they deliver to your hammock, cave or tree house, just like a City of London lunch service. Only cheaper.

• Pig tales •

Back at Arambol, I had a cup of tea in a little café halfway up a cliff overlooking Harmal beach. It was little more than a shack with a fantas-tic view, its kitchen equipped with hardly more than a Bunsen burner. But with these basic facilities, Peter, the owner, was able to produce elaborate and tasty meals (I stayed for dinner as well, which featured chicken, fish and prawns).

I wondered if there was a blot on his idyllic landscape. There is usu-ally trouble in paradise.

Well, he had no trouble with the hippies. The villagers, Peter included, were devout Catholics and they had been offended by hippies bathing naked in front of their homes. But that had now stopped. Peter was not bothered by the hippies' lifestyle. The village as a whole were happy to augment their income by renting out rooms in their houses to budget travellers and running little cafés and bars which fell well short of over-whelming village life.

But yes, there was a cloud on the horizon. There were plans to build a luxury holiday resort practically on top of the village. The sweet water lake and Mike's green valley would become a feature in the grounds of at least one five-star hotel. Or become part of a golf course built for the use of rich Japanese golfers.

Wouldn't that bring prosperity to the village? I ventured.

Peter and his neighbour Philamena thought not. It would destroy the village. The hotels would take the land on which their cashew trees grow. The golf course would take the water from their wells. The beaches would be roped off for rich tourists. Large restaurants would take business from their little *chai* shops. Outsiders would take jobs as waiters. Village girls would become prostitutes …

They were, in short, against it, and said so at length.

In fact they could have gone on all night about the horrors of the modern world being visited upon their way of life, but it was time to go to bed. Peter offered me a room in a house in the village.

The palm-thatched single-storey houses of the village are lined up somewhat randomly amongst scattered palm trees on muddy ground immediately bordering the sea. In addition to fishing, villagers earn their living by toddy-tapping. Toddy is the sap of the coconut palm. It is tapped by cutting into the trunk, in the same way that latex is gathered from a rubber tree. The only difference is that toddy is taken from the top of the tree. Morning and evening, the toddy-tappers shin up to the vertiginous tops of the trees with nothing but a loin cloth and a pot to tap into.

Toddy is highly prized in this part of India, though I must confess it was a bit too coconutty for my taste. I think it is better when it is fermented into a dangerous brew called fenny. This can be made from pure toddy, or mixed with cashew tree sap. Or, on occasion, adulterated with rougher alcoholic spirits.

While Peter led me along the muddy paths, past the water-filled ditches to my room, he introduced me to his father and brother who were going about their toddy-tapping business.

On his way to a room was a young chap from England, who was travelling through India with his girlfriend. They had had many an adventure staying in just these sort of places. He cheerily recalled waking up to find twenty rats around his bed in one village. On another occasion, he and his girlfriend had to protect their landlady from her drunken husband in the middle of the night. He was surprised I was staying in the room Peter had selected for me, as they had rejected it as not coming up to their minimum standard. Actually, the room was fine (bare, with a beaten earth floor), though the lavatory facilities were somewhat out of the ordinary. But what do you expect for forty rupees a night (less than one pound)?

To wash or go to the lavatory, I had to leave my room and walk 30 yards or so down a back alley. The shower was a simple cubicle equipped with a bucket which could be filled with water at the village pump. The lavatory was even more rudimentary, and much more unusual. It consisted of a hole in the ground, plus a pig.

'Pig toilets' are a feature of Goan life and they neatly do away with the need to have an elaborate sewage system because the pigs in Goa eat human waste products. Well, they may be human waste products to you, but they are meat and drink to Goan livestock. And to think I have heard people complain about bacon because they think they can detect in the taste that the pig was fed on fish ... Ecologically sound this may be, but it is rather disconcerting to hear the excitement that your arrival in the lavatory causes amongst the herd of swine stationed strategically underneath. Do they ever get over-enthusiastic and bite the hand, as it were, that feeds them? Is it healthy? There are things like liver flukes whose life cycle would fit rather too readily into these sorts of conditions. Goan pork is regarded as a delicacy, but I decided that I am too delicate for such a delicacy and informed Peter that I did not want bacon for my breakfast.

And what sort of life is it for the pig? Pigs have a famously well-developed sense of smell, and they are capable of nosing out a truffle growing several feet below the ground. I know they are often fed on swill, but here they were literally being shat upon from a short height. And, evidently, lapping it up.

In one of his *Hitchhikers' Guide to the Universe* books, Douglas Adams postulates a restaurant of the future in which diners worried about cruelty to animals are able to eat meat with a clear conscience. A special breed of cows has been developed which not only wants to be eaten but is able to speak to the diners to reassure them of that fact before they order.

I comforted myself with the notion that these pigs must be bred to it and happy in their work, even if they were not able to tell me so in person. In fact I did not give them a chance to get into conversation as I gave them a wide berth whenever I saw them wallowing in ditches or running around the village. After all, I did know where they had been. It was where I had been.

I wonder if Goan parents play with their children's toes. How would their rhyme go?

This little piggy went to market
This little piggy stays at home
This little piggy has human poo
This little piggy has none (lucky thing)
And this little piggy has wee-wee-wee, all the way home …

Mind you, this pig toilet business was not the comfort I am used to. I expect an en-suite bathroom. Next time I am in Arambol I shall demand a Gloucester Old Spot in my room. Or at least a potty and a guinea pig.

Fortified by a share of a bottle of Indian whisky, I settled into my room for the night to enjoy the simple life. Back to nature with nothing but my jungle-strength insect repellent, anti-malaria pills, a copy of *Madame Bovary,* and the BBC World Service on the radio.

The conditions in Arambol seemed medieval at first. Wattle and daub houses, livestock running in and out of everywhere, water drawn from a well. But I suppose country districts all over Britain were not so very different from this right up until the First World War.

Peace came dropping slow, there being nothing to disturb my sleep but the grunting of the pigs, the crowing of cocks, the barking of dogs and all the other noises that an inner city-dweller like me is not used to at night.

The next morning the film crew were on hand to record my waking up, washing and shaving. Naturally, they had not stayed the night in the village – there were no huts left for them. They had had to go off to find a hotel miles away, poor things.

It was not difficult to retain a very warm feeling for Arambol and its people, even in the cold light of dawn. As I shaved I mused that I was the man who so liked the village that he wanted to buy it.

In fact, that title might better belong to a German called Frankie. If he was a hippie it was in a very efficient, Teutonic sort of way. He dressed, always, in a crisp white cotton tennis shirt, of the type Franz Becanbauer might put on to play with his kids at the weekend. He did not wear his hair long any more because he had businesses in India and Germany, and he had to look respectable for meetings. But hippie or not, Franz – I mean, Frankie – had been spending half his time in Arambol for seventeen years and had put a lot of effort into preserving its charm and keeping it clean. It does have a litter problem.

Even people who regard themselves as travellers and not tourists and who want to fit in as much as possible with local people are not prepared to drink water from a well, thereby running the risk of contracting cholera and typhoid and other ethnic diseases of the lower gut. On a hot day they do not want to wait for a toddy-tapper to run up to the tree top for a bucket of coconut juice. They want a cold beer or a mineral water. The trouble is that these drinks come in bottles and tins. And a simple place like Arambol does not have an efficient waste disposal service. At least, not until they can breed a pig that likes to eat plastic, glass and aluminium. (I think the Pigasaurus in the *Flintstones* movie is a step in that direction.)

Frankie told me that he had taken it upon himself to clean up the beach, paying a couple of lads to pick up the bottles and other rubbish which had been spoiling this beauty spot. Although the beach was impressively clean, even with Frankie's help there were distressingly large amounts of plastic containers cluttering up the ditches and pathways around the village.

Frankie is spending money on Arambol, but the man who actually owns the place, and the man who wants to build a hotel development right next to it, is Jitendra Deshprabhu. So he was the man I went to see next.

Jitendra Deshprabhu lives in his family's country mansion just outside Pernem in the far north of Goa. Although they are a Hindu family, the Deshprabhus were always very chummy with the Portuguese rulers of Goa and were relied upon to protect Goa's border with Mathasdra. Their wealth and land holding has survived independence (there is no inheritance tax in India, I was assured) and Jitendra, as the current head of the family, is the owner of a vast estate encompassing something like twenty-seven villages.

From the outside, the mansion is an impressive if somewhat gloomy pile, its classic lines spoiled only by the extra bits of roof stuck on to the walls to deflect the monsoon rains.

Inside I am welcomed into a cool room, its blue glass windows and decor giving it a very Mediterranean (Portuguese, I suppose) feel. The whole house is cool, kept that way by the airy courtyards. The number of courtyards is a sign of status. Someone doing quite well would be able to afford one courtyard to ventilate his home. Someone doing even better would have two; the Deshprabhu mansion has seventeen.

Elegantly dressed in a loose-fitting smock, he has the chubby look of the well-to-do in the Third World which shows they can afford to eat well. (As opposed to, say, rich Californians who are as thin as rakes showing they can afford private trainers, plastic surgery and low-calorie diets.)

Deshprabhu is amiable and aristocratic. He even has an imperial title. The pretender to the Portuguese throne recently invested him with the family's ancient title of Viscount of Pernem. Whether or not that counts for much in the Republic of India, he is certainly a Lord Bountiful. The school which is just outside his grounds was paid for by him and he is given to good works for the poor people who live on his land.

But why is he set upon destroying Arambol and its people with his hideous hotel development? While he answers this question he shows me around the mansion's guest annexe, which contains a few bedrooms, a gallery of portraits of his ancestors and a ballroom that would pass for an Oxbridge college hall.

He assured me that his ideas are not as bad as they have been painted. He is aiming to create a beautiful resort. This would bring wealth and prosperity both to him and to the people of Arambol. They would get jobs in the hotel, supplying food, driving taxis. He would not, as environmentalists claim, be depriving them of their drinking water. The huge amounts of water that 5-star hotel guests need to drink, bath in, see squirting out of fountains and to keep their golf courses green, would all be piped in from miles away. The golf course would not require chemical sprays, it would be fertilized by worm farms.

All this seemed a bit optimistic, and how was it to be paid for?

There were no golf courses in Goa. Surely it could support one or two? Did I know how much the average Japanese golfer spent on golf every year?

No, I didn't. The 4th Viscount had the figure to hand – £9000. With only a proportion of that multiplied by the many hotel rooms and condominiums available for golfers to hire, Desprabhu would be quids in. Aside from getting planning permission, all he has to do is get the millions of quids in as an investment and then he can get started.

The only ones really to lose out would be the hippies. 'Their' green valley, stream, and sweet water lake would become features of the resort. The hippies would be asked to leave, nicely. In any event, they were just squatting on unused land.

He dismissed the opposition of local priests to the hotel development, claiming they resist change of any sort. They fear that any economic development would attract more non-Catholics into the state and break the priests' hold on the local people.

• Let us pray •

Arambol church stands a little way from the village, near the road from the south. It was built about one hundred years ago and is very pleasant, though it offers nothing special to attract the tourists – there are many finer examples of Portuguese colonial architecture in other parts of Goa. But it does attract the local people to its services. Three Masses are held here every Sunday morning, and they are all full. In fact, the church was extended recently to accommodate the congregation. Singing is done to the music of a guitar, lending a sort of Hawaiian lilt to the proceedings.

I thought Sunday would be a good day to find the local priests in the church and, indeed, Fathers Fernandez and Rodriguez were there conducting the service. They confirmed they were definitely against the hotel development. Father Rodriguez had been at a parish in another part of Goa where a similar hotel had been built. He had heard all the same claims about benefits to the local community, and the minimization of harm. But the community had been destroyed: jobs had not gone to locals and all the water had been diverted to the hotel.

The priests did not seem to be following a specifically Christian line on this. More a sort of anti-tourist revolution theology, inviting you to join their congregation in its struggle against unsympathetic development.

Most of all, they were against the golf course, showing me photos of a Japanese women's anti-golfing group which had visited them to show support. The priests, perhaps surprisingly, had no problems with the hippies, despite their (on the face of it) amoral lifestyle. Their only complaint had been the nudism, but that no longer took place in front of the village so hippies were all right. That was the Church's view. But what about the State?

For the official position on hotel development I went to the state capital, Panaji, and there sought out Mr U. D. Kamat, the Director of Tourism. Mr Kamat's office was in a rather shabby-looking building with the underspent, make-do-and-mend feel of government offices the world over.

Actually, that means it was not too bad, as a great deal of Goa appears to run on the principle of make-do-and-don't-mend. (I think this is true of all India.) It seems there is no power point in the country that does not hang off the wall; there is no wall which is not crumbling at the edges; no door which does not swing oddly from the wall. It is as though the place has been put together by one of those DIY enthusiasts who never has the right piece of equipment, and never quite finishes things off.

At two different hotels (admittedly neither were particularly expensive) I found showers equipped with an electric water-heater plugged into an ordinary wall socket. The socket was sited inside the actual shower cubicle, just inches away from the shower head where stray droplets of water were destined to come into contact, eventually, with the wires. Amazingly, I only received an electric shock once and that was because of a wholly separate electrical fault. I dread to think what Esther Rantzen would have said if she had been in the shower with me.

Anyway, Mr Kamat was good enough to see me. Unfortunately he was also good enough to see several other people before I reached the head of the queue. Worse, he was obliged to speak to a couple of dozen callers on the phone while I was trying to keep his undivided attention. Mr Kamat is a busy and important man in Goan tourism. Even when not talking on the phone he was signing documents. Bundles of them: letters, memos, chits ... Who knows what? I hope he does because he had no time to read them. Evidently nothing can happen in his department without his signature. Equally obviously, there were far too many documents for him actually to apply his mind to the actions they were authorizing. A *Yes, Minister* world has arisen around him, and heaven knows how many others in this bureaucratic world, where the responsible person is too busy to be responsible for his actions. (A similar situation emerged at the highest levels of British government in the Scott Inquiry.)

When he was not otherwise engaged, Mr Kamat was very engaging and very enthusiastic about the prospects for tourism in Goa. Luxury 5-star tourism was the way forward. Hippies and backpackers do not bring in enough money. Package tourists might, but only if you allow in millions of them. International high-rollers bring in the money in low numbers. Mr Kamat was not worried that hotels would destroy Goa's coastline, forcing the international traveller to move on to some other Eden. It was true that the number of rich Germans coming to Goa had rather tailed off, but the arrival of vast numbers of British had more than made up for that. The Germans would be back once their recession was over. Strict controls were being enforced to stop buildings being too close to the beach and tourism was going to be the backbone of the Goan economy.

Mr Kamat suggested I visit the Leela Beach resort down towards the south of Goa. That is the future – he has seen it and it has the works.

• Is your visit to Goa really necessary? •

Before going south I went to Mapsa, a busy market town, to hear from the environmentalists who oppose tourist development.

Norma Alvires is a lawyer who runs the Goa Foundation. In her legal practice she regularly appears in court on behalf of the disadvantaged and oppressed. A sort of one-woman legal aid service. The Foundation publishes books and takes up environmental causes in opposition to the individuals and corporations who are out to make as much money as possible with little regard, as she sees it, for the environment.

Her immediate environment is unpretentious – you could say unpre-possessing. On the way to her office, which is in a block above a shop, I had to negotiate a path on which I came across a dead crow and a living cow which, although better than the other way round, are not what you expect to find on your way to see a lawyer. But then you could find yourself walking through a shanty town of homeless people these days in Lincoln's Inn Fields.

The arrangements in Mrs Alvires' outer office were reminiscent of an out-of-the-way shipping office in austerity Britain in about 1947. Two secretaries set about steadily sticking stamps on to packages and letters using a pot of glue and a brush: apparently Indian stamps do not come with adhesive. They have a computer but tend not to use it because of the frequent power cuts. (A couple interrupted our filming.)

In the inner office, sitting at a small wooden desk, Mrs Alvires is both charming and inspiring. She must make an impressive advocate. According to her, luxury hotels disrupt local life. They take water from the land so the water table drops and local agriculture suffers. If too much water is extracted, salt levels rise, killing agriculture possibly for ever. The local people do not always get the jobs it is claimed will be available to them. In any event, life as a waiter or cleaner is less digni-fied than farming the land. The price of food goes up. The hotels try to keep locals off the beach.

Not all of these objections would necessarily stand up in court, but together they sound like quite an indictment.

Mrs Alvires says the Indian legal system is basically sound, the judges are not corrupt and cases are generally given a fair hearing. As far as environmental worries are concerned, the government has put in place well-thought-out legislation. Regulations do exist to prevent hotels being built too close to the shoreline and to restrict the amount of water which can be extracted from underground supplies and so on. So that's all right, then?

Well, no. Rich developers tend to ignore regulations, break promises and generally act as though they are above the law. Politicians lack the political will to bring these powerful operators to book, so it is left to the Goa Foundation to take them to court. Operating as a sort of charitable, private environmental agency, the Foundation obtains judgments against hotels and the equivalent of prerogative orders to make government institutions intervene where the law says they should.

She says that although she opposes tourist development, the tourists who are here have reason to thank her. A tourist in search of paradise may want to stay in a hotel, but he does not want his view spoiled by lots of other hotels.

The Goa Foundation is not the most militant of environmental activists. That title might belong to the Goan Vigilante Force (GVF) which is the IRA to the Goa Foundation's Sinn Fein. (Actually that is not really accurate. The two organizations are not connected, and they do not blow people up, but with any luck you will see what I mean, and they will not sue me.)

Ronan Martin is a leading light in the GVF, and he was about to demonstrate in Mapsa against the tourists who have in recent years invigorated Mapsa market, so I went there to see him. Once a strictly local affair for the selling of fish, fruit and vegetables, the market now attracts stalls selling the clothes, jewellery, baskets, bags and carpets that tourists feel they have to buy to prove they have been to Goa. Many of the stall-holders had also been at Anjuna.

While waiting to film in the market I had my shoes shined. Well, 'shined' might be putting a bit of a gloss on the procedure. I had the dirt on them moved around a bit. Whatever you call it, it was a thoroughly depressing experience.

If you hang around long enough in India, say two seconds at the outside, you will be approached by somebody offering to sell you something, asking for assistance, or begging for money. Bear in mind I was in Goa where this sort of thing is at a minimum. Strolling around the market is enervating for an uptight Englishman like myself. If only the stall-holder would stop offering me stuff I might be able to find some-thing I wanted to buy. If you do not buy anything, salesmen and women crowd after you. If you have not bought yet, they want to make a sale, and if you do buy something they all crowd round you, reckoning that if you have bought once you will be prepared to buy again.

It is much the same with beggars. They hold their babies, they expose their wounds, they tug at your sleeve. Have you a heart of stone? Have you any change left? Give to one, why not give to all? I am a sucker for the beautiful mothers with placid children strapped to their backs, but everyone here looks in desperate need.

Gypsies from Rajasthan and Karnataka have an excellent technique. Whether selling clothes and bags decorated with mirrors, or simply beg-ging, their pitch is to come and sit with you patiently until you hand over some money.

Locals working with us dismiss all these people. They are itinerant nuisances. Not Goans at all. Their husbands all have well-paid jobs. They are professional beggars. Perhaps they are, but they and their long-suf-fering children seem to earn their money just the same.

While all this was going on, the shoe-shine boys tugged at my feet. I am about to appear on-camera, and my shoes are covered in the red mud of India. I have money in my pocket. I am waiting anyway. I am the perfect customer and I agree to the shoe-shine. The boy asks for fifteen rupees. I haggle. Eventually I beat him down to fifteen rupees. I learn later that I am a mug, I should have beaten him down to five rupees (about ten pence). He wants to take my shoes away to do a proper job. This I do not allow. I am not that much of a mug.

He takes out what might be described, quite accurately, as an empty tin of shoe polish and, with his nail finds some vestige of Cherry Blos-som still adhering to the thread in the lid. He uses his fingers to smear this on my shoe and then buffs it off with a moth-eaten piece of brush. The whole exercise leaves my shoes no cleaner than when they started. It is a perfect example of the free market not working in India. The price of a shoe-shine is too low, but he cannot charge more because a thousand other street urchins are there waiting to undercut him. But at the going rate he cannot afford to buy any polish. If he got paid more, the shoe-shine would cost more, but at least my shoes would be shined. And he would be able to make a living wage. As it is, he has gained hardly anything, and I nothing at all.

While I was standing in the market (fighting off the subsequent offers of shoe-shines – reasonably enough, nobody believed I had just had mine done), another modest area of reform came to mind. Street-sweepers in Goa are usually small women bent nearly double using brooms made out of bundles of sticks. I guess the street-sweepers are untouchables or, at any rate, people trapped in low-paid work. But their bundles of sticks are not that good at sweeping up litter, and neither are the sweepers. They swat limply at the rubbish on the street like teenagers set do some task around the house. They cannot refuse to perform, but will not bring themselves to do it with anything that could be mistaken for enthusiasm. Before a pile of rubbish has been formed or put into a bag, it has mostly blown away again, or been kicked along the street. All right, buy some proper brooms. It would cost a little more, but at least the streets would be swept.

Higher wages might help the work rate as well. The sun must be affecting my brain. A few days in India and I'm turning into a Communist.

Ronan Martin wants to turn me into an activist. Or at any rate stop me being a tourist. About four of his army parade around near the market with very well-made signs telling foreign visitors of the damage that our presence brings along with our travellers' cheques.

He insisted that the golf courses with their holiday villages, financed by Japan, would essentially amount to the Japanese exporting their old age pensioners. He would not allow that 'tourist farming', as I wanted to call it, was an acceptable use of natural resources. He would not even countenance the idea that a golf course constructed on waste, barren land could not be, well ... constructive.

In the eyes of the protesters, the tourist industry simply could not win. If they build on farmland they are taking land away from agriculture, but if they build on barren land they are doing something unnatural to the environment; if they spend a lot of money they raise local prices, but if they pay low wages, they exploit local people.

• Playing around •

And what about the golfers? The threatened construction of golf courses seems to excite more ire than virtually any other proposal of the tourist industry. My conscience is clear on this; it is not a game I have ever taken to or been any good at.

On hearing this, the director of the documentary decided to make me play a round of golf with General De Silva. He has retired from the Indian Army and become involved in the public debate about golf in Goa. The idea was that I should interview General De Silva about golf while I was shown making a pig's ear of the game myself.

We played on a small course that General De Silva designed himself. It is part of a luxury Taj hotel development on the coast. This features all the things that the Goan Vigilante Force dislike: restaurants near the beach, green lawns, swimming pools, exclusive beach. I had to force myself to try them out and hate myself for enjoying them all.

On the golf course – not much more than a pitch and putt – and on-camera, General De Silva said he thought it was ridiculous the way golf was being linked with prostitution and drug-taking as a great evil. It was a pleasurable game and Goa and India could do with some courses. True, it was being introduced to Indians by foreigners, but that had been so with cricket, and nobody thought that cricket grounds should be removed because they were alien influences. He had criticisms, too, for the tourist industry. He felt developers were being greedy in hurrying to build expensive golf courses for the benefit of, or the exploitation of, wealthy Japanese people. Courses should be established for local people first. Only that way would a course develop a character which would eventually attract outsiders.

All in all, he was the most agreeable and reasonable person I spoke to about this issue.

Naturally, the General's interview is not in the documentary. Apart from anything else, and by a peculiar operation of sod's law, instead of looking an idiot on the golf course, my shots went annoyingly right. I drove the ball down the fairway, I putted in from 12 feet away from the hole. I could have been, well, if not Nick Faldo, at least Jimmy Tarbuck. Then the film ran out and I reverted to my usual level of golfing ability – slicing, hooking and missing with the worst of them.

• Leela Beach •

According to Ronan Martin, the villain of the tourist piece is Captain Nair, the developer of the Leela Beach. And yet the Leela Beach hotel complex is, according to the Director of Tourism, the very best the Goan tourist industry has to offer. It is some creation. On the coast at Colva Bay, it has 250 luxury hotel rooms surrounded by freshwater lagoons, walls and uniformed guards.

The main buildings are pink. Their architectural style is Suffolk farm-house, teamed with Portuguese Colonial, with just a touch of Disney. In the way of these islands of luxury the design is way over the top, but nothing like as tasteless as a nearby resort which is built in the shape of a Portuguese galleon. It has all the trappings of the luxury tourist hotel, the swimming pools, gymnasium, restaurants. You can choose from Indian, Goan, Chinese and international menus. There are a few tacky examples of poor finishing off, such as stucco walls coming unstuck, but in the main it achieves the effect of leisured opulence.

The guests seem more or less contented. The less contented ones complain about the slow service. One couple had waited an hour for a drink at the poolside. It is all very well being in a Third World country, but they wanted first class service. But another man approached me in the gents to say he found everything absolutely fabulous. And it's a long time since that has happened to me.

It is difficult to tell when they are stripped down to their Lycra swimwear, but these people do not appear to be the filthy-rich independent jet-setters which the travel industry cannot get enough of. Most of the guests seem just like package tourists who everyone agrees it is possible to have too many of. Of course, there are shops within the complex so there is no need for those tiresome shopping trips into the real world. Once here there is no reason to leave.

A sign at the beach advises guests not to eat from stalls and shacks outside the boundaries of the hotel, but promises a 24-hour medical service for those who do. Local people are not completely forgotten, however, as there is a garden decorated with cardboard cut-outs of village houses and village people. They have displays of Goan life in the evenings, but unfortunately I did not get to see it as I was out meeting real Goans in a real Goan village.

Captain Nair is, I think, a self-made man. He certainly made a fortune from textiles and looks as if he is doing all right from the hotel trade. In conjunction with Lufthansa he operates the Leela Kempinski Hotel in Bombay which, by all accounts (not just his), is a magnificent international venue. And the Leela Beach is his next success. He put in sixty per cent of the capital for this venture himself.

Sitting on his private balcony overlooking the lagoon (there are villas and flats available on the site) he is proud of the hotel complex. He has created a garden paradise here, with trees and water and everything, where once there was 'sand, mere sand'. Regulations which prevent him building too close to the shoreline are tiresome nuisances to be overcome like any other problem.

Captain Nair is dismissive of environmental objections generally. He gets water for the hotel by tapping the immense monsoon rainfall which otherwise would run away into the sea and be wasted. He has no time for the notion of leaving Goa as a wilderness. He has the confidence of a wealthy man who is well-connected. Virtually every minister in the Indian government has been to his hotel to enjoy his hospitality.

To say that he was bullish about the future of the Indian tourist industry would not quite capture his obvious enthusiasm. Buffalo-ish might do it.

He said that new free enterprise policies are being followed in India. These, he claims, will have ten times the effect on India that Margaret

Thatcher had in Britain. So it is not the time to sign up as a coal miner in the foothills of the Himalayas.

By the time I interviewed Captain Nair I had visited the Goan village just outside the boundary of the hotel complex. My guide to the way things were on the other side of the tracks was Michael, who runs the improbably named:

A corner of Italy 'Yes That's
VENICE BAR AND RESTAURANT'

There was nothing particularly Italian about Michael's bar. It was a shack that sold beer and served local food. It was one of the few forlorn buildings which formed what was recognizably the same sort of village as the charming Arambol in the north. Except that now it was overlooked by the staff quarters of the hotel. The wall marking the boundary of the hotel seemed to squeeze against the village as though trying to push it into the creek. Barbed-wire fences restricted the villagers' access to groves of coconut trees and the beach. One or two houses in the village were fenced off completely. In short, it had lost its charm. In fact, it was more like visiting a concentration camp.

The villagers here and in Arambol enjoy certain rights as tenants, or *munkars* as they are known. They have a hereditary right to stay in their houses, as long as they can establish good title. This usually requires some written document. Official pieces of paper carry great weight in Indian legal bureaucracy. Although they do not own the trees as such, each *munkar* has the right to tap specific coconut trees for toddy, and may have similar rights to make use of cashew nut trees. In English law, this would be like an easement or profit *a prendre,* under which people in an area are entitled to cut wood or graze animals on the lord of the manor's land.

The problem for Captain Nair and other modernizers is that *munkars* are difficult to get rid of. Some can be bought off, but most wish to stick to their traditional way of life. They realize that a sum of money is soon spent, whereas their rights to a house and trees can, in theory, last forever.

The problem for the *munkars* is that they lack the money to stand up for all their rights, and are powerless to prevent the character of their neighbourhood being destroyed around them.

Looking around the now charmless village the unworthy thought does cross one's mind that a lot of effort is being expended to make life here as unpleasant as possible in order to drive the *munkars* away. With the help of Ronan Martin, a charge had even been brought against Captain Nair that he personally had attempted physically to intimidate a woman called Annie whose house was right next to the hotel.

After dark I was taken round the village by Michael. Right in the middle of the collection of flimsy houses was a pumping station. The pump was leaking or overflowing. And sewage was oozing into the ground, leaving a quite revolting stench hanging in the tropical air. Rich people's sewage escaping right next to poor people's homes. The unacceptable faeces of capitalism. Outside the house, which was practically next door to the pump, no more than 20 feet away, sat an old man, taking the air, and coughing his guts up.

When I interviewed him, Captain Nair would not accept the evidence of my own eyes and nose. Sewage was used to fertilize the coconut palms, he maintained. They had the best disposal system money could buy. He certainly had done nothing to intimidate Annie, who in the past had worked for him. He was expecting to rehouse her once a financial settlement had been reached. The idea that he, friend of the powerful, should be convicted of a criminal offence was obviously quite incredible. I suppose, on this point, he must be right.

The real problem is not Captain Nair. He is just someone trying to make an honest few million bucks. The problems come from the clash between the rich, modern world of tourism and the uncomplicated lifestyle of the folk who have lived in idyllic simplicity for generations. My sympathy was very much with the Goans struggling to hang on to their paradise, but let's face it, my lifestyle is that of the developers and their customers.

That 'each man kills the thing he loves' is certainly true of the tourist. We are all looking for the virgin country we can deflower, the unspoiled beach, so that we can be the people to spoil it. The best time to visit any tourist destination is always ten years before you actually get there. Ten years ago the fishing village still had fishermen, and the local bar still had locals. Now, it is full of people like us.

Tourism, someone told me, is now the biggest industry in the world. Rich cities like New York and countries like Britain and Italy depend upon it. It would be quite remarkable if a beautiful but poor tropical state like Goa were to resist the temptation to sell itself to the tourist.

Obviously, making a TV programme and writing a book about a place like Goa, even though they focus on the problems of tourism, is likely to attract more people there than it repels.

So I am part of the problem and not the solution. But perhaps this is not somewhere to visit for a holiday. It might be better to choose a destination which has a less fragile culture to be destroyed. In fact, nothing of any real worth at all. Somewhere like Eurodisney. After all, Eurodisney needs the money even more than Goa.

OUR MAN IN... HAVANA

CUBA has an unhappy history. Columbus came across it in 1492 and the Spanish thereafter set about conquering the island and eliminating its Indian population. This process was so successful that other Latin Americans claim to be able to identify Cubans by their complete lack of Native American blood. Resistance to the Conquistadors was led by an unusually warlike leader called Hatuey. But after a few months he was captured and burnt at the stake for his pains. He now lives on as the brand-name of a popular Cuban beer: when the heat is really on, have a cool Hatuey.

Cuba's wealth developed on the back of the tobacco and sugar trade and on the backs of the slaves imported from Africa by the Spaniards. Emancipation of slaves was a long time coming to Cuba. There were major uprisings from 1868 onwards, but slavery was not finally abolished until 1880.

Independence from Spain came in 1899. The fight against Spanish domination was supported by the Americans, but this led to half a century of domination by America. In fact it first led to the Spanish-American War in 1898, a conflict sparked by the sinking of an American battleship, USS *Maine,* in the Bay of Havana, combined with the encouragement of tycoon William Randolph Hearst who reckoned that a war would help to sell his newspapers. The idea! It is as though in our times the Gulf War had been waged for commercial interests, or American troops had landed in Somalia for the benefit of TV cameras. As luck would have it, the Spanish-American War led to America acquiring the Philippines, Puerto Rico and other Spanish colonies. It's an ill wind.

America did not gain formal jurisdiction over Cuba but, with the Spaniards gone, American capital was invested heavily in the island, American businessmen controlled its trade and American politicians exerted an overwhelming influence on its general development.

A succession of scarcely democratic governments failed to cope with Cuba's economic problems in the first half of the twentieth century until the military dictator Sergeant, later General, Batista took control in 1952. Under his rule Cuban life was the heady mixture of oppression, corruption, exploitation and prostitution captured in Graham Greene's

Gulf
of
Mexico

FLORIDA

Miami

BAHAMAS

Havana   Varadero

Mariel

Matanzas

CUBA

Caribbean
Sea

```
0        Miles        200
0    Kilometres   200
```

novel which he set on the island and which, by coincidence, he also called *Our Man in Havana*.

Fidel Castro attempted to overthrow the ruthless Batista regime in 1953 when he was only twenty-five. He was captured but, being perhaps not quite ruthless enough, the regime decided to exile rather than execute him. He returned with Che Guevara and eighty other guerrillas in 1956. At one stage Castro's forces were reduced to only twelve but in 1959, with relatively little blood spilt, he finally pulled off a somewhat improbable victory with a combination of skill, charm, determination and good fortune. His luck, if that is what it is, has stayed with him ever since and kept him in control for thirty-five years.

Few ordinary Cubans were sorry to see the back of the Batista regime but Castro's land reforms and appropriation of property hit the rich and affected American economic interests. By seizing their assets he put Americans' backs up and their noses out of joint.

Whether Castro's rule began as a Communist revolution is a moot point. From the word go, Castro was committed to redistributing wealth, but it can be argued that it was only the complete hostility of America that pushed Castro into the arms of the Soviet Union, which was delighted to get a toehold in America's backyard. Castro's revolutionary slogan was changed from *Liberty or Death* to *Socialism or Death*. As a battle-cry, *Socialism or Death* is an inspiring turn of phrase. But after thirty-five years in government, it sounds awfully like a threat.

The idea of a small island, even if it is the largest in the Caribbean, with a population of only 10 million, being able to insist on following a strict Communist line a mere 90 miles away from Miami is, for the rest of the world, a rather amusing joke, albeit one which does have a serious side. For instance, the Soviet Union's attempt to site nuclear missiles in Cuba in 1962, and President Kennedy's reluctance to let that happen, nearly led to a nuclear holocaust. If that had happened, nobody would have remembered where they were when Kennedy died because we would all have died with him.

For thirty-five years America has refused to trade with Cuba; the Soviet bloc which used to trade a great deal with Cuba, and subsidize its economy, is no more; and yet Castro still soldiers on.

So can he be counted as a success? Well, staying in Cuba is certainly one measure of success. But many of his fellow Cubans do not choose to stay there with him. Every year, hundreds of them take to the sea in anything which might keep afloat for 90 miles to escape Castro's socialist paradise. For many it is socialism or death by drowning.

You have to go to Cuba to find out what it is really like. It is impossible to get a clear idea by talking to other people about it. Opinions on

Castro and Cuba are polarized in the extreme. Before I went to Cuba I spoke to lots of Cuban Americans. There are more than a million and a half in Miami alone, most of whom seemed to be gathered for their annual street party, 'Calle Ocho' in 8th Street on 12 March. None of them had a good word for Cuba as it is today. I tried to tempt one of the most affable of their number, a budding politician called Joe Garcia, into saying something – anything good about Castro. He declined. It was, he said, like inviting a Jew to say something good about Hitler.

Well, I suggested, Benito Mussolini at least got the credit for making the trains run on time. Was there nothing like that?

Nothing.

I reminded him that Castro is widely credited with improving literacy rates, building hospitals and schools. Infant mortality rates are amongst the lowest in the world ... Joe was having none of that. Far from being an economic disaster area, when Castro took over Cuba it was out-performing everyone else in the area. Of course there have been improvements in social services since then, but there have been advances everywhere and they are not always accompanied by Cuba's human rights abuses.

In print it is very much the same story. Jorge Mas Canosa, Chairman of the Cuban American National Foundation, writing in 1993 compared Cubans in America with Cubans in Cuba:

> *A spiritually and materially prosperous nation in exile, and an enslaved, destitute, hopeless nation on the island.*

On the other hand, Mary Murray, a journalist who has lived in and written extensively about Cuba, interviewed the Cuban Foreign Minister, Ricardo Alaracón, in 1992. The interview was published in a pamphlet, and included this exchange:

> *Q How is democracy working in Cuba?*
> *A It works better than in the United States. It could work even better than it currently does. We're working on improving it.*

Could they be talking about the same place?

• Take me to Cuba! •

Since America imposes a complete trade boycott with Cuba you might think it would be difficult to fly there from Miami without hijacking an internal flight at the point of a gun. In fact, it is quite easy. America forbids anyone to make money out of Cuba, and certainly does not want Cubans (of the Castro persuasion) making money out of America. So it will not let a Cuban airline fly into the States, but it will allow an American airline fly to Cuba. You get on the flight to Havana by queuing up a few hours before take-off, in good time to have your luggage weighed very carefully. The aircraft cannot cope with suitcases loaded with too many items that are unavailable in Cuba.

The American government only allows its citizens into Cuba on journalistic assignments, and the Cuban government does not like to let many of its citizens go to and from the States, so I rather hoped the plane might be half-empty, but it was full of people paying a visit to their relations in Cuba. One or two were dressed up in several hats and extra layers of clothing, not because it was cold but so they could beat the luggage weight restrictions.

Miami is amongst the most built-up of American cities, rivalling Los Angeles for freeways and skyscrapers and urban sprawl. Everything in Miami is big, flashy and new. Everything in Havana is very different.

On arrival in Cuba the roads are attractively traffic-free. Great to visit, though you might not want to drive there. Here and there are magnificent gas-guzzling American automobiles of the 50s, fantastic machines built just before Detroit went completely space-age crazy with fins and wings. I had been told about these cars before I got there and in fact there were not quite as many as I was expecting. Once the revolution happened the American car-dealers ran out of stock or ran out of town. I suppose I imagined that the street scene would be 1959 America trapped by a Vesuvius of economic sanctions. The truth is that while there are still quite a few automobiles which would not look out of place in an early series of *I Love Lucy*, most of them must have fallen to bits some time in the last thirty-five years. In many ways it is surprising that any remain at all. The survivors could all command a huge price on the international vintage car market, even with the DIY additions and bolt-ons which their enterprising owners have had to resort to over the years to keep them on the road.

The other vehicles on the roads are mostly Ladas. Lada cars, stretch Ladas, Lada taxis. Taken and driven away, no doubt, by Lada louts.

There are almost as many overcrowded buses. Plus lorries and some tractors which are pressed into service to provide public transport. More serious even than the shortage of vehicles is the shortage of fuel to run them on. Everyone has to leave work quite early in the afternoon because just queuing for a bus takes three hours or more for most commuters.

To alleviate this problem, an ingenious ruling requires that all government-provided cars stop for hitch-hikers. This ordinance is no dead letter. There are special people at street corners to hail the passing civil servant, minister or official, and to organize the hitch-hikers into orderly queues.

This is a system we could well adopt in Britain. Virginia Bottomley, say, on her way to close down another hospital would have to share her Minister-ial Rover with a few patients from the waiting list who are waiting at the bus stop and a couple of nurses who are trying to get to work.

We started our look at Havana in *Plaza de la Revolución* – Revolu-tion Square. Revolutionaries like squares. Moscow has its Red Square, Beijing has Tiananmen Square. Even in London, any decent march or demonstration has to go to Trafalgar Square (apart from that 60s anti-Vietnam demo which took place in Grosvenor Square).

This square is a bit bleak. It is large, tarmacked rather than paved and, apart from a monument to Cuba's national hero, José Martí, com-pletely featureless. The buildings which surround it are 50s Stalinist and dull. The front of one, though, is dominated by a massive outline of Che Guevara. I think it is the Ministry of the Interior, though it could be a giant Athena poster shop.

Che Guevara had the right idea. The James Dean of radicals and hero of the revolution, he did not hang around getting old and unpopular in power. After a few years in government in Cuba he went off to join another revolution, this time in Bolivia where he died a martyr's death. Age cannot not weary his radical chic nor his good looks. A glamorous politically correct icon, he remains forever – a cross between Tony Benn and Hugh Grant. Not bad for an asthmatic Argentinian medical student with an allergy to mosquito bites.

Failing to find inspiration in the square, I checked into my hotel, the Sevilla. This was the Seville Biltmore in Graham Greene's *Our Man in Havana*, which was written just before the revolution. Since then the hotel has spent several years in decline but now it has been restored to something of its former glory.

It has eight floors of rooms and three restaurants. On the ground floor is a cool bar in an open-air courtyard. The staff are extremely friendly although the service can be slow. On the ninth floor there is a high-class restaurant in which they have got almost everything right for the international diner. You know the sort of thing: there is a plate laid in front of you which is taken away once you have ordered your meal, to be replaced by the plate your food actually comes on; a phalanx of dif-ferent-sized glasses; lots of waiters with excellent command of English to guide you through the menu and congratulate you on your choice. Everything a high-class restaurant should have, only the food is not par-ticularly good.

Downstairs there is an informal buffet in which the food is largely inedible, though it served a pretty good breakfast which was even popu-lar with a large party of French holiday-makers.

Graham Greene said that the Spanish made much more of an effort to build magnificent cities in their Caribbean possessions, comparing the ramshackle townships of the British West Indies with the flamboyant architecture of proper cities like Havana. I do not know what Graham Greene would make of Havana today. Most of the Spanish Colonial buildings he knew are still standing. No, that is not true. Most of them are falling down. Some have fallen down already. Here and there are what look like bombsites. They are the remains of elegant apartment blocks, or whatever, which have collapsed under the accumulation of years of neglect. Some surviving, elegant facades are held up with crude wooden supports; other buildings manfully stay upright against the odds, subdivided as many times as possible into flats for the citizens of Havana.

The view from my hotel room is astonishing. A few years ago the Americans started to develop the neutron bomb, which was going to kill all the people in a battle but leave the buildings standing. This city looks as though it has been hit by a bomb with the reverse effect. Perhaps it would be a proton bomb. No people have been killed but the fabric of the place has been completely destroyed.

I found the sight of a city crumbling around its inhabitants profoundly depressing and also quite inexplicable. The explanations everyone gives for this mess are that, after the revolution, the priority was to build hospitals and schools in the country, not to titivate the capital city … And they are short of hard currency … And then there is the American blockade … None of which quite accounts for thirty-five years' lack of routine maintenance, however worthy the other aims of the regime might be. UNESCO has apparently stepped in. My guidebook tells me they are doing painstaking restoration work in an attempt to save something from the wreckage. Just next door to the hotel is a good example of a magnificent, delicately decorated building being well-maintained and put to good use. The Cento Provincial de Entreramento was built as a fencing school, and is now used mainly for gymnastics. There are two floors of long galleries linked by winding stone staircases. Everyone trains here, from the smallest school children to Cuba's highly successful Olympic-champion gymnasts.

The long airy galleries are ideal for setting up parallel bars, or doing floor exercises. Even the flights of stairs provide excellent indoor training runs for the children. Using a beautiful building, once available only to a privileged élite, for the benefit of the highly successful national sports effort is a symbol of what might have been achieved.

The building opens out on to the Prado (or the Paseo de Martí, as it is officially called). The Prado is a famous city street which has a paved promenade down its centre. In Batista's day it must been a great place to walk, to be watched by secret policemen, and to get hassled by prostitutes and cigar-sellers. Nowadays it is a great place to walk, to be watched by secret policemen, and to get hassled by prostitutes and cigar-sellers.

The Malecón is an even more famous highway, a wide road which sweeps around Havana's waterfront. Here the buildings seem to have fared particularly badly. Perhaps if Cuba was still under American influence the buildings would have gone by now anyway, replaced by high-rise hotel developments or at any rate obliterated by advertisements for McDonald's hamburgers – the disagreeable facets of capitalism. Crumbling buildings, though, make very poor advertisements for Communism.

If the buildings were in a much worse state than I had expected, at first sight the people on the street seemed much better. Cuban Americans had warned me that, cut off from good food, cosmetics and the high life, Cuban Cubans walked around with gloomy faces, poor skin and shabby clothes. In fact Cuba retains a very vivacious atmosphere. Everyone walks around dressed as sexily as possible, the men admiring the girls in their Lycra shorts or revealing dresses. It is all a bit macho in a Latin American way, but at any rate not gloomy. A country of crumbling buildings and beautiful women. Which is, I suppose, better than the other way round.

But it does not require a much closer look to realize that life is actually pretty grim for the average Cuban. The average Cuban queues up not only to get on a bus, but also to buy goods in a shop, when they are available. Basic foodstuffs are rationed. Shops for the average Cuban are dreary counters where your allowance of rice and cooking oil is doled out to you. In one shop I went into, only one product was displayed on the shelves – tins of dull-looking beans. I commiserated with the shopkeeper. It was a shame that was all she had to sell. Actually, she explained, things were worse than that. The tins were empty. They were just there for decoration.

In contrast to the average Cuban, the above-average Cuban, or at any rate the unusual Cuban, can do better. In Cuba if you want to buy luxury items like fashionable clothes, or soap or toothpaste, you have to have hard currency. And 'hard currency' means American dollars. Such is its global power that the American dollar rushes in even where Americans fear to tread. And it does mean that factory workers, doctors, even government officials, struggle to eke out an existence on Cuban pesos, while more and more Cubans turn to prostitution, taxi-driving and selling cigars on the street to foreign tourists. One black-market taxi-driver we spoke to had, only a year before, been one of Havana's most successful businessmen, but he had been driven to taxi-driving by the need to make money that can actually buy something.

It was time to start filming some of this and time, therefore, to make contact with our government minder. His name was Raphael Padilla, Press Attaché at the Ministry of Foreign Affairs. A really jolly good sort, Raphael's mastery of English idiom, ancient and modern, suggested he must have been attached to Cuba's London Embassy since early childhood. In fact he has never been to England, so is a walking tribute to the Cuban education system. He was very bright and breezy, loyal to the regime and anxious to do everything to assist our filming except appear on-camera himself. He did provide a translator/guide for this purpose, a forceful Jamaican woman called Louisa who years before had made her home in Cuba.

The first interview Raphael arranged for us was with Carlos Azugurray, a high-ranking government official: the Advisor to the Foreign Minister on Global Affairs. I met him in the magnificent Foreign Office Building. Foreign Offices always have the best premises, they are the best parlours that all governments keep to impress visitors. This building was a rich man's folly which had been built in the 30s and then donated to the nation.

Mr Azugurray's English was very good as well, though more formal than Raphael's, at least in the setting of a televised interview. With him I essayed some criticism of Cuba's condition. He agreed that economically they were in a bad way, but not in terminal decline. The way forward was still with socialist principles, despite the collapse of the Soviet Empire in Eastern Europe.

But what about the shortage of food, the lack of transport, the collapsing buildings?

Well, that was the Americans' fault for not trading with them.

We got into an interesting discussion about political prisoners. I had yet to speak to any opponents of the regime, but it is the Cubans' human rights record by which, above all, the Americans justify their economic sanctions. There are supposed to be thousands of arrests, hundreds of political prisoners.

The Advisor assured me that Cuba did not have hundreds of political prisoners. When pressed for a figure he suggested that fifty political prisoners might be about it. He stoutly maintained there was freedom of expression – the only thing which was discouraged was support for America – and Cuba most certainly was a democracy.

Wait a minute, democracies usually have different parties, and governments are voted in and out of office. Fidel Castro was President for Life.

No, the Advisor maintained that Cuba was a democracy, even though it was not readily recognized as such by other democracies. Castro is a great man. Not that there was anything like a cult of personality.

• Take me to your leader •

Well, whether he was a cult or not, Castro was the personality I wanted to meet or, at any rate, see in the flesh. And as chance would have it there was a possibility for me to do just that. Recently there had been rumours that Castro might be ill or even dead. It has to be said that there are more of these rumours than there are political prisoners in Cuba's gaols, but there was going to be a big opportunity for Fidel to appear in front of the world's media to show he was still alive.

A shipment of goods was to be landed that day at Mariel Harbour by a group of people called Pastors for Peace. This was a group of American clerics who, appalled by their own government's policy of cutting off supplies of American food and drugs and other essentials, were prepared to break the embargo as a gesture of goodwill. Castro himself had turned up to receive the first boat-load of goods, and he was rumoured to be doing so again today.

We hurried over to Mariel Harbour, which is about an hour's drive from Havana. The trouble with Castro is that he is often scheduled to be at a certain place but then simply does not turn up. Actually, 'scheduled' is the wrong word. Rumours just circulate that he is going to make an appearance, so I suppose he cannot be criticized when the story turns out to be false. Whether the fact that he makes very few public appearances is due to pressure of work, a security measure or because he suffers from Alzheimer's disease is anybody's guess, or prejudice.

The omens were reasonably good at Mariel Harbour. There was enough checking of press accreditation and fussing around by security staff to suggest they really were expecting the great man. There were plenty of news-cameras and reporters. The Reuters reporter was fairly certain Castro would not wish to pass up the chance for excellent publicity. The *Morning Star's* man in Havana agreed.

The Pastors for Peace boat was tied up to the harbour. On board was a yellow school bus and a variety of other necessities. I would imagine a shipload, though impressive, would be little more than a token gesture but the Pastors were well received by the crowd. A very orderly crowd, mainly school children, stood maybe fifty deep along the dockside while the arriving Pastors glad-handed the front rows and received their cheers like political candidates on a walkabout.

The Pastors were an eclectic mixture of religious worthies, the American equivalent of Hampstead intellectuals, student activists and aid workers. A middle-aged lady assured me that her neighbours all thought it was marvellous that she was coming on this trip. Perhaps she was one of the ones from Hampstead.

The excitement built as the speeches began. The Pastors were led by the Rev. Lucius Walker – the new Dr Martin Luther King, according to a sympathetic member of the Press corps. He addressed the crowd in English and his speech was simultaneously translated into Spanish by one of the several people standing on the platform. The line of them up there facing an open-air crowd made the whole thing feel like a proper old-style political rally.

The Rev. Walker's speech started well. He berated America for maintaining a blockade of Cuba, pointing out that America sees itself as the land of the free. He went on to praise the great work that Cubans were doing here, and to call for the assistance of God in promoting the work that had brought him and the boat here. His speech kept reaching a climax and then starting up again, a tactic by which we were teased along for an hour-and-a-half of rhetoric, bombast and oratory. Was this his usual style, or was he just playing for time? Had Castro been delayed?

The speech degenerated into telling us the ages of the people on the boat (youngest twelve, oldest eighty-six, if I remember correctly). The climaxes got weaker and weaker and finally we came to an anti-climax: the realization that Castro was not going to make an appearance after all.

The Press corps sensed this and started to drift away. Enthusiasts in the crowd hung on ready to cheer Fidel's famous bearded face. In the end any beard would have done. We would have cheered David Bellamy. Or anyone with particularly heavy designer stubble.

• Ordinary people •

No luck with the leader, but Raphael was able to set up an interview with some ordinary people. Well, fairly ordinary. Francis is the president of his housing block's CDR – Committee for the Defence of the Revolution. He is in his sixties and lives with his wife in Calle Obispo. Their flat is fairly typical for central Havana. Entered via a gloomy staircase, its high-ceilinged rooms have been divided horizontally to create bedrooms above the living room. Perhaps the strain of these subdivisions has contributed to the collapse of so many buildings over the years.

Francis and his wife are enthusiasts for the revolution and are anxious that we show exactly how bad things are in Cuba, to demonstrate the evil effects of the American boycott.

Although I had some idea of what a CDR was I had assumed it was rather like a Neighbourhood Watch scheme: a small group of community-minded locals keen to do their bit. No, Francis told me, everybody in the block is a member of the committee, except one old woman who is slightly too long in the tooth. And they all report to each other about counter-revolutionary behaviour, which they generally sort out amongst themselves. Only with very serious matters, usually people coming in from other districts, do they have to involve the police. Working through my official translator I never managed to get him to explain what he meant exactly by counter-revolutionary behaviour or counter-revolutionary elements. One abstract expression was always explained by reference to another.

These committees could be seen as the basis of Cuban democracy. Or the basis of all-pervasive social and political control.

What I could see in the shops was certainly further evidence of the desperate conditions of the people. No one appears to be starving, but there is practically nothing for sale. Francis's wife took me to a local store. It was arranged like an indoor market, but the goods on offer would have been left behind at a lacklustre car-boot sale. An old man cheered things up with a tune on his guitar as we inspected a strange selection of bicycle pedals, plastic jewellery and plastic flowers.

Notwithstanding the views of Cuban Americans, Cuba has a very high international reputation for its medical service, but its pharmacies have no drugs. Francis took me to his local chemist's. It is very picturesque with interesting bottles on wooden shelves, an old-fashioned apothecary's. But it has nothing to dispense. Nothing behind the counter except the staff, who continue to work there despite having nothing to do.

Since it was the end of the afternoon we decided to call in at the Café Paris which is not far from Francis's home. This is a lively, trendy place which serves tourists, plus the Cubans who can afford its prices. We had been here before for lunch, which was fine. This afternoon, though, they had run out of coffee and tea. Forced, then, to have a beer, we sat as boys approached us from the other side of the lattice-work windows begging for chewing gum, or cash. 'One dollar' is the street cry of Old Havana. Tourists often hand out pens so the boys even demanded the biro I was using to write up my notes.

• And a packet of Embassies •

The next day we experimented with travelling around Havana in something other than a taxi. Buses seemed rather slow so we eventually came up with the idea of hiring a motorbike. Apart from the police, who have Italian machines, motorcyclists in Cuba make do with rather clumpy Russian bikes, usually with a sidecar. I assured Louisa I was a competent motorcyclist and she sat in the side car urging me to slow down as I fought to move the bike's clumsy gearshift. We managed a tour past the extraordinary edifice which houses the Russian Embassy – it looks rather like an airport control tower. Some people say that, now the Russian presence has been scaled down, the building is going to be converted into a hotel and conference centre. But then some people said Castro was going to be at Mariel Harbour.

While Louisa recovered from the experience of riding with me, I decided to call in at the British Embassy. This proved to be more diffcult than it sounds because it has moved from where the guidebook said it was supposed to be. My tour up and down the lift in the rather run-down block where His Excellency, Our Man in Havana, used to hang out was filmed for its humorous effect but there was, I suppose, a serious point to be made. Surely there should at least be a sign on the door to tell the distraught British visitor where his Embassy has transferred to?

By the time we found the new, temporary, Embassy building it was after-hours. We eventually established that the Ambassador was away and that no one really wanted to comment on Cuba from the British Government's point of view.

• A queue of Cubans •

The Cuban Government, however, wanted us to talk to the crowds queuing up outside the American Embassy, trying to get entry visas.

Actually, it is not the American Embassy. Since America and Cuba do not enjoy political relations, America is only represented in Havana by the American Special Interests section of the Swiss Embassy. But if it were an Embassy, it would be the biggest in Cuba.

You might think that the Cubans would be reluctant to show that dozens of people wait every day for an all-important interview in an attempt to get out of Cuba and into the hated America, but they do have a point to make.

America is no more generous in granting entry visas to Cubans than it is to any other nationality. However, if a Cuban sails to America in a home-made boat, he is automatically granted entry as a political refugee. A clear practical inducement to take to the water.

Anyway, we were supposed to do *vox pops* outside the Embassy with some people who were going to say it was not the Cubans who stopped people leaving Cuba but the Americans who stopped them getting into America. So we sought out people who had been kept waiting by American officials, refused entry, or required to come back month after month or even year after year to have their applications considered.

As it happens, though, we were waylaid by a political protest. An impassioned man, eyes bulging, screamed that it was absolute nonsense to say that the Americans were to blame. America was the only country in the world to take a stand on the human rights abuse in Cuba. It was not America's fault that so many Cubans wanted to leave their own country. He expected to be punished for speaking on-camera, but he no longer cared. He had been condemned to death thirty years before but not executed because he was too young at the time. He had received many death threats since then.

Louisa found all this too difficult to translate, but I got the gist. As did the rest of the crowd who, disgruntled with the United States, should have howled him down. Instead they all cheered him.

• Street life •

On another day I thought I had stumbled on evidence of genuine political discussion and exercise of free speech. In a square called Parc Centrale, a group of men appeared to be having an open-air meeting. Thirty or more of them were yelling and screaming. Now they were all one crowd, then they would divide into smaller groups. Were they political agitators? They were certainly very agitated. Perhaps it was the equivalent of Speaker's Corner? Here Louisa was able to help me. They were arguing about baseball. Baseball may be an all-American sport but it excites real Cuban emotion as well, and is played extensively throughout the island. These men were all beyond the age of actually playing. They had reached that age of man when he is only fit to argue the toss with the likes of Desmond Lynam and Jimmy Hill. So here they come every day, apparently, shouting each other down and putting the world of sport to rights. Lacking a working knowledge of both Spanish and baseball, I confined myself to advocating a change in the LBW law in Test cricket. Most of the crowd looked at me in astonishment, but several vociferously argued that the rules should be left well alone.

• Eat, drink and be merry •

We thought we had better investigate the unofficial side of life in Cuba. Being TV folk we naturally first thought of dinner. Regular restaurants in Havana are not particularly impressive, but we learnt that you can eat well enough on the black market.

I shall be discreet to protect my sources. Not far from one of the most touristy parts of Havana, Hasselbacher [not his real name] runs a restaurant in his house. You get to it through a front courtyard and it consists of a combined kitchen and dining room (and living room for Hasselbacher's family) leading on to another courtyard at the back, where they keep a pig. In the steaming kitchen Hasselbacher presides over his stoves, oblivious to boiling water and fat splashing on to his naked torso, while his wife and other relations sort out the plates and serve local take-away customers who come to the front courtyard.

The children wandered around the table legs and the family's puppy weed on the floor, but in these frankly squalid circumstances we ate the best meal of our stay in Cuba: a huge lobster served in a fantastic broth. (I cannot give you the recipe, Hasselbacher is protecting his sauces.)

All this is illegal for some reason – possibly because you have to pay in US dollars (I suppose the Health Inspectors could probably shut the restaurant down anyway) and Hasselbacher has even been to prison for his crime of providing what people want. He certainly would not let his restaurant appear on-camera, but if you go to Havana, I would recommend you find Hasselbacher's real name and address.

Since it was a family home, the family television was on in the corner. Cubans pick up American programmes using a variety of dustbin lids and tin foil dishes which would sadden the heart of any BSkyB salesman. But Cuba's own TV stations are pretty good as well. We were in Hasselbacher's a night or two after we had been to Mariel Harbour, and watched a live broadcast of Fidel Castro meeting the Pastors for Peace in a TV studio. Various Pastors we had met at the harbour were there being greeted by the Great Leader. So he was still alive.

Or was he? It may have been a trick of the light, or the effect of too much wine with the lobster, but the more I looked at him the more Castro looked like Frankie Howerd wearing a false beard. Now there's a conspiracy theory for you.

It was time to wend our way home, shrugging off the late-night shift of cigar salesmen, rum suppliers and girls anxious to show us the delights of Old Havana in their apartments.

There was another illicit night spot to visit. Yoya is a singer and hostess of her own salsa bar in central Havana. I was told that her bar was in some way illicit or unauthorized so I expected a sort of speakeasy with maybe a hatch to talk through. In fact the bar (again, really the front room of a house) opened directly on to the street so the sounds of its five-piece band (trumpets, guitar, drums) spilled out into the dark night. Clearly it was not regarded as a threat to the authorities.

Yoya herself was a large version of Eartha Kitt. As far as I know she only entertains in this little bar crammed with no more than thirty people, but she exuded star-quality, clasping me to her like an old friend, leading the singing and dancing and winking at the camera. There was no shortage of rum to drink but not quite enough glasses to drink it from. There was no talk of politics – the ostensible reason for our visit. Politics was not on anybody's mind. This was not Communist Cuba, or capitalist Cuba, but the Cuba of a good time and music.

• The morning after •

What could be better for the morning after than a religious experience?

On my first night in Havana I had been introduced to a Venezuelan called Hector. He was dressed all in white because he was being inducted into the Cuban religion known as *Santería*. This is a system of beliefs brought to Cuba by the African slaves. It recognizes a variety of spirits, gods and goddesses which over the centuries became identified with Christian saints, largely, it would seem, to avoid suppression by the Catholic authorities. It has an exotic voodoo quality to it and is increasingly popular in these troubled times. Even Fidel Castro himself is said to be a believer.

The day after my visit to Yoya's, Hector took me to the house of his mentor, Pupi Brinks. A *Santería* shrine was set up there. Up some rather crumbling outside stairs was another shrine to a related faith of Palo, or the Congo religion as Hector called it (the Congo is where this faith originated). This shrine was surrounded by offerings of foodstuffs and chicken and dolls' heads. Hector gave me a special, possibly holy, spirit to drink. There was not much room for the liquid in the bottle as it was crammed with a variety of chillies, peppers, herbs and spices, plus gunpowder. One spark and it would be holy smoke.

I did not have enough time to understand many of the tenets of this religion, but the music was easy enough to get into. Pupi instructs a collection of followers in the discipline of African-style drumming and the dancing which goes with it. So here was yet another crumbling, private house crammed full of sensuous excitement, this time in the morning as they were rehearsing for a performance. But rehearsing with gusto. Half-a-dozen drummers, bongo players and percussionists beat out powerful rhythms, while men, girls and boys danced enthusiastically to the beat. It was all quite intoxicating, although that might have been the spirit.

• Leaving on a Lada •

It was time to go on holiday. Varadero is a little peninsula or spit of land which sticks out into the Caribbean from the north coast of Cuba, about 80 miles east of Havana. It always was a holiday resort but in the new drive for tourist dollars it has been rapidly developed. I was driven there in a Lada taxi along the dual carriageway called the Via Blanca. There are not many other cars on the road. The whole thing looks like a fifties bypass serving thirties levels of traffic.

Along the first few miles there are fields of oil derricks or nodding donkeys with which the Cuban government is hoping to strike lucky.

They already produce some oil but they would like to produce more. There is a smell of sulphur in the air – almost as strong as the smell in Havana when the power station smoke blows in the wrong direction – so perhaps there is some progress being made. Most of the nodding donkeys, though, seem to have forgotten how to nod and stand around rather forlornly in the fields.

Not far from a magnificent bridge I made the mistake of stopping at what looked like a motorway service station, a restaurant called the Moderno. I can only ask for beer, sandwiches and water in Spanish, but I might as well have been asking for *pâté de fois gras*. It was lunchtime but the café had nothing to eat or drink. It was open, and the staff were there, but there was nothing for them to serve. My mistake was in calling at a café for Cubans. Further along the road was a café with plenty to eat. That one is for foreigners.

Varadero is a holiday paradise with hotels and beaches which look exactly like hotels and beaches the world over. The sea here is crystal clear, the sky particularly blue and the sunshine fabulous. It is like every other holiday resort, except for the eerie absence of Americans. But there are plenty of other people – Canadians, Germans, even some Britons – lining up to come here. Eammon Donnelly, the Irish general manager of the Bella Costa Hotel, is very enthusiastic about the trading conditions in Cuba: strong central government, very well-educated and well-behaved staff. This was the positive side of the Cubans' complaints that they were producing the most literate head-waiters in the world and the brainiest whores.

Either way it illustrates the grim paradox. Only by having a well-developed socialist system do you produce staff with the education and attitude to serve in a capitalist palace.

And capitalist palace it is. Here the bloated tourist can eat until he bursts on an island where the bulk of the population is rationed to a few pounds of rice a month. The socialist revolution is being sustained by providing a playground for visitors from the free-enterprise world. The whole area of Varadero is notorious for the number of prostitutes who are attracted to the rich foreign visitors. But is Cuba prostituting itself and its revolution by getting its foreign income in this way?

I made my excuses and left, and went back to Havana to talk to the civil rights movement.

• Going underground •

Angela Herrera is the President of the Cuban Democratic Coalition, one of the many internal opposition groups in Cuba. When contacting her we tried to be as discreet as possible. We did not think we had any reason to fear for ourselves, but there are plenty of stories of people speaking to foreign media who are picked up once the media have left.

Angela Herrera is used to trouble from the authorities. According to Cuban American literature, her home is under continuous siege by the secret police. It was not as bad as that, but we assumed that her local CDR would notice a British TV team paying her a visit. To reduce our numbers we did without our official translator and, indeed, our film camera (we had the sort of video camera that any tourist might carry).

She lived in one of the apparently ubiquitous gloomy Havana flats. Angela has been arrested on countless occasions over the years and imprisoned, usually for short periods, but at one point had the prospect of a seven-year prison sentence hanging over her head. The previous year she had been on hunger strike. In court, Angela is not represented by lawyers – there would be no point.

Angela is very popular with Cuban American groups, especially because she is black. Cubans come in all shades of black and white and all points in-between, and as a national group they seem tolerably well integrated. But the vast majority of Cuban Americans lobbying in Washington are from the lighter end of the spectrum, which sustains the belief that it is only the rich and the white who object to Castro. He is said to remain most popular with blacks despite the fact that he is white and his chosen companions are more or less exclusively white as well.

Right from the word go, Angela objected to the revolution. 'Batista was nothing compared to Castro', and she is angry about the oppression she and her family suffer for claiming what she regards as the basic human right of self-expression. Identified as an 'opposition' family, they found life even harder than everyone else did. They were convinced that Angela's grandson was excluded from his school basketball team because of the family's political stance. Angela was prepared to speak in public and has paid the penalty many times for having done so. How many others are too scared to speak their mind?

We filmed another scene on a video camera. Three young guys wanted to talk to us, on-camera, but they wanted their identities kept secret. None of them claimed to be political activists but they were all desperate to get away from Cuba. One had tried to escape in a little boat but had managed no more than 10 miles of the 90-mile journey. A baby had fallen overboard and the whole thing had been a dreadful farce. Another guy had made two attempts but had been arrested on both occasions and gone to gaol. The third said he would never dare try to escape. He had spent some time working in Czechoslovakia and was therefore a rich man in Cuba as he had been able to bring back a motorbike and sell it.

Mr Azuguarry had assured me that Cubans were free to leave the country, but to these men that was a joke.

Did they blame the Americans for the poor economic conditions within Cuba? No, the system here in Cuba was the problem. They had no future. All there was to do, said one in broken English, was to 'drink rum, if you had the money, and fock'. He claimed that everybody hated Castro and wanted to leave, including his own family. (One of Castro's daughters made a highly publicized exit from the country. Castro's brother Raúl remains in power as he has done for 35 years.)

Since these men were not in any way political activists their remarks seemed all the more poignant. The broken-English speaker was kind enough to say that it was a pleasure to talk to me because he was able to express himself freely for a short while. Normally he felt like a slave. I put it to him that the Government asserts there is free speech and democracy in Cuba. The suggestion was met with scorn.

• Special interests •

It was nearly time to leave Cuba. On our last day we finally got permission to interview an official in the American Special Interests section of the Swiss Embassy.

There is nothing very Swiss about the American Special Interests section. Opposite the building the Cubans have thoughtfully sited a billboard on which they can post one of their many anti-Yankee messages for the benefit of the Americans over the road. Inside, the offices are guarded by a detachment of Marines. A popular posting for marines?

Not really, as apparently there is a strict non-fraternization rule. A difficult rule to obey for a fit young Marine in a country where there are plenty of women keen on fraternizing, especially with anyone who has hard currency in his pocket.

Gene Bigler, the First Secretary, is tall, large and bearded. A great cuddly bear of a man who had been an academic before joining the Diplomatic Corps. Strangely, it had been almost as hard to get an interview with him as it had been to catch sight of Castro, but in the event he was as relaxed as all Americans seem to be on-camera.

I reminded Mr Bigler of the absurd efforts America had made to get rid of Castro over the previous thirty-five years. The CIA-backed Bay of Pigs Invasion mounted in 1961 by a collection of Cuban Americans had been an utter failure; the blowing up of an airliner had been murderous; the attempts to use thallium salts to make Castro's beard fall out, to poison him with a tuberculosis-impregnated diving suit, to send him exploding cigars, to kill him using *femmes fatales* and other nonsense had been utter farce.

Mr Bigler wryly agreed this must have provided some comic relief for students of international relations, but maintained that Cuba's human rights record justified America's opposition to Castro's government.

Wasn't it, I wondered, simply the longest sulk in history? American businesses had been nationalized and America could not stand this impudent left-wing upstart who was right on its doorstep. Why else would a blockade be maintained against Cuba, and yet China be granted most-favoured-nation status?

No, the United States was entitled to object to its citizens' capital being seized and to refuse to trade with a country whose policies it disapproved of, and anyway it was not a blockade, just an embargo.

Either way, does not America's refusal to trade with Cuba provide Castro with the perfect excuse for his country's woes?

Not at all. The ports of Mexico and South America were as close to Cuba as Miami. It was the Communist system which was at fault. The American embargo scarcely affects Cuba's comic well-being.

If that was so, one wonders why they bother imposing the embargo in the first place. Also such a theory ignores the overwhelming influence America has on world trade and the fact that under the Cuba Democracy Act (The Torricelli Bill) it is attempting to force foreign businesses and countries to break their links with Cuba as well.

I also put the point to him that, by allowing Cubans automatic political refugee status if they fetched up in American jurisdiction but no special deals in the issuing of visas, the US Government was inadvertently encouraging Cubans to risk their lives in little boats or even deliberately for the propaganda value.

No, that was the result of two separate policy considerations. In general, Mr Bigler addressed the issues expertly and diplomatically, but I wonder if behind it all there is considerable embarrassment at the position America finds itself in with relation to Cuba. For all its influence in the world, America is trapped on this issue. The sanctions America uses against Cuba, whether you call them a blockade or an embargo, look like a sledge-hammer to crack a nut. And the fact of the matter is that the nut is still there. China is too big to shut out, but Cuba is too close for comfort.

While Castro remains in power, America looks impotent, but if Cuba's economy collapses altogether, will Communism or America get the blame?

One important factor in maintaining America's total opposition to Castro and all his works is that the million or more Cuban Americans are an extremely powerful and vocal political force. So my next step was to go back to Miami to meet some of them.

I have already mentioned Jorge Mas Conosa, the grandfather or perhaps godfather of the Cuban American Community. He agreed to see me in his office in the middle of the day on which his company was completing a take-over of some size. Mr Mas Conosa is not a large man but he is very powerful. He delivers lectures rather than answers questions and must be a formidable force in Washington where he argues the Cuban American's case from a right-wing perspective. He has been an exile for a long time. An opponent of Batista, he was an exile even before Castro came to power. He is fiercely anti-Communist and anti-Castro.

Castro, he insisted, has turned Cuba from one of the richest Latin American countries to one of the poorest. He will not have it that Cuba under Castro has achieved anything remarkable in the social or medical sphere. Costa Rica has done just as well and, in any case, was an improvement in medical care worth the arrests and imprisonment and exiles? More than one-fifth of Cubans now live in exile.

He did not think it anomalous that America imposed trade sanctions on Cuba. He rattled off a list of other countries to which these restrictions had applied. And why, he asked, was it all right for England to have imposed sanctions on South Africa because of its human rights record, but not all right to do the same to Cuba?

Like many Cuban Americans, he has become very successful in America but is keen to go back to rebuild Cuba. Strangely, if he ever gets his chance, he would probably rebuild it in America's likeness, so the long-term effect of Castro's revolution may be to make Cuba even more Americanized than it was when he took over.

A more impressive anti-Castro witness was the security guard just coming on duty in the office block as I was leaving. He told me he had been a political prisoner in Cuba, where he had been closely confined in a cell with other prisoners. They all had to urinate and defecate where they stood. He and his fellow prisoners were fed practically nothing. If their wives or girlfriends brought food when they visited them at the prison they would be subjected to intimate and offensive searches. He had eventually been released in the Mariel boat-lift, when Castro emptied his prisons and allowed America to take a motley collection of political prisoners like himself, plus pimps, drug-runners and mental patients. More than 100 000 people in all. But, he said rather quietly, even here in America where he has found freedom, people do not really want to listen when you tell them of experiences like that. They do not believe you.

• I want to be in America •

The next day I flew with *Hermanos Al Rescate*, or Brothers to the Rescue. This is a group of volunteer Cuban Americans who fly little four-seater planes from the coast of Florida out over the sea to spot people fleeing Cuba in their home-made boats. The US Coastguard does not have the resources to maintain sufficient patrols but does respond when it is informed of sinking boats or people washed up on a rocky island. (Brothers to the Rescue do not do any of the picking-up themselves.)

There is some danger in this activity. On the day I flew with them, a senior member of the group was suffering from a broken leg which he had sustained in a recent accident, and another young man was getting used to a wheelchair, having been paralysed from the waist down from another crash. As he checked our plane, Carlos, my pilot, wished to assure me that these were both incidents caused by mechanical failure rather than pilot error.

Brothers to the Rescue fly over the ocean looking for a raft. This can be as pathetic as a few planks of wood tied together, or even only a couple of tractor tyres. Some rafts have outboard motors, some just drift with the current. Some make it, some do not. Some get picked up by Cuban gunboats before they reach Florida. Some sink.

Only 90 miles separate Cuba from Miami, but that is oceans of ocean to get lost in. But if these people make it, they have really made it.

As we flew on, looking for a raft of people to whom we could throw a message and a marker flare, it struck me that this was a satisfying activity for these volunteers. Not as self-indulgent as merely island-hopping would be, not as dangerous as going off to war. Self-sacrifice and good fun in one package. It was hard not to get carried along by their enthusiasm, and equally hard not to have a good time flying around in the sky.

In the aircraft hangar there is a woman called Maggie who organizes things back at base while the aircraft are in the air. She can remember, as a young girl, being really excited by Castro's revolution. She reckoned that Castro had the support of 90 per cent of the Cuban population, but within a year everything had gone sour. She was glad to get away, as were the people spotted in the sea that day.

For years I can remember Cuba being held up as an example of what Communism can achieve, and Castro was heralded as a leader who remained popular with his people. Opponents of Communism explained this away as being the result of the subsidies and help that Cuba received from the Soviet Union. Now the boot is on the other foot. And it is Castro's failures which now have to be explained away, usually by referring to the American blockade or boycott. The only thing worse than trading with the enemy is not trading with the enemy.

The sad thing about the Cuban revolution is that, even in its own terms, it has failed. The buildings are falling down, the people are desperately poor, desperate to get away or simply desperate. Political prisoners are in the gaols, prostitutes are on the streets, the American dollar is in demand: the very conditions that inspired the revolution in the first place. But perhaps it is true that all revolutions eventually bring things full-circle.

I had an hour or two left to walk along the smart streets of Miami Beach. As I strolled past its shops crammed with stylish clothes, its restaurants and fast-food stores and bars offering every sort of delight, it struck me what a paradise in material terms this must seem to a half-starved Cuban refugee who washes up here after several days at sea and several years on subsistence-level rationing. In 500 yards, though, I was approached by four beggars asking me if I could spare any change.

At least I wasn't mugged.

OUR
MAN
IN... DOMINICA

AS island paradises go, Dominica is not well-known. Its name does not help. Christopher Columbus spotted the island on 3 November 1493, which happened to be a Sunday, and it has been called after the Latin word for the Sabbath more or less ever since.

Explorers were always doing that sort of thing – Easter Island, Man Friday, Sheffield Wednesday – but it is not always useful. Certainly with Dominica, the name does not really capture the essence of the place. It implies a special connection with the Lord's Day or Latin America, when in reality it has neither. It is actually a former British colony, with an English-speaking population retaining strong links with the Commonwealth and the United Kingdom.

But mispronounce Dominica, as many people do, and it is easy to confuse it with its much larger Caribbean neighbour, the Spanish-speaking Dominican Republic (Haiti's other half in the island of Hispaniola). Worse than that, pronounce it correctly, as Domi-nee-ca, and it is easy to confuse it with the greatest hit record of the Singing Nun.

It is not much better writing it down. A good deal of mail intended for Dominica gets misdirected to the Dominican Republic, even if you use its correct title, 'The Commonwealth of Dominica'.

Quite apart from the problems of its own name, Dominica is an island in a sea of confusing nomenclature. The Caribbean Islands, especially those once owned by Britain, are often referred to as the West Indies. (Another of Columbus's contributions; he thought he had got to India when actually he had sailed West across the Atlantic. St Columbus is the patron saint of baggage handlers.)

The term 'West Indies' lives on chiefly as the name of the cricket team assembled from players who come from a variety of now quite separate independent countries brought together to humiliate the all-England team of Robin Smith, Allan Lamb and Graeme Hick. Plus Philip De Freitas, who was in fact born in Dominica.

Dominica forms part of a chain of islands called the Antilles, or more specifically the Lesser Antilles, as any atlas will tell you. In my experience you seldom come across the term 'Lesser Antilles' or 'Greater

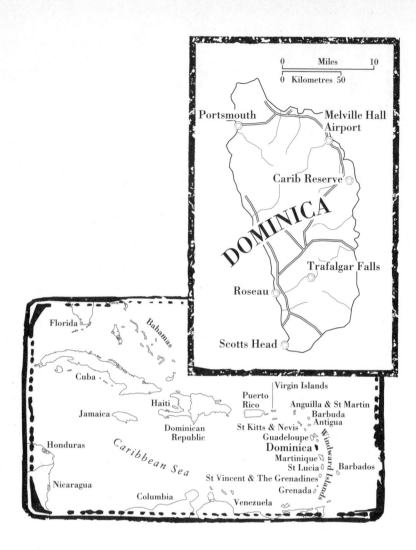

Antilles' in everyday life. Within the Lesser Antilles, Dominica is part of the Windward Islands. Dominican bananas are normally sold as Windward Island Bananas, although, as it happens, until the Second World War Dominica was regarded as one of the Leeward Islands. Perhaps the wind of change was blowing around the area at the time.

The complication of all these geographical terms is matched by the untidy colonial history of the region. Looking down the Antilles in an atlas, one finds islands with allegiances, or former allegiances, to Britain, France, Spain, Holland and the United States of America. It is an apparently random pattern of political and linguistic attachments produced by the ebb and flow of military and maritime fortunes two or three hundred years ago. The epitome of this illogicality must be the tiny island of St Martin (also known as Sint Maarten) which, despite having an area of less than 25 square miles, is divided in jurisdiction between Holland and France. Why they don't just give it to Belgium and have done with it, goodness only knows.

Dominica is not quite as complicated as that. It was fought over by the French and the British right up to the beginning of the nineteenth century. Britain ultimately prevailed, but there is a local French-based patois and quite a number of French words which have found their way into everyday (English) speech.

In fact, Dominica is now located between what are officially two French departments, Martinique and Guadeloupe. The French notion of decolonization is to alter the status of a colony to a county, and then insist that no one notices that these departments are to be found thousands of miles from the mainland.

Dominica was one of the last of the Caribbean islands to be conquered, colonized or otherwise taken from the Carib people by the European powers after the New World was 'discovered'. Approaching Dominica, especially by air, one can immediately see why. It is almost entirely made of densely wooded, steeply sloped mountains and valleys. There are practically no beaches to provide easy landing points. Altogether very difficult territory to invade. No doubt as a result of that, there is an area of Dominica in which the last survivors of the Carib people are still living. To have a reservation on one island in a sea named after them may not be much, but I suppose it is something.

Dominica is a challenging place to invade, and also a challenging place to make an economic success. Its lack of beaches limits its attraction to tourists, so it has avoided the destructive force of tourism. But it also misses out on the income now enjoyed by St Lucia, and almost all of the nearby islands, which comes from holiday-makers heading for a paradise which has to include a white sand beach where you can lie in the sun before or after or instead of swimming in the sea.

At different times in its history, Dominica has enjoyed some fairly prosperous periods growing sugar, limes or vanilla, but for the past forty years it has made its living from bananas. This banana trade is, however, under threat. Bananas grown here are produced by independent farmers on remote mountain small-holdings. Bigger, fatter and cheaper bananas are produced on bigger, flatter and more profitable plantations in Costa Rica and other Latin American countries. How serious is the threat to Dominica's banana trade, and how serious would it be for Dominica if the trade were to collapse altogether?

Finding out was the reason for my visit.

• Just off the banana boat •

The trade in bananas with Dominica, and all the Windward Islands, is conducted by one company: Geest.

A leisurely way to arrive in the Windward Islands is to get there by a Geest banana boat. Setting off from Southampton, it takes eight days to cross the Atlantic, eight days to go from island to island, and eight days to sail home again.

There is room for twelve passengers. And they make the crossing in style: black tie for dinner, gin slings and Scrabble for recreation. Plus food of the highest order. It is all redolent of an age when there was more pink on the map than on Barbara Cartland's cocktail dress. There are dozens of cruise ships which ply their trade up and down the Caribbean, but this one is different. A banana boat is not like a cruise ship (cruise ships are really far too Billy Butlin, according to virtually all twelve of Geest's passengers) and has the disadvantage of not being as stable in rough weather. I joined the Geest boat to get to Dominica, but only after it had reached the Caribbean and had already weathered several storms in the Atlantic. It had been a particularly rough crossing, but by the time I joined the passengers they had recovered their composure and were, on the face of it, having a very good time indeed.

They were certainly all in a healthy frame of mind to tuck into a five-course dinner which featured some excellent crab backs (a local delicacy), and Beef Wellington, a suitably imperial reminder of home. They took in their stride the intrusion of me and my film crew, and I was berated on all sides one for being so easy to confuse with Clive James – same name, same lack of hair, eyes and neck. I am pretty sure they could have kept up joshing of this sort for the entire twenty-four days if I had been with them for the whole voyage.

A banana boat is not a cheap way to travel and not everyone would enjoy being tossed around for nearly a month in the company of eleven other well-heeled fellow travellers. Your travel plans do sometimes have to be changed at short notice to accommodate the demands of the bananas, but Geest have no difficulty in filling their very well-appointed cabins.

It is all very old-fashioned, quirky and British. And like everything else which is old-fashioned, quirky and British, it is not going to last.

To me the ways of business are strange: Geest make a profit on their passengers, which must, you would think, be a comfort when the income from bananas can go down as well as up, and sometimes threatens to disappear altogether. However, as and when they replace their banana boats, the people at Geest who decide these things are getting rid of the passenger accommodation. Apparently it costs a lot to fit out a ship with cabins and so forth, and takes eight years to recoup that money from the fares. And that is not fast enough. Compared with the time it will take to make money on the Channel Tunnel, or most skyscrapers in London, eight years must be a drop in the ocean, but there you have it. Next week a big-businessman will explain why it made sense to keep London's Centre Point empty for twenty years.

Anyway, bidding a fond farewell to Captain Flannagan, and the passengers with whom he dines every night, I jumped ship in Dominica. In the meantime, bananas were getting on board. They were being brought from all over the island, checked, weighed, graded and loaded.

Boxes are put on to pallets and pallets are put on to the ship using cranes. Occasionally there is a crash, and some bananas setting out on the long journey to an English fruit bowl fall at the first hurdle. The dock-workers, like dockers and packers the world over, bear these occasional accidents with equanimity, and are allowed to take a few damaged bananas home with them.

• Banana splits •

Dominica has been an independent nation since 1978. Its trading arrangements as far as bananas are concerned go back to colonial times, and its critics say they still smack of the days of the Empire.

In the thirties, bananas which grew well in the Caribbean (they need lots of sunshine and rain) were chosen as a crop to bring cash to the Windward Islands and fruit to Britain. The Second World War rather disrupted things but afterwards the trade resumed and in 1954 Geest took over the shipping of bananas, and things really began to prosper.

Geest was a successful British horticultural firm, founded by two Dutch brothers, whose original business was importing bulbs from Holland. Its move into importing bananas from the Windward Islands was a spectacular success. Geest came to outstrip Fyffes and Jamaica Producers (both of whom import bananas from Jamaica) as banana suppliers to Britain. Geest currently imports about 60 per cent of the UK's bananas.

Under more or less paternalistic arrangements, the Windward Islands were allowed a protected market. The Windwards and Geest have profited from the deal. And the contract with Geest was renewed after Dominica's independence. Under this contract, Geest buy all the bananas from Dominica's producers and ship them to Britain. (The same arrangement applies on the other Windward islands.) Geest gets the best price it can from the retailers in the UK and pays the farmers, but only after it has deducted the cost of shipping, ripening and marketing the bananas, and taken its own profit on all those operations. The ordinary farmer has to bear his own costs, such as paying for fertilizer and vehicles. The farmer might receive about 10 per cent of the retail price of the banana.

It is anything but a free market. Dominica's farmers and Geest's profits rely upon the preferential tariff protection of the British government. There is much to recommend the arrangement. It is difficult for a small island like Dominica to produce anything in large enough quantities to make it economical to transport it to the rest of the world. Having one product and a guaranteed market solves many of these problems. But there are obvious dangers. Being dependent on one crop, dependent on one company, dependent on one foreign government's preferential tariff protection makes the Dominicans, well over-dependent.

Disease, or a hurricane, might ruin the banana crop, but as it is the dangers on the horizon are the Single European Market and the GATT Trade Deal. There is not a great deal that Dominicans can do about either of these things, but they are increasingly doubting whether it is a great deal that they get from Geest.

Mind you, Shelford Scotland, the first man I talked to on the island, was not minded to criticize the arrangements. He thought the forty-year old contract with Geest was an excellent one. Up and down the island he sees people able to afford 4-wheel drive pick-ups and cars, there is food in the shops and wealthy-looking people. All right, it is forty years with one company. But if you are with a wife for forty years, and you're happy with her, why change her?

Well, Scottie, as he is known, has worked for Geest for most of the forty years they have been trading. He is now the manager of their dockside operations in Dominica. So I suppose he would say that, but I went off to explore the island and to see if his view was in the majority.

The main town of Dominica is Roseau. It is a sleepy little place made up for the most part of streets of little wooden buildings with brightly painted balconies. It has a dour Roman Catholic cathedral and a large Anglican church. There are some other public buildings but mostly it is small-scale and low-key. It has a waterfront promenade which looks very familiar, as well it might, having been built recently by McAlpine. It is one corner of a foreign field which is forever Frinton. Nearby is an unusual plaque which says:

The British were here, thank God.

I say it is unusual. Perhaps there is one like it in Dublin.

As a rule I am not one for feeling guilt about the actions of my countrymen before I was born. Nor, to be fair, would I claim any credit for their success. But there is something dreadful about realizing that almost the entire population of an island like Dominica is there only because their ancestors were slaves brought on British and other European ships. It is particularly dreadful because, even by the standards of the day, I would suggest it was an entirely immoral thing to do. Certainly slavery was not recognized or lawful within England itself, as a slave-owner discovered to his cost in 1772. He brought his slave home from the West Indies, whereupon the slave, James Sommersett, brought an action for *habeas corpus*. The judge, Lord Mansfield, found in the slave's favour, ending his judgment with the resounding cry, 'The Black must be discharged.' (Sommersett's Case, 20 St. Tr. 1.)

Nowadays, Roseau looks a simple sort of place, not rich but not stricken with poverty. Undeveloped rather than underdeveloped. And quiet. Except that when I arrived it was carnival time.

Carnival celebrates the beginning of Lent or the end of slavery or something like that. You get carnivals all over the Caribbean and in Dominica you get them all over the island. On Monday and Shrove Tuesday there are two days of dancing in the streets, drinking to excess, music to burst the eardrums, costumes, displays and parades. In England, we make pancakes.

Actually, it is obvious that the British influence is still strong as the whole thing is clearly modelled on the Notting Hill Carnival.

Mostly, the carnival consists of a procession of large lorries carrying even larger sound systems. There are a few live bands but recorded music predominates. Either way the music is loud enough to make your heart cavity vibrate to the bass beat. Presumably the flimsy wooden buildings can only survive this annual onslaught because they are built to withstand hurricane-force winds.

During the day, groups of youngsters and oldsters dress up in co-ordinated costumes: as angels, Egyptians, local firemen or London policemen; but as the day wears on it is the individuals with their individual idea of what to wear who catch the eye. One guy washes himself from time to time, covering his body in soap suds at key points on the procession route, others wear Wellington boots and swimming trunks. It is as though the whole island has suddenly dived into a dressing-up box. A large number of men dress in women's clothes. They do not seem to be camping it up, or even playing for laughs like pantomime dames. Nobody could explain to me why this is so popular. Maybe they are related to Tory MPs.

Most of the time the sun shines on what is undoubtedly a carnival atmosphere, but every now and then there is a rain shower which lasts for a few minutes. However, this is ignored by the crowd and it just goes away.

As the evening wears on, the crowds in the narrow streets develop a sort of rhythmic shuffle. Not so much a dance as a very energetic bus queue. Young and old people join in, the really energetic having started at 4 a.m. on the Monday with the opening event (this is called *Jové* and is when things are really wild).

The jump-up continues that afternoon and evening and all day Tuesday. The action ends at 8 p.m. by order of the police. This is to prevent the wild behaviour and violence which apparently happened on previous years. The ordinance is not popular but is obeyed with more or less a good grace.

The population of Dominica is about 70 000. That is less than it takes to fill Wembley Stadium. But while the carnival is on, it is as noisy as Wembley with a Cup Final taking place plus three or four rock concerts happening at the same time.

The music is highly repetitive with two or three high-volume calypsos coming round and round again. One, called *Kool Pipe*, has a message about Aids and safe sex. (There is a dangerously erotic feel to carnival music.) More popular is *Tiwé Yo*. The words are local patois for 'take them out'. This means throw away the rotten fruit and, by extension, kick out those responsible for the running of the banana trade. Ultimately this means get rid of the ruling Dominica Freedom Party and its leader Prime Minister, Dame Eugenia Charles.

• The iron lady •

Dame Eugenia Charles has a flat right on the route of the carnival. She recently moved there from her family home which was in a leafy valley out of town.

As leader of the Dominica Freedom Party (DLF), she has been Prime Minister of the island since 1980. She is conservative, favours co-operation with Britain and America (she was active in promoting America's intervention in Grenada) and is opposed by the more radical United Worker's Party, and another opposition party, the Labour Party.

Dame Eugenia is dignified and wise and not a little weary, I would guess, at trailing across the Atlantic to London (and nowadays Brussels) trying to put deals together to keep her nation's economy afloat.

Her flat is unpretentious, neat and tasteful. It could belong to a retired civil servant in Hove. Whatever criticisms the voters of Dominica may have of her (and these days they have many), her home is clear testimony that there has been no corruption or personal gain from her years in power.

She studied law in Canada and England, where she was called to the Bar, returning to Dominica to practise law before embarking on her political career, in which she has been so successful. But is she now too deferential to Geest, Britain, America, to rich white capitalists generally?

Dame Eugenia meets such allegations with a weary shrug and a sharp analysis of her country's position. The position is not good. For forty years Britain has conducted a policy of buying bananas from Dominica and the other Windward Islands. By restricting the market in Britain the price to the customer is higher than it would be in a free market. But Britain is now part of Europe and Europe is supposed to be a single market. So how are Windward Island bananas supposed to compete with cheaper bananas that are already imported into the continent of Europe from Latin America? The answer is only by a lot of personal contact and special pleading.

For example, take a look at the delightfully titled Banana Protocol of the Fourth Lomé Convention.

Lomé is in Togo, and there every five years a group of African, Caribbean and Pacific nations (ACP) meet the European Union to negotiate trading arrangements in the light of closer European integration. In general the single European market requires the abandonment of the special deals which ACP states have with former colonial powers. But at the fourth meeting (Lomé IV), it was agreed that, with respect to bananas, each ACP country would be allowed to retain its established access to its traditional markets.

The French are OK on this as they have their former colonies to think of. But the Germans are a problem. They have no imperial debts to pay. The German housewife, apparently, likes her bananas big and cheap rather than small and juicy, which is what we go for in Britain. But if Germans import cheaper bananas from other parts of the world, what is to stop them finding their way to England?

And there is GATT. Bananas stick out like sore thumbs in the global liberalization of trade under the General Agreement on Tariffs and Trade.

One of your main activities, if you are Prime Minister of a place like Dominica, is to fly to Britain and Brussels on a regular basis to argue that the elaborate structure of tariffs and trade deals should be left in place. The only real argument is that, without all this support, the island economy would collapse altogether.

To add a touch of drama to the TV documentary, it is edited to suggest that I followed Dame Eugenia to London to cover a meeting she had with Baroness Chalker at the House of Lords. This will no doubt annoy the hard-pressed licence-fee payer.

> *Dear BBC, Why, oh why did Clive James have to fly to London,*
> *at our expense may I add, in the middle of his film about the*
> *Dominican Republic? Wouldn't it have been possible to film a*
> *meeting at a time when he was already in London?*
> *Yours,*
> *(Name and address withheld because I haven't paid my licence*
> *fee yet.)*

Actually, it was possible, and I did meet Dame Eugenia and Baroness Chalker before setting off for the Caribbean. On a personal level they clearly get on like a house on fire. Baroness Chalker is also very much the politician, praising to the heavens Dame Eugenia's sterling qualities which have enabled her to battle on behalf of her island's bananas for many years.

The trouble is that, however benignly Britain may continue to look upon the West Indies, the maintenance of preferential tariffs or subsidies for the benefit of Dominican banana farmers is quite difficult to justify, especially when criticizing the Common Agricultural Policy for subsidizing French, German or Italian farmers, since they at least have a vote in European elections.

In London and in Dominica, Dame Eugenia dryly recounts that she has explained to the German representatives that if Dominica loses its banana trade it would have nothing to turn to but drugs. And it would not be impossible to make it legal to export cannabis to Germany, or the departments of France which are but a rowing boat ride away, in order to keep Dominica afloat. (Dominican cannabis is, she has heard, like its bananas, amongst the best in the world.) She cannot be serious. Or can she?

We decide I should interview Commissioner Blanchard, head of the Dominican police, to discover something about drugs trafficking on the Island.

Commissioner Blanchard is known to the criminal classes as 'The Fox', and just talking to him I could sense why. He was not to be bested in any verbal exchanges:

'It must be unusual for you to be answering the questions, Commissioner … I dare say you normally ask the questions here?'

'We don't normally do the questioning in my office.'

'Perhaps it's done lower down in the dungeons, in the depths, below these offices?'

'In this police headquarters, everything is above board and above ground.'

He could not imagine drugs being legalized. Dominica has a drugs problem, but no more so than anywhere else in the world. His department was lacking in resources to apprehend those growing cannabis in the mountains or landing it, or harder drugs, at remote points on the coast.

They had recently detained someone who had escaped from a prison in Guadeloupe and were working out what to do with him. There is no extradition treaty between France and Dominica. He also showed me a huge pile of cannabis which had been confiscated the night before in a raid. One of the men who had been caught with it had tried to fight Mr Blanchard's officers. He had lost.

Wiping my hands clean of traces of the drug I had been invited to touch (you cannot be too careful if there is any chance of forensic science being employed against you), I got on to the main subject of my enquiries, the banana.

• Broadcast views •

Wanting to hear the views of the ordinary working Dominican, I naturally went straight to the Dominican Broadcasting Corporation. I met there a radio producer and presenter, Ken Richards. On the basis of phone calls to his station he was able to say that people were agitated about the price of bananas. Over in St Lucia there had been riots about it, and, unlike Dominica, the St Lucians had a highly developed tourist trade to turn to.

Ken agreed to drive me around the island to meet some farmers, even though he was a little fragile having been up the night before at the carnival. In fact I had seen him, wearing a dress, dancing in the street. And he had continued carnivalling well after the 8 p.m. curfew which had only been enforced in Roseau, not in the more remote towns and villages.

To meet the farmers you have to go up into the hills, which is where the farms are. But it is not difficult to find the hills because they are everywhere. Roads are generally narrow and very bendy, with just enough room for vehicles to pass when going in opposite directions. It takes about an hour and a half to drive from Roseau to the opposite end of the island where the main airport (Melville Hall) is situated. The whole island is a gem. The jagged hillsides which, in Scotland, say, would be cold and windswept and covered with tussocks of grass and heather, here support tropical rainforests. Areas under cultivation are covered in banana plantations, which are themselves lush and green, here and there interrupted by groves of citrus trees that someone once thought would be a commercial success. It seemed that wherever we stopped to ask directions, to film part of the journey, to take a look at the view, it was possible to reach over to a tree and grab a grapefruit or a banana or a breadfruit that would otherwise be going to waste. A paradise indeed. But man cannot live by breadfruit alone. What about the people?

The first person Ken took me to see was Clement Ferreira, who farms towards the north of the island near the Layou River. (The largest of Dominica's rivers, according to a sign provided 'courtesy of the British Government'.)

Clement loves bananas. As a crop they are 'always willing', as he put it. In the largely unchanging tropical climate there is always enough sun, always enough rain. Every fortnight all the year round you can harvest something. There is sometimes too much wind. Hurricanes destroy the whole crop, but regular heavy winds can damage enough leaves to reduce yields. There are not enough nutrients in the ground, so fertilizers have to be applied and they soon run off the steep slopes. But the banana is, taken as a whole, always willing.

Many of the bunches around the island are grown inside blue plastic bags. It looks as though they produce their own wrapping ready for Sainsburys' shelves. In fact the bags are put on to accelerate growth, in the same way that an English cold frame works. Clement does not trouble to do this, reckoning the labour cost of putting on the bags outweighs the economic gain of faster growing times.

Botanically, the banana plant is a monocotyledon, a term which describes how many leaves it produces when its seed germinates. This puts it in the same category as grass. Banana trees grow to a height of 10 feet or more, but basically they are just overgrown bits of lawn. Although that is rather like dismissing a tiger as a jumped-up tabby cat, or a Great Dane as nothing more than a dachshund with high suspension.

As arranged on Dominica, banana plantations are agreeable and relaxing. Work is quite labour-intensive, with banana hands having to hack back leaves and branches with machetes and in due course pick the grown fruit. But for a great deal of the time the banana trees just lap up the sun and the rain showers and produce bananas by the handful.

Clement Ferreira cannot see himself staying in bananas much longer, however much he likes them. The banana is willing, but the price is weak. At the price they are fetching at the moment, he is not making a profit at all. But he has no alternative way to make a living. Dame Eugenia had outlined a number of schemes to improve things including one to organize the workers into entrepreneurial units, travelling round the farms hiring out their labour and using their own pick-up trucks. She seemed to pin some hopes on this to raise the living standards of the workers while lowering labour costs to the farmers. But Clement dismissed this notion out of hand. He would still have to run his own pick-up truck to travel round the island and get his bananas to the ship. Why would he want to pay for the use of someone else's pick-up as well?

No, he would be out of bananas by next April, if things did not improve. I wonder for how many years he has been saying that. And whether this year it may turn out to be true.

Cletina Benjamin has got out of bananas. She started in bananas by carrying boxes of them at the dockside, supporting herself when she was fifteen and pregnant with her first child. She progressed over the years to the position where she was able to buy 4 acres of banana plantation when Geest were selling off the land they owned on Dominica (they no longer own any here). She explains she had to sell one of her acres to a housing development to pay for the land she had bought. In fact, she got as much for that single acre as she had paid for the whole lot, which sounds like a good deal, but it just was not practicable for her to support herself on her remaining 3 acres. And as she explained as she sat outside her small wooden house, Geest no longer pick up bananas from Portsmouth (her local town), so she would have to transport them to Roseau. This is more expensive both in fuel and in the almost inevitable damage to the easily bruised bananas as they bounce around in the back of a pick-up.

Cletina can still eat her own bananas and sell some coconuts from her few coconut trees, but she does not farm the bananas as such. In fact I could not quite grasp how she makes a living. Her daughter, Anne Marie, is not interested in bananas at all. She appears to spend all her time at the moment travelling to and from Barbados in an attempt to get a visa to study in America.

In a particularly remote part of the island we tracked down Vanoulst John Charles. Everybody knows Vanoulst, which is just as well as his banana farm is high up in the hills where the long and winding roads have given way to tracks and ordinary vehicles have given way to

Land Rovers. Signposts are not a strong point anywhere on the island; up in the hills they are non-existent. But everyone we spoke to on the way knew where we could find Vanoulst, even though we had to be given direations five or six times before we were able to track him down.

He is a self- (and rather well-) educated man. Tall and thin and in his sixties, he has been in bananas and Dominican politics all his life. He was a founder member of Dame Eugenia's Dominican Freedom Party, but later fell out with her and her party's policies. He had served as the President of Winban, the quango set up to represent the Windward Island banana industry. He maintained that the various Prime Ministers of the various Windward Islands had not been firm enough with Geest over the years. Dame Eugenia (and others), for all her iron lady image, had not got rid of the old colonial attitudes which still paid too much respect to people and institutions from overseas.

Vanoulst resented the profit that Geest made from his bananas. The Windwards did not need Geest: they should have their own ships, do their own marketing and so on. I pointed out that farmers always resent money being made out of their crop by those who package it, transport it, retail it. An English farmer does not normally own the lorries which take his crop from the countryside to the city, nor does he make any money from its retail and distribution. Why should Dominican farmers be any different? And with banana prices low and getting lower, was this really the time for these islands to start investing in banana boats and ripening sheds in England, risking even more money in the process?

He dismissed all those arguments with a grin. This should have been done years ago. The Third World just gets worse and worse off. The price of bananas and all other agricultural commodities goes up, or more usually down, because of economic conditions in the First World. The price of vehicles and chemicals such as fertilizers goes down, or more usually up, because of economic conditions in the First World. The Third World does not get a look-in. It is then granted aid representing only a fraction of the cost that these changes have imposed. And what is more, the Third World countries do not co-operate with each other, but compete. The good price of Dominican bananas was being undercut by Latin American banana growers whose workers were paid a pittance. So if they take all the banana trade, the Third World, will, overall, have grown even poorer.

This rather depressing analysis was said in a charming and good-natured way. Vanoulst is never without a twinkle in his eye. He seemed certain that Geest had done too well out of the Windward Islands and that the farmers had been ripped off. His whole livelihood is under threat, but he is content to discuss the problem with less rancour than a couple of cricket fans analysing a Test Match defeat.

Vanoulst's large estate is high up in the hills. His trees are therefore particularly exposed to wind damage but their lofty position does make his corner of paradise particularly beautiful. Stretching to the horizon is a Jurassic Parkland of jagged mountain peaks and emerald forests decorated with puffs of white clouds and swirling mists.

As we spoke, a few of Vanoulst's workers sheltered from the gentle rain in one of the many shacks dotted around the countryside while they packed bananas in their boxes ready to be driven off and put on the next boat to England. Playing at Vanoulst's feet was a pretty two-year-old girl – his latest and thirteenth child. The child's mother, an equally pretty twenty-year-old, helped with the packing. It just shows what bananas can do for you.

• Yes, but what if we have no bananas? •

Early next day I flew to St Lucia to see Willie Rapier, Geest's head man in the Windward Islands. Geest's headquarters in the Windwards are now in Castries, which is St Lucia's main town.

Island-hopping in a small plane in the Caribbean must be one of the most joyous activities possible. I dare say nautical types would insist that it is better by boat. And railway buffs would resent not having some solid track beneath their feet. But to fly like a bird, oh me, oh my ...

As you skirt round Dominica, you can understand why it has no beaches. The steep line of the hills appears to keep going straight down to the water's edge. Here and there you spot a few fringes of sand but nothing much to write, or to send a postcard, home about.

The sea is overpoweringly blue. Alongside the various greens of the hills, the whole place looks like a new paintbox before a child has got to it and messed it up to produce the muddier tones we are used to in Britain.

The one-hour flight takes us over Martinique. Of course I am cheating because I know it is French, but Martinique definitely looks French from the air. You cannot actually see the croissants in the cafés but you know they are there. It has large, flat, open fields like you get for miles and miles around Paris. It does not have the mountains of Dominica, and if it once had a rainforest it is long gone. The island is more built-up, developed I suppose is the word, and much, much drier.

We do not have a chance to see a great deal of St Lucia from the air, but its landscape is approximately a cross between Dominica and Martinique. It does have inviting white sand beaches and is pretty well built-up. But there are also green hills and forests towards the centre of the island.

I had been to St Lucia a few years before, and it seemed to me that Castries had doubled in size in less than ten years. Having said that, on my previous visit I had not sought out Geest's headquarters in an unprepossessing office building in an industrial corner of the town, so I may be getting a different impression this time round.

Willie Rapier is tall and stoops down to talk to ordinary-sized mortals. His shape, plus a slightly yellowy skin, invites the thought that he is growing, just slightly, to look like the fruit he has been trading in all his working life. He speaks with a soft, slightly West Indian accent. He points out that the contract with Geest has been in existence for forty years and it is only now, when times are hard, that people are claiming that the contract is no good.

It is true that Geest have a monopoly under the deal, but the deal is to take *all* the bananas that the farmers produce. Not such a bad deal. If two or three competitors called each week or month, none of them would be able to give this guarantee. Geest have been very successful in building up their ripening sheds in Britain, as well as good trading contacts throughout the country to ensure a market for the Windward Islanders' crop. Perhaps Geest cannot expect to be thanked, but it is a bit much to be criticized for having done their part of the job well over the years.

Yes, yes, but are Geest going to abandon Dominica now? Willie says Geest will always take bananas if Dominica is producing them.

This expert phrase is, I suppose, intended to be an assurance, but it means very little. If the Dominicans cannot make money out of bananas, they will stop growing them, and that in itself would leave Geest free to go elsewhere. Indeed they are already going somewhere else, having acquired banana plantations in Central America.

This, Willie Rapier maintains, is just by way of increasing volume, so that Geest's overall strength is improved. They are not preparing a bolt hole in case the Windward Islands trade goes belly-up. They are not, of course, mutually exclusive.

Throughout our conversation, Willie Rapier was charm personified. But a worrying picture is emerging. Geest own no estates on Dominica, although they do in Latin America. They are not building any more boats to cruise passengers around this pattern of islands. They do not have to trade in Dominican bananas; the Dominicans do.

The fact is that Geest are in business to make money, and for forty years they have done just that. No doubt they would be happy to continue to do that in the Windward Islands for another forty years, but only if conditions remain favourable.

And what are the alternatives to dealing with Geest?

Geest are a big company in the Windward Islands and in Britain, but in the world – even in the world of bananas – they are tiny. They ship only 1.6 per cent of world banana exports. Most of the world banana trade is controlled by the three American companies: United Brands, Standard Fruit and Del Monte. And nobody claims any of those would treat the Windward Islands more generously than Geest. These companies' records over many years make Geest look benign in the extreme.

At Dominica's most renowned beauty spot, the Trafalgar Falls, I chatted to Atherton Martin. As an ecologist, he reckons that a monocrop is always doomed to failure, whether from disease, disaster or disruption of some sort. Diversification is the answer.

But would it be worth the while of Geest, or anyone else, sending a refrigerated banana boat to pick up only a fraction of the bananas produced today? Could anything other than concentration on bananas have provided the steadily growing prosperity that the island has enjoyed since the war? Could small amounts of citrus fruits compete on the open market?

There is an established coconut products industry. And there is certainly room for the Caribbean islands to supply each other's wants, rather than each of them seeking markets in America and Europe to earn money to import basic requirements back home again. Because of its underdeveloped tourist industry, Dominica does not have an international airport. By that, I mean one to which you can fly direct in a jumbo jet. Atherton makes the point that it is quite unnecessary for every island to have its own full size runway. No community of 70 000 people in Europe would expect such a thing. To take a random example, the London Borough of Islington has a population twice that size but is content to share the few airports in and around London with the other thirty-two London boroughs and the rest of the South East of England.

Atherton Martin was at least optimistic. Unusual in an ecologist, in my experience. Dominica has a good water supply and a cheap hydro-electric power supply. It has not been spoiled by tourism in the past and so, oddly enough, can look forward to a future in nature tourism for people who come to walk or swim in the natural world without doing as much damage to the environment as a package tourist.

A lady called Grace Tung had an even more outlandish way for Dominica to make money. She is Chinese and has introduced a scheme whereby Taiwanese or people from Hong Kong can invest a minimum of US$35 000 in the island and acquire Dominican citizenship. This sounds like selling your birthright, but over dinner in a Chinese restaurant in Roseau – in fact, the only Chinese restaurant in Roseau – Grace

Tung explained it was not that, nor even selling passports. Other countries, even Canada, went in for something along those lines, but this scheme involved investing in a particular project, and then getting a passport. It was not like selling a passport at all. It all sounded a bit desperate, though I understand that residents of Hong Kong find it easier to get into Britain if they arrive with a pile of money, so it may be that nobody is in a position to criticize.

• Queen for an hour •

By happy chance the Queen chose to visit Dominica just as I was leaving.

In fact she was only going to touch down at Melville Hall Airport in order to refuel. She was on her way, with the Duke of Edinburgh, from Anguilla to Guyana on a Caribbean tour. With no sign of a Dimbleby in sight I attempted a commentary for our film, but it was all very low-key. Very British, in fact, even down to the shower of rain which threatened to, but did not quite ruin, the whole thing. I was able to point out that the Queen was wearing a blue outfit (she even had a matching blue sling to support an arm injured in a riding accident), and the Duke of Edinburgh was in grey.

She met Prime Minister Dame Eugenia Charles, plus Dominica's President, as well as Commissioner Blanchard and several other dignitaries. There was just enough time for tea and sandwiches and a full tank of aviation spirit, and she was off again. I think it was Billy Connolly who noted that the Queen must think that Britain smells of fresh paint. She certainly must imagine that the entire Commonwealth is populated by politicians, policemen in white gloves and school children whose main hobby is waving little Union Jacks. She did not notice me among the cheering children, but I am almost sure that Baroness Chalker, who was with the royal party, nodded briefly at me as she went past.

Anyway, it was time for me to leave too. Since I had found everybody so charming on this pretty island I rather hoped they could hang on to their banana trade. I arrived home in England determined to eat only Dominican bananas as far as possible. A protected market in bananas seems the Dominicans' only hope, unless and until Atherton Martin's notion of a diversified economic base takes root.

In my local supermarket in London I was still reflecting on how difficult it must be to export foodstuffs, or any other products, from remote islands given the transport costs and so on. But I was pleased to find Windward Islands bananas on sale and, for the moment, still going strong. And onions grown in Tasmania.

OUR MAN IN... THE MAASAI MARA

KENYA has been a favourite of mine since I spent a few months there between school and university more than twenty years ago. A careless remark by an acquaintance of my father's led to my stay in Mr and Mrs Ron Pirie's comfortable house in a leafy suburb of Nairobi. A welcoming home-from-home from which I was able to explore the whole country: hitch-hiking here, travelling by third-class sleeper there, borrowing a car when I could I stayed with hippies on the island of Lamu, ran out of money in Mombasa and survived on sweetcorn and pineapple bought from street-vendors, went on a boat round Lake Victoria, watched big game in the bush, and got a car stuck in the mud beside some lions. Looking back, I wonder how I had the nerve to do it. Not the bumming around – I mean arriving to stay with people I had never met. Anyway, thank you Mr and Mrs Pirie, I hope I will be as generous if a layabout student lands on me some day.

A few years later I returned to visit my wife, who was in Kenya on a medical assignment. She was also staying in a well-appointed house in Karen, a suburb of Nairobi, but working in some of the city's most squalid shanty towns. On this trip I had an equally great time, marred only by coming down with some sort of dread African food poisoning on New Year's Eve. You may know the sort of thing. Stuff pours out of you from top and bottom – well, mouth and bottom to be more accurate – until you think you are going to die. This soon gives way to a feeling that you want to die, until finally, dehydrated and weakened, the conviction grows that you have already died.

The whole incident left me with an inferiority complex about my digestive system's ability to cope with foreign travel. It also raised question marks in my mind about medical practitioners. Each of the several doctors I happened to be with at the time had different suggestions as to what to do when I started to get ill, none of which did any good at all. As I got worse they all left me to my fate, apart from my wife who, if I recall correctly, prescribed Fanta lemonade to aid my recovery. Mind you, I may have been hallucinating by then, or possibly fantasizing.

Anyway, what it did not do was diminish my affection for Kenya. In the highlands, the cool hillsides and mountains provide a pleasant cli-

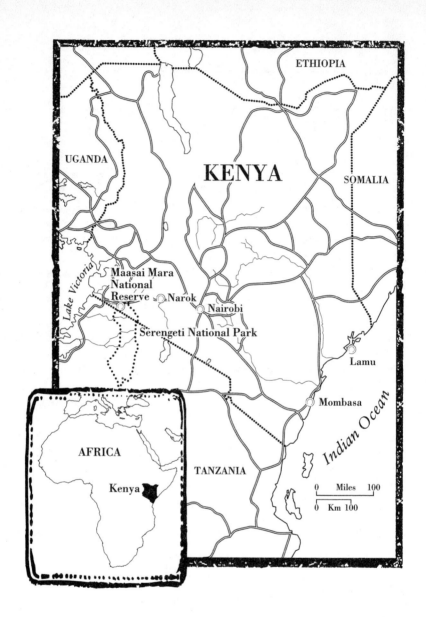

UGANDA

ETHIOPIA

KENYA

SOMALIA

Lake Victoria

Maasai Mara
National
Reserve ○ Narok

○ Nairobi

Serengeti National Park

Lamu

Mombasa

Indian Ocean

AFRICA

Kenya

TANZANIA

| 0 | Miles | 100 |
| 0 | Km | 100 |

mate right on the Equator. In addition there are wide African plains, extraordinary wildlife, the spectacular Great Rift Valley, a fantastic coastline on the Indian Ocean, tea plantations, forests, deserts and lakes. Kenya's population is an engaging mixture of black Africans from a variety of tribes, spiced with Arab traders at the coast, Asian traders in the towns, topped up with an intriguing collection of ex-pat and resident whites. It accords with my idea of paradise and so I jumped at the chance to go back there to make a documentary.

As it happens, I do not think my own experience of the country is particularly unusual. White people visiting East Africa have always gone looking for wildlife, the great outdoors, excitement and adventure, but usually manage to find some home comforts to fall back on. Karen Blixen had a farm in Africa, but like everyone else she had house-boys and farm-hands to do the actual work.

Like everywhere else, Kenya is not what it was. But some things never change. A generation or two ago white people went there as colonial administrators, big game hunters and missionaries. Now, thirty years after independence, they are UN representatives, photojournalists and charity workers. The same collection of do-gooders doing pretty well, and ne'er-do-wells doing even better.

The film was to be about the Maasailand. The Maasai Mara is a marvellous area of classic African grassland, dotted with acacia trees, lying about 150 miles to the west of Nairobi. Part of the Mara is set aside as a National Park which, with the Serengeti just across the border in Tanzania, constitutes an important area for African wildlife.

The Maasai people who live in the Mara – nowadays, outside the National Park – are semi-nomadic pastoralists who are just the sort of people to inspire awe and affection in British Empire-builders, anthropologists and modern-day tourists. More than most of the other tribes in East Africa, they have clung to their traditional lifestyle. This for them means avoiding such naff things as growing crops. The traditional Maasai life centres on herding cattle. The more cattle you have, the better you are doing. You drink cows' milk, sometimes cows' blood, and you eat cows' meat.

The Maasai have a reputation as being brave fighters. They have fought other tribes, fought the colonizers from Europe, and fought civil wars between themselves. What the Maasai have never done is kill the wildlife. A few lions have been engaged in mortal combat to prove bravery or to protect livestock. But the zebra, the elephant, the wildebeest and the antelope have been left alone, regarded as God's cattle. This has meant that in the Maasai area of the country the wildlife has continued to flourish, even outside the National Park itself.

But will this last? Over the last few years some of the Maasai have changed their ways and have started to see the advantages of the modern world of agriculture and money. Some groups, who usually own land in common, have sold or leased their lands to people of other tribes for use in agriculture. Other villages have taken to growing crops themselves. In these areas, the herds of wild animals have ceased to be God's cattle, sharing the grazing with man's cattle. They have become pests, which threaten to trample the corn, ruin the harvest and steal the farmers' profits.

Was the Maasai lifestyle disappearing, and would the wildlife go with it? I headed towards the Mara to find out.

• Up country •

I drove to the Mara Safari Club in a Land-Rover, all the way from the nearby airfield, pausing only to draw a map of Africa in the earth for the benefit of the cameras. This I did with only the assistance of a stick and a printed map. Not only do I do my own stunts, I also do my own cartography.

The Mara Safari Club is one of the tourist resorts which are the modern epitome of the adventure-with-comfort philosophy I was referring to. It is outside the National Park. Ostensibly it is a campsite in which you are sleeping under canvas miles from anywhere, right out in the African bush. Strictly speaking, all that is true, but the tents are permanent fixtures, each with running water and electric light. They even have en-suite bathrooms. The food is excellent in a British sort of way. The camper's day starts when he is woken at first light by a waiter bringing tea and biscuits to the tent veranda. If he wants the biscuits, he has to hurry up and eat them or the birds will get there first. Off he goes on a game drive, a tour round the locality in a Land-Cruiser, his driver finding wild animals to look at, hopefully without too many other vehicles full of tourists round them as well. Back to the camp for a full cooked breakfast, then off on a late-morning drive to see anything he missed the first time round. A curry lunch taken outside in the hot sunshine is very acceptable, after which the afternoon could be spent relaxing by the swimming pool until it is time for afternoon tea. Then back out on safari at twilight and home again for early-evening drinks and a five-course dinner. The whole thing is not cheap but nor is it to be missed by anyone who is not roughing it on a real safari. On a real safari you go off on your own with only your driver, guide and bearers to help you.

The various lodges have slightly different styles. From a previous visit I remember Governor's Camp, which is in the Mara as well but inside the Park, being very impressive and slightly wilder. The Mara Safari Club is just a little over-fenced (they do not allow lions to wander in at night and kill the clientele as it is bad for repeat business). And it has what is basically a crazy-paving path leading to the tents. Set in the close-cropped grass it is slightly too redolent of English suburbia. What it does have, though, are hippopotamuses.

The tents are strung along the banks of the Mara river, a squelchy brown watercourse which meanders around the edge of the camp. In it, 20 or 30 feet down the bank, live the hippos. Dozens of them. They spend the day wallowing in the muddy water. They are ideal animals to accompany tourists. Fat, ugly, messy creatures, lying around bathing all day. And the hippos are much the same.

I know it is wrong to judge animals on how they appear to us. Different species look the way they do because of the requirements of their life cycle. And they should not be praised or condemned on the basis of anthropomorphic aesthetic considerations. Having said that, hippopotamuses really are ugly. From the Greek, their name means river horse, but river pig would be more like it. They have hideously obese bodies, nasty pink eyes and mouths which they open wide to emit fearsome noises which are somewhere between a roar and a belch. If their hairless sludge-coloured skins were not enough to put you off, hippos have an unattractive way of emptying their bowels. As huge amounts of waste material emerge from their vast rear ends, they fan it with their tails, spreading it around the river they live in. The original shit hitting the fan, in fact. No wonder the water is so brown.

The hippos spend the whole day in the river, engaged in face-to-face yawning and snarling contests over their favourite stretches of the sluggish waterway. They have contests which threaten to get really nasty but never seem to develop into actual violence. Perhaps they are just discussing their royalties on the song that Flanders and Swann used to sing about them.

Oh, all right. I loved them really. I could have spent hours watching them wallowing in the muddy water. In fact, I think I did.

At night the hippos heave themselves out of the water and go off foraging for the huge amounts of food it takes to get them to full size. Come the early morning they grunt and groan their way back to the river, into which they dive with all the grace of Robert Maxwell falling off his yacht. You must be able to hear them miles away. You can certainly hear them yards away in your tent.

In addition to the hippos along the river there is an occasional crocodile, a giant floating lizard with malice aforethought. On the opposite bank baboons chatter and swing in the trees while a line of mongooses urgently go about their business. Weaver birds weave, fly catchers catch flies and kingfishers fish for kings.

There are different Creation myths, but personally I believe that when God created Africa, he was on drugs. The rest of the world does not have animals the size of dumper trucks wallowing in its rivers, so what was He up to with hippos? Stoned. The rest of the world has tall trees, but it does not, like Africa, have frankly ludicrous creatures like giraffes with unfeasibly long necks so they can eat the topmost leaves. The rest of the world makes do with squirrels, and monkeys and things which take the trouble to learn how to climb trees and so do not have to walk round looking like a street lamp inspection crane in fun fur. Rhinoceroses are, just like hippos, pointlessly large, but not so fortunate. Unluckily for them, they have been endowed with an impressive horn at the front, a quite unnecessary piece of decoration which is as pointless as the wings on 60s American cars. They eat grass, for goodness' sake. Why do they need to carry an offensive weapon on their top lip? Rhinos have been hunted to the point of extinction because their horn is supposed to put a bit more lead into gullible Chinese pencils. And what about elephants? Who in their right mind would come up with another giant animal, this time one which can perform almost every activity with its nose? I know God can do anything, but coke-head or what?

• Female of the species •

Having been filmed settling into my luxury bivouac, it was time to meet my translator and guide. For my benefit, someone had been hired who had spent years in this part of Africa, spoke Maasai, Swahili and several other languages, and who was used to the difficulties of life up-country.

When my old-Africa-hand arrived, she was something of a surprise. Carolyn Roumeguere is a beautiful, dynamic, French twenty-something who has had a particularly exotic upbringing. Her mother was a social anthropologist who came to study the Maasai and loved them so much she decided to leave her French husband to marry a Maasai Chief. She still shares her life with him, and he shares his life with her and the six other wives he has since acquired.

Carolyn was a small child when this happened and was brought up amongst the Maasai in their villages until she was sent to Nairobi to be educated in the ways of the Western world by an English governess. Later she attended university in Paris, earned her living as a fashion model, and now makes her money exporting jackets and jewellery to Europe. But she is most at home roaming around the plains of Africa. Not quite Saunders of the River, but someone you would genuinely want to go into thejungle with.

• Don't fence me in •

We set off to visit a village near Narok. Narok is the local big town, but it is a couple of hours' drive down the bumpy mud roads and tracks from the Mara. Even longer for us, since we had to stop from time to time to film the countryside we were passing through.

The open country of the Mara was looking very green. For several months there had been drought and the land had burnt dry, robbing the animals of water and then food as the grasses withered away. This is part of the annual cycle of events but droughts seem to be getting longer in Africa nowadays. But by this time the rains had come and the grass was putting out new growth. Dotted with trees, the fresh green shoots made the grass look like English parkland. This sort of scenery might well have appealed to British colonizers, but it was not so welcome to British film-makers. It is no good coming all this way if it is going to look like Richmond Park. Mind you, you do not see as many herds of wildebeest, zebra and antelope in Richmond Park as you do here.

As we got nearer to Narok the landscape changed. It was much drier, the rains had only really come to the high ground and, in place of bush country dotted with trees and circles of huts, there were huge open fields, fenced off, cleared of scrub and planted with maize. This did not look like English parkland – more like Canadian prairies. This was evidence of the change of use which is stealing over this land.

Near Narok we visited a Maasai village which had gone over to agriculture. A confident young man called Simon showed us round. I am not sure if he was the head man of the village, but he was clearly its spokesman. He was not by any means the oldest, nor was he the richest nor necessarily the bravest. He had his position because of his skills as an orator, a skill valued in Maasai tradition as in our own. Anyway, this village John Major was now the village's representative on Narok County Council and was dressed in a formal suit to welcome us to the village.

The village was a simple sort of affair with thatched huts strung in a line. Carolyn hurrumphed that it was not a proper Maasai village at all. The houses were the wrong shape and made of the wrong material. They were not arranged in a circle and the place was messy. Worst of all, the village was surrounded by fields sprouting maize and other crops.

Simon explained that the village had gone over to growing crops because they brought in an income. Crops took them out of the subsistence-level life they had previously enjoyed. The main drawback they now experienced was trouble from wild animals. Elephants especially had a nasty tendency to break down fences and munch their way through a few acres during the night. What they did not eat they trampled underfoot. Elephants and other animals sometimes even killed people; Simon showed me a girl whose mother had been killed by a buffalo, and who was still awaiting compensation for her death. Ordinary people were not entitled to kill the wild animals which threatened their new livelihoods. That had to be done by the Kenya Wildlife Service (KWS). The KWS was responsible for preserving the wildlife and also protecting people from the wilder wildlife. But, according to Simon, although the KWS was quick to punish any poaching of animals, it was slow to protect the farmers from the marauding animals.

But did not the Maasai traditionally welcome the wildlife? And did not the wildlife attract tourists to the area? Simon was not interested in that argument. The animals should be confined to the Game Reserves, not allowed into his people's fields.

Thus this village had broken with its past, but not completely. The mothers of the village, including Simon's own very young-looking wife, gathered in traditional dress to sing me songs of welcome. They started with some religious songs and, goaded by my sadistic director, Simon demanded a response from me. So on an African hillside I launched into *Amazing Grace*. As soon as I started I remembered I do not have much of a singing voice. It did not take too long for it to become obvious to everybody else.

The mothers had more of their songs to sing. They sing as a group, with two or three lead singers backed up by ten or twelve others. Their voices have a whining haunting quality not unlike bagpipe music or a collection of Kate Bushes. This is a living tradition: they were not singing ancient folk songs but ones which were recently made up about topical subjects and matters of local concern. For example, they sang a song praising Simon for his efforts in arguing for the elephants to be chased away. This was all too up-to-date for me: I was racking my brains to think of a recent *Spitting Image* number I could belt out, but sadly I was not called upon a second time.

We were a bit gloomy during the long drive back to the lodge. Other people have no right to expect that the Maasai should refrain from taking the step from pastoralism to agriculture, just because of the romance of their traditional lifestyle. But it is sad nonetheless to see a way of life disappearing. There is something very attractive about nomadic people generally. Perhaps we respond to some atavistic urges lost within us. Perhaps it is their arrogance we admire. The Maasai were traditionally disdainful of other tribes which grubbed around in the dirt to produce food, but now they are literally being brought down to earth.

The rains fell as we made our way back the lodge on roads made almost impassable by the downpour. The roads are built of mud and round here mud comes in two forms – red, which is difficult to drive on when wet, and black, which is totally impossible. In the dark there are the further hazards of trucks which have skidded to a halt across the road and the odd baby elephant appearing in the headlamps. Baby elephants are not like the baby rabbits you might bump into in Britain. You cannot just drive over them. They are to be avoided at all costs, especially as they are usually accompanied by mummy elephants.

Somehow the driver of our 4x4 managed to get us home. Amazing when you think that these off-road vehicles are really designed for shopping in Knightsbridge.

• Out of Africa •

The next day Carolyn took me to a traditional Maasai village to see the real thing. It was easy to see how markedly the agricultural Maasai of the day before had departed from the ancient ways of the tribe. In this conventional village, or *enkang*, the houses were arranged in a circle enclosing an area the shape and size of a very large roundabout. Branches and bushes are arranged around it to provide a hedge. At night the cattle are herded into the central enclosure through the three or four gaps between the houses, which are mainly joined together in groups of five or six, forming short, curved terraces. As a result, the ground within the village is covered with squished-down cow dung which forms a soggy, springy floor for men and women to walk on, and children to play in. The Maasai generally go bare-legged, wearing brick- or blood-red blankets. Perhaps this is why. A central plaza of cow dung seems weird at first but it is surprising how quickly one gets used to it, and to the flies.

Cow dung is central to the village physically and central to village life generally. The houses are low single-storey huts made of wood plastered with cow dung. The roofs were not the pitched roofs of the previous day's village but rounded and slightly convex, made also of cow dung. Cow dung, even when dried, does not sound like the perfect roof covering but the night before there had been rain of monsoon-like intensity and the roofs in this village had not been washed away or sprung any leaks.

It struck me that the restaurant and bars at the lodge, which are permanent buildings, have roofs decorated with a straw thatch to make them look authentic but really they ought to be covered in cow dung.

We were invited inside these genuine houses and, indeed, filmed inside one where I was welcomed by the woman who lived there. Filming was not easy as the space is limited and there is very little light. The houses do not have windows as such, just one or two little openings to let some daylight in and some smoke out. The smoke comes from an open fire which is used to heat the house (scarcely necessary on the day we were there) and to cook food. Smoke from the wood fire hangs around inside until it can find one of the little openings to slink out of.

The Maasai set great store by their milk. It is collected in a calabash, a misshapen bottle sized container made from a hollowed-out gourd. We thought it would be good fun for me to drink the milk from a calabash, but when it came to it the woman who was kind enough to give me the milk insisted on pouring it into a glass first. The milk has a slightly smoky, herby taste imparted by the inside of the calabash which is cleaned out and, I hoped, sterilized by burning embers.

A calabash is also used to collect cows' blood. The jugular vein is punctured by an arrow and sealed afterwards with cow dung. Thus the Maasai are able to milk their cattle of blood without having to kill them. But, as it happens, I was not offered cow's blood to drink. Luckily I had ordered gold top, not red top.

Certainly, a glass of Maasai milk on its own was not enough to turn me into a Maasai. That, in their highly structured society, is a long job. Boys go through several stages before they reach full status as an elder of the village. At puberty the boys are lined up to be circumcised in public. This is obviously painful (it can take up to five minutes) but the idea is not to cry out in pain or call Childline or anything. Crying is a sign of cowardice and takes some living-down afterwards. The boys then become *morans* – young warriors. They grow their hair long and smear it in red ochre. *Morans* are supposed to go off into the bush, kill lions, steal cattle and do a whole lot of other things, most of which are next to impossible in the modern world. *Morans* are heroic figures who enjoy a few years of excitement before they are ready to come back to the village to marry, settle down and become elders.

Girls are also circumcised at about the time of puberty. Female circumcision, which is a feature of many peoples around this part of Africa, is somewhat of a euphemism, as it involves rather more radical surgery than the removal of the male's foreskin. The girl is held down while her clitoris and labia minora are cut away. The girls are at least allowed to undergo this ritual in private and are not obliged to refrain from screaming in agony while it takes place.

Lost in admiration for Maasai life as I may be, circumcision for males or females strikes me as a very strange practice. I wonder who first came up with the idea. *Hey, guys, never mind inventing the wheel, let's cut bits and pieces off our bits and pieces. In fact, let's do it to all our children ... Then they can do it to theirs, and so on to the end of time ...*

I had always understood that female circumcision was fundamentally intended to suppress a wife's enjoyment of sexual intercourse in order to discourage unfaithfulness. This, however, does not seem to accord with what actually happens in Maasai society. Men are allowed to have more than one wife, but it is also accepted practice for a woman to take lovers. She is not supposed to choose them outside her husband's age group, but otherwise she has a free hand. All the children she bears are always accepted as offspring of her husband, although it is preferable to have at least some who resemble him more than his chums. Girls and boys have sexual intercourse from a young age, although it is considered bad form for an uncircumcised girl to get pregnant.

Most of this I discovered from talking to Carolyn or doing background reading. In a spirit of enquiry I tried raising questions of sexual behaviour with the Maasai women themselves while sitting inside the cramped quarters of the village house we were filming in, but I was given precious little information. But then, being squeezed into your own home with some complete strangers and a camera pointing at your face is not conducive to intimate disclosures in any culture.

What I did establish was that each house has two beds fixed into position on either side of the fire. The mother sleeps in one with her children, unless she is being visited by her husband or a lover. Anyone else who may be in the house sleeps in the other. I am afraid I did not stay the night to check all this out.

Some of the older villagers remembered Carolyn from her early days in the district and berated her for still being unmarried. To what extent, I wondered, had Carolyn been inculcated into the life of the Maasai in the raw? As a small girl she told me, she had been held down and a couple of (milk) teeth pulled out, which is the standard East African way to ensure a channel for feeding in the event of lockjaw. But that was the worst thing that had been done to her.

How genuine was all this? Forewarned of our arrival, the village mothers had given us another sung greeting (puzzlingly, none of our team was asked to sing on this occasion) and on display was a variety of spears, clothes, jewellery and other Maasai trinkets which the villagers sell to tourists.

The Maasai used to enjoy a ferocious reputation. Their belief was that all cattle in the world belonged to them, so stealing cows from other tribes was not larceny. Was the choice open to them either to abandon all their old ways, or to preserve themselves and some traditions as living curios, pale imitations of a once-proud race?

We considered the problem over our pre-dinner drinks back at the lodge. Pre-dinner entertainment consisted of half-a-dozen waiters and security guards dressed in all the finery of *morans*. They danced in the high leaping style of the Maasai warriors in a very impressive and convincing way. But their long red ochre hair was false – wigs put on to give us cocktail drinkers an idea of what Maasai life is like. Maasai life is a cabaret, old chum.

• Live and let die •

The next day, a cynical city slicker called Maina Mwangi told us we were mad to worry about the Maasai way of life. Maina is an Oxford-educated Kikuyu (the dominant Bantu people of Kenya) from Nairobi and has no time for any sentimental noble savage stuff. As he put it, nobody comes to Africa to take his photograph, but he is as African as any Maasai. They are going to be pushed aside by inevitable changes, just as English rustic life has changed over the centuries. And just because he is Kenyan does not mean he is in love with African animals. Quite the reverse. If he wants to see wild animals (which is rarely), he is happy to see them in the zoo.

We appealed to the romantic side to his nature. What about the magnificent herds of animals? What about the culture which was disappearing? What, once the animals were no more, about David Attenborough's TV career? Maina remained unmoved and suggested that the sooner the Kikuyu farmers moved into the area the better.

We told him that the animals are a unique resource, able to attract tourist revenues, whereas crops are duplicated the world over, and in the long-term likely to turn the plains into a dust bowl. Overall, it was a risk he was prepared to take. Humans come before animals. Whatever the economics dictate, that is the route to be followed, and the Devil take the hartebeest.

We could have gone on chewing the fat much longer, but there was a danger that Carolyn might have strangled him.

• Pachyderm patrol •

At the moment there are still animals in Kenya, and farmers. And trying to keep them apart is the job of the Kenya Wildlife Service (KWS). If farmers are not to be allowed to kill the wild animals, then the Wildlife service must prevent the animals interfering with agricultural land. Elephants are emerging as the main cause for concern so we arranged to tag along with a KWS patrol to see how they scared elephants away.

We set off at about four in the morning with a detachment of eight KWS men led by their officer, Joyce Wafula. She explained that foraging elephants would come out of forested land during the night and make for maize fields, generally taking the crop just before it was ready for harvest. As dawn came up they would retreat into the trees. To frighten the herd off cultivated areas, first find your elephants. This is not quite as easy as it sounds, as they do drift away pretty quickly. It is impossible to track them at night, and they keep in the trees in the full of the day, which is why this scaring-off tends to be done at first light.

Joyce took us to an area which was divided up into *shambas*, small-holdings worked by individual farmers. This was Maasai land which had been leased to members of another tribe. The earth was suitable for crop growing but because it was surrounded by forest and bush it was liable to constant encroachment by elephants. In fact, if Maina will forgive me for saying so, it was the humans who were doing the encroaching because, until the farmers moved in, this had been part of the elephants' range.

Farmers in England have trouble scaring crows away. An elephant is even less likely to be put off by Wurzel Gummidge. Once you have found your elephants you have to put the wind up them with explosions, thunder-flashes and gunfire. In this way you can frighten more elephants than you can shake a stick at. Since they are intelligent animals they should begin to associate the farmers' fields with the nasty bangs and decide to stay in the uncultivated forest for a bit of peace and quiet. Unfortunately, their intelligence means they eventually notice that the explosions, thunder-flashes and guns are not actually hurting them so from time to time you have to kill one, *pour encourager les autres*.

With the patrol we made the important discovery that it is possible to lose a herd of elephants in a matter of seconds. They are well-camouflaged against the tree trunks and move very fast when they want to. We might have got close enough to the herd to worry them a little, but certainly nowhere near enough to film them. It was nonetheless great running full-stretch across the rough ground trying to keep up with the fit young men of the KWS, who were trying to keep up with the fit old elephants.

We decided we could not give up as easily as that and set off to track the elephants through the woods. How difficult can it be to stalk elephants? The KWS employ all the techniques of animal tracking that I had learnt with the 4th Harrow Weald Scout Troop. Techniques which had proved to be so utterly useless in suburban London, but which were invaluable here in Africa. Elephants leave very shallow, dinner-plate-size footprints on the ground which are fairly easy to spot when:

(1) you have understood the configuration to look out for and
(2) there is a KWS patrolman standing next to one and pointing it out to you.

Then there are the branches and bits of grass, which are bent over in the direction that the elephants travel. To spot these you really do need to be a member of the KWS. Being a Boy Scout Patrol Leader (Retired), I can report, does not help at all.

And finally there are elephant droppings to go by. These are substantial at the best of times, but particularly so – elephantine, in fact – when the elephants are scared by pursuing humans and on the run, so to speak. To make sure you are close behind the elephants you have to check that the droppings are fresh. The easiest way to do that is to stick your finger in the dropping to take its temperature. If it has gone cold the elephant is long gone. If it is still warm, the elephant cannot be far away. If it is warm and getting warmer, the elephant is probably standing over you and still doing it.

After several hours of elephant-tracking we realized it was totally pointless as the elephants knew we were after them and were perfectly capable of keeping out of range. But I can recommend a day's walk in the Kenyan forests. It was not jungly and overgrown with creepers – in fact it was rather like a walk in Sherwood Forest but with no danger of coming across CenterParcs. If there was any danger from animals or snakes, all I can say is the KWS did not mention it.

• Elephant man •

The next day we tried again, this time with more success. We were able to surprise a small group of elephants at the edge of some woods. The KWS chased them this way and that, while the director chased me this way and that, hoping to get me near the herd and on-camera. Since both the elephants and I were convinced we were going to get our faces blown off by the explosives, we actually found ourselves going in the right direction from time to time. I do not know if all these shock tactics keep the elephants away, but I did not go back again.

One problem we had with filming this sequence came from our government minder. Peter was a townie himself and when he first joined us he and his city clothes looked a bit out of place in the bush. In supervising us on behalf of the government, he did not interfere with our activities except to object vociferously once when we accidentally went off to do some filming without him. This threatened to be a problem until we were able to smooth things over with him. By the time of the elephant run, he had rather got into life in the great outdoors. Reluctant to stay in the background he insisted on keeping up with the KWS and me. I mention this in case, when you watch the documentary, you notice amongst the muted greens and khakis a figure in a bright red tracksuit and inappropriate loafers. That is Peter.

• Magic lantern •

Back at the Mara Safari Club, I attended a lecture by their resident naturalist. This took the form of an old-fashioned illustrated lecture given by the appropriately bearded and well-informed Mike Clifton. From him I discovered that the Maasai had not merely tolerated wildlife, but their activities actually encouraged it. If left alone, the plains in the Mara would gradually become overgrown by a tough grass which absolutely nothing can eat. In the absence of human activity this would choke out the other grasses and plants, and even bushes, considerably reducing grazing for the wild herbivores. After several years there would inevitably be a fire. The tall dry grass would burn ferociously, scorching the earth which would then take years to recover. The Maasai land management involved burning off this grass on a regular basis when it was much shorter. The set fires would cause much less damage to the land and ensure better grazing for the cattle and the wild herbivores alike.

Mike also described the massive migration of wildebeest which takes them up and down Africa, in and out of the Mara and the Serengeti. I had seen this sort of thing many times on television, but I had not before understood that zebras have a strange way of joining the migration, appearing to supervise and control the very stupid wildebeest as they cross rivers and other obstacles. *Don't risk going over the river on your own. Always use a zebra crossing.*

And why do zebras have stripes? Mike Clifton suggested that their markings do not make them invisible to predators such as lions but that very possibly they put off the tsetse flies, whose multi-faceted eyes are disturbed by stripes. I made a note that next time I am in Africa I must bring a wardrobe of Newcastle United shirts and pin-stripe suits.

• Up in the air •

But is there any future for the Maasai and the wildlife?

One possible way forward has been identified by an organization snappily called the Ol Choro Oiroua Wildlife Management and Conservation Association. My next step was to meet Willie Roberts, the Association's Executive Director. Willie is a white Kenyan who lives in a private camp a mile or two down muddy tracks from the Safari Club. Originally he came to this area to farm but became disillusioned with the steps you have to take to keep wildlife off farmland. He tried electric fences, but the elephants learnt that the fence posts were not live and so would trample them down. He tried staying up all night to scare the elephants away, but the human flesh weakened before the elephant spirit wilted. He was advised to kill a couple of elephants and drag their bodies around the boundaries to put the smell of death about the place. It was at this point that he decided there must be a better way.

The key point that he and the Association realized was that the move towards agriculture was being hastened because the landowners around the National Park – the Maasai themselves – were earning little or nothing from tourists who came to see the wildlife, but could earn quite a lot by turning their land over to agriculture.

Of course tourists do pay to come to this area – they pay a great deal, but the money earned in admission fees and taxes is collected by hotel-owners, the national government and local government. If the Maasai landowners received the proportion of this tourist revenue to which they were already entitled, they would have a direct financial interest in the survival of the wildlife. And there would be much less pressure to enclose the land for crops.

In the Association are Paramount Chief Ole Ndutu and other Maasai landowners, Willie himself and a Nairobi lawyer called Stephen Mwensi. They operate what they call a Group Ranch scheme. Various owners pool their resources and so control a sizeable area of land. With the benefit of Stephen's legal advice they have been able to pursue a variety of court actions in order to ensure that they receive their rightful cut of the tourist revenue cake. If their scheme is successful a number of problems are solved. The Maasai can continue to raise cattle in their traditional way, live in harmony with the wildlife, but still receive an income equal to or more than what they would earn by going over to crop-growing.

From the conservationist's point of view, obviously the more land that is left for wildlife the better. As Willie explained when I chatted to him at his camp, the wildlife cannot live on the National Parks alone. The animals have to roam large areas in response to changes in the weather and the availability of grazing. The animals are unlikely to be given more land for their exclusive use, so it would be folly to get rid of areas where man and beast can get along together.

Willie's camp epitomizes the joy of the white settler's lifestyle. He and his wife have a large living room which, although it is covered by a tent, could be a comfortable sitting room anywhere in the English-speaking world. Sleeping-quarters are a string of other tents. In addition there is an extraordinary outdoor bathroom. Surrounded by a wooden palisade is a free-standing Victorian bath which has to be filled with water heated by a wood-burning stove. It is Robinson Crusoe made over by *Homes and Gardens*. Naturally I had to have a bath in these unusual circumstances. The water is as brown as the water in the River Mara, as is the water in my bath at the lodge. Mud in the water is probably good for you, but is there just a whiff of hippo?

Naturally I could not persuade the director to leave me alone, and the cameraman crept up on my bathtime, trying to catch me playing with my rubber crocodile.

As the night fell at Willie's camp I sat round the campfire listening to the lions roaring in the woods. All creatures great and small can be glimpsed or imagined in the African bush. The next morning, across the lawn came wart hogs to feed on the scraps which are put out for them as though they were blue tits. No wonder Willie loves it here and has given up trying to be a farmer.

Willie has a dry sense of humour which came to the fore when he took me up in his light aeroplane so I could see the change in land use from the air. He has being flying for decades in a sort of gung ho way that leaves you slightly in doubt as to whether his improvised repairs will keep you in the air. As he demonstrated his aeronautical skills he seemed slightly disappointed that his diving, banking and looping were not making me feel ill.

'Not sick yet, Clive?' was his merry cry as he went into another turn. Not me. If only he knew – one taste of underdone chicken and I would have been finished for days.

Willie was depressed as he showed me the encroachment of more and more shambas into previously open country. Even more worrying are the large fields of commercial proportions. It is extremely doubtful whether this tropical, indeed equatorial, environment can sustain the clearing, ploughing and soil disturbance that it takes to grow cash crops. Near-desert can turn very easily into near-disaster. In the 30s the Americans managed to turn their Great Plains into a dust bowl by over-grazing and over-farming land which had supported roaming herds of buffalo for time immemorial.

Here and there are fields on which farming has been abandoned, and the bush is making an attempt to reclaim the land. If it is successful, perhaps the wildlife will find its way back as well.

It is equally obvious from the air that tourism puts its own strain on the land. Tourist buses keep going even during the rainy weather and leave ugly tyre marks over the soggy ground as they track and circle the big animal attractions. Sensible management and control, confining tourists to set areas, and building roads, would help preserve the land, but that would make the place even less 'wild'.

But Willie and the Association are convinced this is the way forward. Who disagrees?

Well, the reason it is so important to include the lawyer in their set-up is that the Association has had quite a legal battle with Narok County Council to obtain its share of the tourist money. More than that, the Association has been asking what has happened to the money the Council has collected over many years. Are there hospitals and schools which have been built with the money? Where are the accounts?

This mixture of money and politics, with just a suggestion of corruption, is as potent a brew here in Kenya as anywhere else.

• Party political •

Kenya has done pretty well since independence in 1963. Very well, compared to the other countries in the region. If you consider the disasters and upheavals which have befallen the Sudan, Uganda, Rwanda, Burundi and Ethiopia, the stability of Kenya is remarkable. As a democracy it is far from perfect. Its great first leader, Jomo Kenyatta, turned the country into a one-party state. His likely successor, Tom Mboya, was assassinated in 1969, simply, it is widely assumed, because he was not a Kikuyu. His actual successor, Daniel Arap Moi, has ruled very firmly, and had to counter an attempted *coup d'état* by the Air Force in 1982. In elections held in 1992, his success was assisted by the simple device of doubling everyone's money just before polling day. The inevitable inflation developed only afterwards. Had they stuck with a Westminster-style democracy, of course, he would instead have had a pre-election tax-cutting budget and engineered a mini-boom, but there you are. Still, to most people, Kenya is the acceptable face of capitalism in Africa.

But politics can be a rough old trade in rough young countries. And a doughty battler on the political scene is the Honourable William Ntimama. And the Association have him to contend with.

William Ntimama was the Chairman of Narok County Council for a while before joining the cabinet as Minister for Local Government, a position he has held for several years. The title Minister for Local Government conjures up the picture of a rather anaemic figure. John Gummer, perhaps, crossed with Gillian Shepherd. In the flesh, the Kenyan Minister is much more robust and partisan than that: Michael Portillo out of Ian Paisley.

He agreed to meet us on a Saturday when he was going to be in his constituency, Narok North. He mentioned he would be meeting some constituents, and we imagined this was going to be something like an MP's surgery. In the event it was a large public meeting with some of the qualities of a royal garden party.

William Ntimama's fine house has a substantial garden with an area of lawn the size of a school sports field. When we arrived, the garden was full of hundreds of his political supporters. Town councillors, elders of the community, women in traditional dress, and anybody else who wanted to come and 'pay homage' to the Minister, as he put it in a casual aside to me.

Several hundred of the guests queued up to greet their host and a few of his close associates. I was invited to join the receiving line, like the bride's father who happened to turn up at the last minute. Older people shook hands with us. Actually, the custom here is to touch hands, as I noticed only after I had crushed the fingers of the first twenty people in the line.

Children and young people bowed and presented their heads to be touched. This is standard Maasai etiquette for showing your respect to anyone old enough to be your parent, a system which works fine in a society where age is venerated, but which might cause havoc in Hollywood. Imagine the clash of heads between Joan Collins and Elizabeth Taylor.

At the end of the greeting process Ntimama was presented with a couple of goats. Politicians clearly do better here than in Britain, where the best they can hope for at a constituency gathering is a piece of rubber chicken.

Later on, Ntimama addressed the crowd in the Maa language of the Maasai. One of his daughters, who were home for the holidays from an English public school, languorously translated parts of his speech for me. The daughters were dressed like Maasai princesses but spoke like Sloane Rangers. They had obviously seen Daddy in action before and were not going to get excited by a few people who had come for Saturday lunch on the lawn.

Ntimama is evidently a good orator. Speaking off the cuff, his jokes and remarks went down well with the crowd. As well they might. Poking mild fun at us, 'some white men who were interested in wildlife', along the way he said the Maasai should be able to expand their population if they wished. Birth control was unnecessary as they were only recovering lost ground. He also said it had now been declared that, if an animal kills, it shall be killed. The Maasai did not want to finish the animals off but did seek to prevent the animals finishing them off.

He also expressed great delight about the removal of Dr Richard Leakey as the head of the Kenya Wildlife Service. This referred to a very public, very bitter feud in which Ntimama had led a campaign against Leakey, the world-famous environmentalist and palaeontologist. Although respected internationally, Leakey's forceful style had made him many enemies within Kenya, none more ferocious than Ntimama. One Kenyan magazine likened their feud to a battle between two elephants.

In effect, Ntimama puts himself forward as a leader of the Maasai people. The Maasai have genuine grounds for complaint. However admired they were as noble savages, they were excluded from the development of the country in colonial times and many have continued to be left out of things since independence. As with other tribes in Kenya, some of their lands were taken by white colonizers. And as with other nomadic people, title to their land has sometimes been difficult to maintain against the more organized claims of settled people. National Parks, land set aside for animals, have made further inroads into the area available to them and, understandably, furthered their resentment of animal conservationists, especially those from abroad who have not preserved natural habitats for wildlife in their own country.

This well of anger is exploited by Ntimama, and his outrageous, inflammatory remarks both in and out of Parliament have made him notorious in the Kenyan Press and in political life. What he embodies, though, is the argument that the Maasai should compete in the modern world with the other tribes in Africa. They should seek material improvement in their conditions by moving away from a 'primitive' lifestyle as noble savages. I suppose it could be argued that it is more noble to be a farmer growing your own food than to become an exhibit in an African theme park. Ntimama, though, is not totally against wildlife tourism: he is part owner of the Governor's Camp Safari Lodges in the National Park.

After his speech there were songs from the women of a succession of villages. As before, the women were in traditional dress. Their orange, red and white cottons and intricately beaded necklaces were in bright contrast to most of the men who were in duller, more Western clothing. The whole event was a powerful combination of old and new, ancient tribal loyalties being deployed in pursuit of modern political ends.

I sat on a low bench with dozens of elders and councillors (including Stephen from the agricultural village). Ntimama sat on a chair which had been ceremonially carried out into the field.

Ntimama was eventually free to be interviewed. He laughed off my suggestions that he was being controversial in his speech, inviting people to have babies and kill elephants. No, he said, he was a politician and had to speak in soundbites to attract attention. He was in favour of the Maasai improving upon their milk-and-blood diet and going into agriculture. He was concerned about the two years of drought this part of the country had suffered, but did not think the farming they were now doing was likely to turn the area into a dust bowl.

I had understood that he was very much opposed to the Association's group ranch schemes, fighting tooth and nail to protect the interests of the Narok County Council and its revenues. But on-camera he expressed affable support for their efforts, although he thought other ranches closer to the National Park might do even better. He cheerily agreed that the Council should be publishing accounts dealing with the revenue it had received, and said that they probably would be doing just that in the not too distant future.

His bark on this occasion was much less worse than his normal sound-bite.

• End of the road •

My time in Kenya was coming to an end. There was a little time left for me to take a proper look at the wildlife. Despite the anxiety for its future, there is plenty to be seen.

I practically ran over a herd of elephants when I was being filmed driving through a thunderstorm. A family of cheetahs, a mother and three young females, took up residence just by our lodge. As is their way, prides of lions sat patiently in open ground ignoring any vehicles which come to watch them digest their food.

Ol Choro Oiroua are even seeking to reintroduce rhinos to their area. They have a bad-tempered pair which they have imported from South Africa ready to release into the wild. But at the moment they are being kept safe from poachers with a round-the-clock guard. Perhaps more than anything they symbolize the future, because so much of the natural world now only exists with the protection of mankind. There is no wilderness left.

Finally at the lodge I interviewed Paramount Chief Ole Ndutu in company with Willie Roberts and Stephen Mwensi. It is odd that the way forward for this part of Africa might be found in an alliance between an old Maasai Chief, a farmer turned environmentalist and a smart city lawyer.

Ndutu is an old man and in poor health, but still has the energy to worry about the future. One way or another, one cannot help thinking that the Maasai way of life is on its way out. If encroaching agriculture does not destroy it, money from tourist revenue will. Many young Maasai are already employed in Nairobi as security guards, protecting rich people from burglars, rather than their own villages from lions.

Chief Ndutu could not be sure that in fifty years' time there would still be Maasai herdsman tending their cattle in the Maasailand, but he was confident there would still be lions chasing wildebeest. In that, at least, I hope he is right.

OUR
MAN
IN... THE TIMBERLANDS

WHEN Europeans first started arriving in North America they must have found it astounding. A whole new continent with hotter summers, colder winters and wider open spaces than anything most of the tired, poor, huddled masses had left behind in the Old World. Here was a New World full of natural resources just waiting to be explored and exploited by anyone in pursuit of a better life or a quick buck. In many ways it was a paradise. True there were Red Indians living there already, but it was relatively easy to push them aside. Not to say slaughter, corrupt and betray them. By hook or by crook, the Land of the Free was not going to remain the Home of the Braves for very long.

The modern map of the United States reflects the path of the European immigrants. On the Eastern Seaboard there are twiddly little states like Connecticut, New Hampshire, Rhode Island and Maryland, with boundaries which take account of the topography and history of their area. But as the pioneers went westwards they could not be bothered with all that and drew straight lines on the maps with rulers to mark out great blocks of territory in the shape of oblongs and squares which eventually became fully paid-up member states of the Union.

For my visit to Timberland I was going west to the end of the Oregon Trail, which is, of course, Oregon. In the 1840s the Oregon Trail, a notional route across the country, brought land-hungry homesteaders to the far North West, lured by the promise of free land. The American government offered 640 acres to each man who cared to claim it. Later this was amended to 320 acres for each man, plus an extra 320 acres if he was married. There was nothing at all for a single female. This was a subtle inducement to matrimony. Many preferred to head south to the gold fields of California, but in due course Oregon attracted enough settlers to establish it as the thirty-third state of the Union.

Oregon (which is known as the Beaver State), is an area of mountains and rivers and lakes, but above all an area of trees. The trees are big round here, and so is tree-felling. Oregon has lived off its mainly coniferous forests – Douglas fir, spruce, cedar, pine and hemlock – for one hundred years. Some of the trees have been here for much longer than

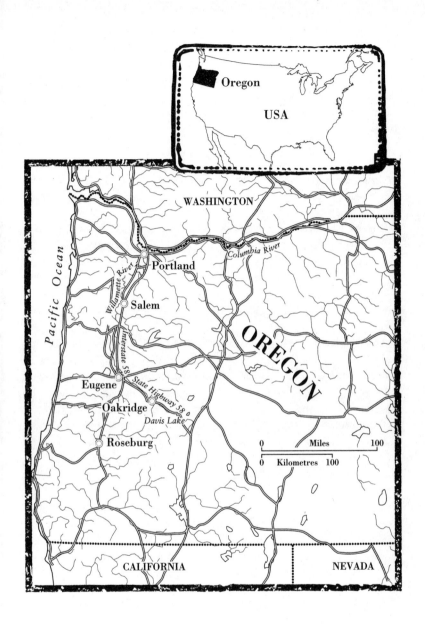

Oregon

USA

WASHINGTON

Pacific Ocean

Columbia River

Willamette River

Portland

Salem

Interstate 5

OREGON

Eugene

State Highway 58

Oakridge

Davis Lake

Roseburg

Miles
0   100
Kilometres
0   100

CALIFORNIA

NEVADA

that. But environmentalists are worried that too many ancient wood-lands have been chopped down by the timber industry, and that such tree-felling has to stop. And they have decided to use every means pos-sible to prevent the ancient forests being destroyed, enlisting in their support the Northern Spotted Owl.

And so I set off on the trail of the beaver, the Spotted Owl and the lonesome pine.

• Go West, young man •

Salem is the state capital of Oregon, and Portland is its largest city, but I was heading somewhere nearer the trees – the logging and university city of Eugene.

Eugene is a pleasant, home-town kind of place. Like most American home towns, when you first get there it seems kind of empty. Everything is spread out, as you might expect from a place which started with everyone being issued with 640 acres apiece. Mostly it seems empty because of the motor car. In America nobody walks much from A to B unless A is where he is now and B is where he left his car when he got here.

America has drive-in cinemas, drive-in banks, even drive-in wedding chapels, and, of course, the drive-in hotel, the motel. Motels still exist all over the States, motels just like the one in *Psycho*, only, with any luck, nothing more distressing is waiting for you in the shower than the remains of the previous occupant's soap-on-a-rope.

The motel I checked into in Eugene was the Parkway Inn, two floors of basic hotel rooms alongside a convenient parking lot. No restaurant, no bar, just the bare essentials: a bedroom, a bathroom and a TV set. Pizzas you can have delivered.

The manager of the Parkway was called Troy. He had longish blond hair and black-framed glasses. He did not look like anything out of *Psycho*. In fact he looked like Garth out of *Wayne's World*. Troy was real friendly and he was very much at home in the Parkway. He does not get paid a fortune by the owners of the joint, but that does not stop him lav-ishing upon it all the care and attention of a fanatical do-it-yourself home improver.

Troy's pride and joy is the 'Love Room'. It has a heart-shaped bed, a heart-shaped doorway and a heart-shaped Jacuzzi. Bright red plaster cupids fly above the bed. It is built for that romantic night with the woman of your dreams. In case the woman of your dreams does not turn up in person, there is an extensive selection of pornography to watch on the television to help you make it through the night.

Duty calls, however and I had to bone up on trees. By coincidence, there was an item on the local television station, KMTR, about the conflict between environmentalists and the logging industry. Actually it was not particularly fortuitous, as this is the big issue round here and KMTR covers it more or less every night.

The latest bulletin announces that the Greens have come up with a few more animals and plants whose existence is said to be threatened by logging in Oregon. The Northern Spotted Owl has always been on the list but now it has been joined by the Marbled Murrelet (a bird, apparently), the Short-Nosed Sucker (don't ask), the Red Spotted Pocket Mouse, plus a selection of newts, bats, voles and other critters. Plus some crazy stuff called wild parsley, which I assumed was something you might add as a garnish to magic mushrooms.

The loggers, meanwhile, have found an academic who claims that more of Oregon is covered by trees now than it was one hundred years ago. I did not hear much more about him during the rest of my visit. He sounds exactly the sort of person that would get a column in *The Sunday Times*.

The next morning I decided to check up on the story at KMTR. I also decided to check out of the Parkway Inn, and check in to the Eugene Hilton.

KMTR is housed in a neat but rather anonymous building on the edge of town. An introduction is reasonably easy to arrange. Everyone has heard of the BBC. In fact, it is quite amazing the number of Americans who claim to watch nothing but BBC programmes on America's non-commercial Public Broadcasting Service (PBS). With such massive popularity, you would think that PBS has the biggest viewing figures in the country instead of languishing, as it does, somewhere between the 24-hour weather forecast and the shopping channel. Also, it has to be said, the classy BBC productions that Americans particularly love generally turn out to involve Benny Hill. It has been my sad duty to inform dozens of Americans that Benny Hill is no longer with us. (He left the BBC years ago and life on earth rather more recently.)

Anyway, Jim Brown, the deep-voiced newscaster at KMTR, whose set I wandered on to at the end of another Oregon update, said I should check out the rendezvous that Earth First! was holding that weekend up in the Deschutes National Forest. If I went there I could get the story from the environmental activists' point of view. He told me to be prepared to eat lentils and take a tent. Jim Brown appeared to be charming and sincere. Appearing to be charming and sincere are, of course, the major subjects at American newscasters' school (along with nodding your head now and then when speaking on camera *and* emphasizing *the* wrong words *in* a sentence). But I thought I could act on his advice.

It was the sports correspondent who was the real delight. After giving the baseball scores and the results of the High School Athletics Meeting, he stood up to reveal that, although his jacket and tie were visible above the desk, he wore nothing but a pair of shorts below. Benny Hill would have been proud.

• Drive time •

Earth First! is a nationwide group of environmentalist activists who have an annual get-together in the Oregon Forests, and they were to be found by the side of the Davis Lake, which is just down the road from Eugene. This being America, 'just down the road' means getting on for 100 miles away. The road takes you through Oakridge, which is exactly what a town way out west ought to be called, alongside the Willamette River, which is not exactly what a river way out west should be called. It sounds more like a character in an Australian soap opera – 'Charlene, have you heard? Shane has left Draylon and run off with Willamette. I think she must be pregnant!'

In fact, the Willamette is the principal river of Oregon. Here and there it has been dammed to form reservoirs which are now part of the very fresh-looking landscape of water, woods and hills: Scotland without the mist, Austria without the people. The road, however, is pure Americana. American roads go on forever. Along them drive enormous American trucks which go on forever as well, axle succeeding axle, bearing loads the size of Liechtenstein. They are great. But American cars leave me cold. They have pointlessly large engines, soggy suspensions, ghastly plastic interiors and a complete absence of style. Detroit car-makers deserve all the trouble they get from Germany and Japan. Yet American trucks are unbeatable. Chrome-plated radiators, chrome-plated exhaust chimneys, chrome-plated bonnets, chrome-plated chrome. An American truck cab is a work of art, a truly regal throne in which sits the king of the road, the truck driver.

The truck driver is the all-American hero, travelling all over America, heroically keeping open the arteries down which flows the life blood of Uncle Sam. While heroically clogging his own arteries with fried food bought at the ubiquitous McDonalds and Wendys and Taco Bells.

The timber trade makes its contribution to the highway. Twenty tree trunks the size of, well, tree trunks are hauled down from the hills into the lumber yards in great big articulated trucks. The trade is supposed to be threatened by the environmentalists but, even so, great Birnam Woods travel to their Dunsinanes every day in impressive lorry-loads.

In fact, ordinary cars are a rarity along these Oregon roads. The Oregonian driver prefers to travel in a pick-up with a weird roof, trailer or other bespoke customization. Fashionable at the moment are monster-mobiles with high, fat wheels to lift the chassis several feet off the ground. Perhaps *Mad Max II* has just hit the state? Those heading for the hills travel by 'recreational vehicles'. These giant motor caravans allow you to take everything – including at least two kitchen sinks, a lavatory, air-conditioning, television and sound system – as you drive off to get away from it all. 'You can't take it with you' may be true of life in general, but it is not true of the American holiday-maker in particular. A crash between two of these movable monstrosities would keep a Third World shanty town in household equipment for ever.

Lunch is eaten in a roadside diner in Oakridge. It has everything. Fellow diners are characters out of *Twin Peaks*, all denim dungarees and weird-looking eyes. You cannot tell if they are gentle, sad country folk or serial killers. There are no red necks in these parts as everyone wears their hair short at the front and long at the back – the early 80s style kept alive in England by Ian Botham.

The waitress cracks gags for all the world as if she were in an American road movie as we order. I plump for an elkburger, made from real local elk. Very edible but bland. Exactly like a hamburger, in fact.

In fact, exactly like 99 per cent of American food. Nowhere else in the world are you offered so many different choices of foodstuffs, all of which taste of nothing at all, unless you cover them in the sauce of your choice, in which case they taste of sugar and salt. Travelling in a large party makes ordering fast food a slow process. Selecting your main course is just the start of it. A meal always comes with side-orders and add-ons. By the time each of you has specified the type of bread, the type of salad, the type of salad dressing and the type of coffee, you have forgotten what it was you ordered in the first place.

After a two-hour snack we had to press on to the lakeside rendezvous. We turned off Interstate 58 and on to a couple of back roads, then on to a forest track. We were on our way to meet a group of people who were desperately worried about the loss of trees, yet all we could see were trees, mile after mile of Christmas trees, conifers, pines, spruces.

Now, I love trees. Old English oaks, Brazilian rainforests, palm trees, shoe trees, all of them. My credit card even supports the Woodland Trust. But at first sight these conifers are just a touch boring. Growing straight up, they lack character. Telegraph poles with a garnish of green leaves.

Was this the forest that they were trying to protect, or the plantations which were replacing it? The brightest feature of some of the roads was the bright yellow flowers of the European broom. They call it Scotch broom round here, where it is regarded as a pest. Introduced from, presumably, Scotland, it threatens to take over the whole place as its seeds lie dormant for years, ever ready to spring up as soon as land is cleared. Nothing seems to kill it, and it is displacing native species. Revenge on America for the grey squirrel, perhaps?

• Wood stock •

There was no sign of any Earth Firsters along the empty forest tracks until at last we came across a very orderly line of parked vehicles. There were about fifty of them, all parked tidily on the one side of the road. These people were supposed to be anarchists, for goodness' sake. Had they no sense of disorder?

You could tell they were not hunters or fishermen because of the bumper stickers – *Save the Forest; Save the Owl; Save the Whale; Save the Bumper Sticker; Nuclear Power, No Thanks; No More Roads; Kill your Television.* If a car did not have one bumper sticker like that, it had several.

The cars all appeared to be about ten years old. Perhaps the theory is that cars get more environmentally friendly as they get older?

In the woods, the Earth Firsters were getting organized in a non-organizational way. In the absence of a hierarchy, orders were being given and received on a voluntary basis only. We met Tim Ingelsbee first. He is not the leader of Earth First! There are no leaders. But he does talk to the media quite a lot. He is tall, gentle and determined, and he knows what he is talking about. Equally importantly, his long brown hair braided into plaits provides an ideal frame for apocalyptic soundbites about the destruction of our planet through big business and bad management.

Earth Firsters were getting things set up for their weekend. Groups were forming to have teach-ins and seminars on nature studies, law, sex and sexuality, that kind of thing. Here and there were supplies of food and a lot of fresh drinking water in plastic containers. Not ecologically sound but, hey, at least you stay alive.

For the weekend, hippie dress is the standard clothing for the environmental activist: ponchos made from old army blankets for the men, long flowery skirts and monkey boots for the women – the hempen homespun uniform of the disaffected radical the world over.

As we strolled by the lake, Tim talked me through his concerns. Since the White Man came to the North West United States (and Canada, for that matter) he has been steadily working his way through the trees. As well as forests cleared for agriculture and housing, tree-felling for the timber industry has been gradually cutting into the naturally occurring woodland, the rate of destruction increasing since the war and the introduction of the chain saw. In theory, the timber industry replants as it goes along and, of course, given time, the forest can regenerate itself, but in practice the environment has been seriously damaged. Commercial pressures on corporate owners of private land force them to maximize their profits as fast as they can, so they tend to fell as many trees as possible as quickly as possible. The Federal Government owns a great deal of land from which it sells the timber on a regular basis. It should act more responsibly than private owners and to some extent does, but even in these Federal forests, the call of the mighty dollar rings out loud and clear. Politicians are not immune to the blandishments of big business and the desire of voters to keep their jobs.

When it comes to replanting, the diversity of the original forest is usually replaced by the single fastest-growing species. The result is what Tim calls a tree farm. It is not a real forest which has a mixture of ancient and modern trees of different species and supports countless other plants and animals as well.

The industry's preferred method for extracting timber is to clear-cut, which means to remove all the trees from a substantial area. This looks very ugly when it has just happened and can cause serious long-term damage. If you remove the trees completely the subsoil gets washed away by heavy rainfall. The streams get clogged with mud and the salmon die off (causing job losses further down the river). If enough subsoil is washed away the trees cannot grow back at all, and you have created a desert. No good for the environmentalist, and no good, in the long-term, for the logging industry either. Nowadays the loggers do not touch the trees which grow beside the streams and rivers, in order to help retain the banks and aid the recovery of the land. But would they have done that without the pressure from environmentalists?

Since ultimately they both want to protect trees, there should be plenty for the loggers and the greens to agree on, but in fact they are at loggerheads. Earth First! claims Oregon is down to the last 5 or 10 per cent of old-growth forest. But the loggers dispute this and reckon that quite enough land has been set aside as wilderness already. They are worried about losing their jobs – and, indeed, their whole industry – if muddle-headed concerns about imaginary threats to the environment unnecessarily prevent legitimate use of a renewable resource.

Earth First! makes the point that the wilderness areas are the least productive for man and nature. It says that there is no point in continuing to cut down the old woods to the very last ancient tree. The industry would come to an end then anyway, so you might as well stop before you have spoiled the land for good.

Tim is used to arguing these points with the logging industry, and in the media. But this weekend there are no arguments. He is camping with the converted. Earth Firsters have all the virtues – and vices – of hippies, Friends of the Earth, Woodcraft Folk, Luddites and Boy Scouts rolled into one. In fact, they chiefly resemble religious fanatics. Earth First! is a pantheist faith believing that the Earth as a whole is of far greater importance than mankind. Like religious zealots, Earth Firsters preach higher moral standards and foretell Doomsday. Unless we mend our ways Armageddon will come as rivers are poisoned and the ground is turned sour by our sins of commission and pollution. Or something like that. The End, at any rate, is Nigh.

Unlike most religious zealots in America, Earth Firsters are regarded as highly subversive. I chatted to a woman called Judi Bari. She was able to walk, just, with a stick. A bomb had gone off in her car when she was organizing protests against the cutting of redwood trees in California. To add insult to injury, literally, while she was recovering in hospital she was charged with being in possession of the bomb when it was in her car, just before it exploded and smashed her pelvis. The charge must have been based on the suggestion that she was going to plant the bomb somewhere herself, but she denies this and is convinced that someone in the timber industry was out to kill her, and that the FBI were out to frame her. Can things really have got this serious?

This weekend, though, is a retreat and a chance to commune with nature. Lake Davis is 4000 feet above sea level. Its area has shrunk over the last few years – the rainfall has lowered because of the reduction in tree cover, Tim tells me – and therefore has a flat area of land covered in springy turf alongside it which used to be part of the lake bed. From here the view is of hills covered with woods, one or two mountain tops covered with snow, and the remains of some ancient volcano still covered in solidified lava. However much tree cutting has gone on since they arrived, it must have been just this sort of landscape that the White Men gazed upon in wonder when they first got here.

'To make it complete, some Indians should come swooping down from the hills,' I remarked to Tim.

'No, we are the Indians,' he replied, somewhat delphically.

After nightfall there is a campfire. The plan is to film me chatting to people as they gather round the flames, but getting permission to do so is not easy. Some Earth Firsters have apparently had nasty experiences with television reporters. In any case a TV camera epitomizes the world of consumerism to which they all object. But the chief problem is that there is no leadership as such, no formal structure at all. All Indians and no Chiefs. (Perhaps that is what Tim meant.) So no person or persons can give permission on behalf of anyone else. Asking a group of fifty people whether we can film is a process fraught with difficulty. Eventually we establish the idea that we will be filming and anyone who does not wish to be caught on-camera should keep out of the way. That seems to be acceptable to most people, but one petulant voice demands:

'Hey, what if you don't want to be filmed, but you do want to hang out by the fire?'

In the end we were allowed to film. A certain amount of fat was chewed, breeze was shot, and toss was argued. A couple of guys started playing their guitars and a couple of girls stripped to the waist. We did little to establish whether their environmentalism was merely a fashionable stick with which to beat the consumer society or a real breakthrough in political thinking. Most concern was expressed at the shortage of beer. The guy who was organizing it was apparently engaged in ecological discussions with his girlfriend in a distant tent.

In the darkness a voice asked me, off-camera, what my real views were on Earth First! I had been warned that FBI agents infiltrated the organization so I went carefully, even though the questioner was from New Zealand. Well, I evaded, I have only just got here, I do not know enough yet to make up my mind.

'I thought you guys in Britain would have done massive research before you arrived,' my questioner sneered.

'I thought New Zealanders were polite,' I tried as a riposte.

Some other voices, not knowing that I was still there, roundly abused the BBC as our crew bus drove off. It was time for bed.

The camera crew were off to stay in a warm hotel back in Oakridge. But to get the full flavour of a night in the woods, and to retain credibility with the Earth Firsters, I was sleeping under canvas. While it was light I had pitched, with the maximum of fuss for the cameras, a Hillary bell tent which I hoped was named after Sir Edmund Hillary, the first man up Everest, rather than Hillary Clinton the First Lady in the White House. Now that it was night and pitch dark, it was difficult to find the tent. It was not far from the lake, near some trees, a description which would apply to no more than 1000 square miles of this continent. It had been quite a cold day and threatened to be an even colder night. Why was I doing this? It was by no means certain that the tent was even waterproof. Television programmes are normally made in nice warm studios with a quiet dressing room beforehand and hospitality afterwards. I wanted to win a BAFTA, not a Duke of Edinburgh's, Award. Did the director (himself on his way back to Oakridge) secretly want me to get frostbite in the documentary?

In the event the night was not too bad and I managed to survive it with a sleeping bag for bedclothes, a Barbour for a ground sheet and a warm researcher for company. The only interruption during the hours of darkness came from some revelling Earth Firsters playfully attempting to let the tent down. No real malice, just a test of our good sportsmanship, which was rewarded with a bottle of Jack Daniels. So at four in the morning I found myself teaching the night visitors games from *Whose Line Is It Anyway?* which eventually drove them back to their own tents.

Next morning the scene was magical. The subtle grey of the early morning sky blended with the pastel colours of the hills to be reflected in the still water of the lake. The cry of the occasional bird flapping over the lake's surface rang out as clear as a bell from half a mile away. I was one of the first up but gradually the voices of other early-risers could be heard celebrating the dawn. I had not been camping like this for more than twenty years. I decided I must do it again. In perhaps another twenty years' time.

I picked my way through the trees to find the carefully dug latrines. The campers here were radical, anarchist hippies to a person, but Baden-Powell would have been proud of them. Everything here was done exactly as set out in Scouting for Boys. I wondered if there would be Church Parade on Sunday.

My thoughts having wandered to and from the Relief of Mafeking, I awaited the arrival of my troop to record for posterity my early-morning awakening in this corner of paradise. This was duly filmed at about 11 o'clock when they made it back from their corner of bed and breakfast luxury in civilization, the cameras capturing the moment when I emerged from my tent on the way to lunch.

This morning everyone seemed friendlier. Perhaps it was because I had shared the experience of one night in the open with them.

My next interviewee was a very committed activist called Peg Millett. In fact she had been committed to prison for two years for taking part in an activity called monkey-wrenching.

This does not involve monkeys but does involve literally throwing spanners, or monkey wrenches, into the works of industrial activity thought to threaten the environment. Monkey-wrenchers reckon that if you vandalize or otherwise interfere with the actions of big business you will be able to render unprofitable certain economic activities you disapprove of.

The best-known example of monkey-wrenching in the tree-felling business is to hammer metal spikes into tree trunks. A hidden metal spike in a tree can wreak havoc with the sawing equipment at a sawing mill. At the worst it can threaten the lives of mill workers, at the least it might require every tree to be X-rayed before it is cut into planks. At any rate, the very threat of these metal spikes makes the lumber industry less profitable. Monkey-wrenchers get up to other activities as well, including the removal of markers in the forest set up to show which trees have been sold at auction. They block drains on forest roads built to allow access for heavy equipment, hoping that a big storm will flood the road or even wash it away.

These methods are all set out in a book called *Ecodefense*, edited by Dave Foreman and Bill Haywood. It is printed on recycled paper, naturally. But also with soya-based ink. I am ashamed to admit I have no idea what ordinary ink is made from. It isn't seal cub blood or anything nasty like that, is it?

The First Amendment to America's Constitution makes it impossible to prevent the publication of a book which manifestly encourages illegal activity. In Britain you could probably only publish it if the words were removed and dubbed on later by an actor speaking in an Irish accent.

Anyway, whether or not she had been encouraged by the book's methods, Peg Millett had been convicted of destroying an electricity pylon in an attempt to disrupt uranium mining in Arizona. She was caught when a friend she had known for years informed against her. It turned out that the so-called friend had been an FBI agent all along, and had only got to know her to turn her in to the authorities. Sometimes you just don't know who to trust.

• Woodman spare that tree •

An area which throws the dispute between the conservationists and the loggers into sharpest relief is Warner Creek. In October 1991 a fire swept through about 9000 acres of prime Spotted Owl habitat on which tree-felling had been banned. The fire stripped the trees of every leaf and twig, scorched the earth and killed all the wildlife. Presumably the owls flew away. Only the tree trunks remained standing, blackened and unbowed, but dead.

Tim took us to the creek. It is an eerie place. The blackened trunks of thousands of dead trees stand where they perished. If left alone they would remain upright for many decades. The fire here has acted like a neutron bomb and destroyed all life while leaving the structures in place.

All the evidence indicates that this was a man-made fire. Tim is convinced it was arson deliberately committed by loggers. This may seem like paranoia, but there are some grounds for his suspicion. Although the area has been destroyed as a forest, the wood in the trees would still be usable if it were removed. Indeed, the logging industry has pressed for the right to extract the timber now that the area has been ruined anyway. Conservationists make the point that whether or not the fire was started with this end in view, to allow logging now would be an open invitation for loggers to set fire to inconveniently protected areas all over the country. The loggers are incensed that there is good timber here which is just going to waste. And so we are back to the fundamental difference between the two sides. To the logger, a tree which falls down and rots away is an utter waste. To the environmentalist, a tree which rots is part of the life cycle of the forest. So even dead tree trunks should be allowed to sink slowly back into the ground.

To me, dead trees standing on a blackened hillside look like a bad result for everyone. The baby chopped in half before Solomon has given judgement.

• I am not a lumberjack and I am not OK •

To speak to the loggers we went to see Wilbur Heath who used to run Heath Logging. Actually, he still does, but now the company is called Mountain Resource Management. Wilbur, a giant redwood of a man himself, wryly acknowledges that his activities have had to be renamed. He is no longer clear-cutting sections of the forest, but engaged in 'view enhancement'; his business is no longer called logging but conducting 'ecosystem management'. He is not chopping down trees but 'harvesting renewable natural resources'. His parody of politically correct language, although a joke, does represent a victory for environmentalists. Their concerns are now setting the agenda.

But Wilbur claims that the loggers are the real environmentalists. He says the so-called environmentalists are preservationists – they do not want to see anything altered or used for the benefit of mankind. Be they environmentalists, or preservationists, they do seem to be winning many of the battles. The Endangered Species Act was passed in 1972 to conserve threatened wildlife by, amongst other things, protecting their habitat. In the modern American way, a steady stream of legal actions has identified more and more species dependent on the forest. And so it has become more and more difficult to chop down trees.

The Northern Spotted Owl is the most famous, or notorious, of these protected creatures. Wilbur says the 1972 legislation has been unfairly exploited by environmental groups who seek to bring to an end to logging, which was never the intention of Congress when they passed the Act.

Nor are the owls completely innocent. Wilbur reckons they are cleverer than most people realize. He says one of their favourite prey species is the tree rat, great numbers of which are brought to earth by tree-felling. Owls are therefore attracted to areas where tree-felling is taking place. Consequently it always looks as though there is a high population of owls in areas where tree-felling is occurring. Tree-felling is thus blamed for destroying the owl's habitat.

To Wilbur, this is madness. He argues that the trees are a renewable resource. In that sense, the timber industry is not like coal mining or oil extraction. And even with the best growing methods there are about eighty years before a crop of trees is harvested, which should be quite long enough for the natural world to enjoy them. In addition there are wilderness areas set aside which are not interfered with at all. Wilbur's main ire is directed at Earth First! which he regards as a smelly, slimy terrorist group. The book on eco-terrorism has not gone unnoticed by people like Wilbur who have invested their lives in logging and their money in logging equipment.

He showed me the work which is done by him and his men. The men prefer not to be called lumberjacks. They say 'lumberjack' is a Canadian term. Or maybe it was the Monty Python song that put them off. They are tree-fellers.

The actual business of tree-felling is relatively straightforward. First you use a chain saw to cut into your tree on the side you want it to fall, until you reach about the middle. Then you cut in from the opposite side until the tree topples over, perhaps helping it in the right direction with a wedge or two, hammered into the trunk with the blunt side of an axe. As you reach the point when the tree cannot hold itself up any longer, there is a sad creaking noise – the death cry of a king of the forest, or two bits of wood rubbing against each other, depending upon your sensibilities. This is followed by a resounding crash as a magnificent specimen hits the ground or a depressing splat if the tree turns out to be rotten.

On the forest floor, the trunk is trimmed of branches and cut into 30-foot lengths. The whole process takes a matter of minutes. While this part of logging cannot be anything like as physically demanding as it was before the invention of the chain saw, it is clearly no work for a wimp. You have to watch out for the tree kicking back as it keels over and bringing you to the ground with it. You must be careful not to massacre yourself with the chain saw. And you need a sure foot to pick your way over the damp ground strewn with felled trees and branches all tangled up with the undergrowth. Getting the trees to fall in the right direction is made to look easy by the tree-fellers. The only stage I was allowed to help with was to shout 'Timber!' when a tree was about to fall. They really do shout 'Timber!' when a tree is coming down. Unless there are environmentalists around, in which case they shout, 'Hey, you like trees! Why don't you stand over there and see if you can catch this one?' They are uncomplicated folk, genuinely puzzled by the opposition to their going about the forest doing an honest day's work for an honest day's pay.

Tree-felling has a simple charm, but getting the logs out of the forest and loaded on to trucks is epic. At the edge of a forest clearing, Wilbur Heath's men have positioned an enormous tower which forms part of a temporary funicular railway. A wire stretches about 80 yards from the tower into the recently denuded forest. Workers attach chains to the 30-foot sections of wood which are dragged down the hillsides by the engine which runs along the wire to the tower.

Once there, the logs are detached and then picked up one by one by a mechanical grabber, a lobster from the land that time forgot. Its metal claws are directed skilfully by its driver, who stacks the logs neatly on the back of an eight-axled truck which then drives down the specially built forest road to town.

The whole process is noisy, dangerous and impressive. Real man's work. Even the various engines involved must, you feel, run on testosterone. It is work that belongs to a time when man went nobly into battle with the wilderness. Has too much of the wilderness vanished? What will Wilbur Heath do with his logging equipment if there is no logging left?

Much the same question faces Jim Hallstrom. He is the owner of the Zip-o-Mill in Eugene. Here seasoned trees, when they can get them, are turned into planks of wood. Trunks travel along conveyor belts towards giant saws, like so many James Bonds left for dead by a sadistic baddie.

The mill is working on trees bought three years before. Since then, timber sales have been held up in a legal gridlock. Or perhaps that should be log jam. The Clinton Administration has tried to work out a compromise between the environment and the economy. (They had got to Option 9 at the time of my visit to Oregon.) But that would allow for only 20 per cent of the former levels of timber extraction from Federal forests. Better than the zero option which has applied for three years, but still likely to be disastrous for the little mills like this one which depend upon government timber sales. And disastrous for employment in the state of Oregon.

The mill used to employ more than one hundred people, but now that number has dropped to fifty. Of the six mills that were in the immediate area, Zip-o is the only one still in operation. The remaining workers are kitted out in blue denim dungarees, wear baseball caps and eat their lunch from tin boxes. They look the way American blue-collar workers have looked since the early days of the Flintstones. It is difficult to see what they would do if the mill ground to a halt.

Mert Minges who lives out on the Oakridge Road used to be a logger and did very well for himself in a small way. But his sub-contracting business was too small to survive in these difficult times, and his logging equipment lies rusting beside his single-storey wooden house.

He still uses his chain saw. But nowadays he uses it to carve wooden statues out of tree stumps and logs. Mostly he does bears, about 3 or 4 feet high. They are pretty good. Even when he shows you how he does the delicate work with a tool designed to hack through a trunk as fast as possible, you cannot really see how it is done. He can carve all sorts of forest animals and he knows exactly what the bears and the racoons and the elk look like because loggers, these so-called despoilers and destroyers of the forest, actually love going there. All of them go there to hunt and fish and enjoy the natural world. It is strange how much loggers and long-hairs have in common.

Mert blames the clamp-down on sales of timber from government land on the owners of private land who have felled their own forests in the reckless pursuit of profits. Mert is lucky because he has his skill as a chain-saw artist to fall back on, but he would rather be logging. In the meantime he is carving out a niche for himself in the economic environment.

• Spotted Owl spotting •

The niche that the Northern Spotted Owl has carved for itself is a highly inconvenient and irritating one for the logging industry. A breeding pair of owls needs about 1000 acres of roughly two-hundred-year-old Douglas fir forest in which to live. The owls nest in hollows at the tops of the trees and feed on the various vole, squirrel and other mammalian species which live lower down. They tolerate a few bare patches of ground and some young trees, but they have to have plenty of tall old trees. The dark dank forest keeps them cool in summer and protects them from the snow in winter. Of course, 1000 acres of ancient Douglas fir is exactly what the logger is desperate to get his hands, and his chopper, on as well. So the identification of the owl as a protected species has made it public enemy number one amongst the logging community.

Most of the loggers I spoke to claim they have never spotted a spotted owl in many years of working in the woods, so I assumed it must be hard to track them down. Actually, it is very easy. All you need to do is go to the right stretch of forest with the right guide. We went to a protected woodland with Frank Oliver of the Bureau of Land Managment.

How does the Bureau of Land Management differ from the US Forest Service? Well, I am not absolutely sure. One is so used to thinking of America as the land of free enterprise and unbridled capitalism that one can forget it has a bewildering array of bureaucratic agencies, departments and offices regulating and controlling all aspects of the American dream. The US Forest Service is basically part of the Department of Agriculture and seeks, so its critics would have it, to assist the exploitation of the forests for profit at the expense of a work of nature. With the Bureau of Land Management, which is more like an arm of a ministry of the environment, it is the other way around.

Anyway, Frank Oliver knew how to attract owls. You make an owl-like call near one of their nest sites and take along a supply of live mice. Immediately we arrived in the woods we saw an owl sitting on a branch. It recognized Frank's call and was licking its beak at the prospect of a few bite-size rodent snackettes (hold the salad). We got really excited and insisted on filming the owl from every angle, anxious that it might fly away before we had got some decent footage.

Frank clucked at us and said film crews were always like this and not to panic, the owl would not be going anywhere. The owl is a placid, trusting kind of critter. It is not put off by film crews in the slightest. An avian Tony Slattery, it is happy to appear on television at any time.

For the mice it is less fun, more like a snuff movie. A mouse is put on a twig which you hold out in front of you and the owl makes its way down from the tree tops, flying from branch to branch until it is within swooping range of the unsuspecting little mammal. Released from its carrying box, the mouse has just started exploring the sights and smells of a real twig when the owl suddenly glides in and grabs it with its claws. It flies on to another branch and bites the mouse's head off. Nature red in beak and claw. Where is Ted Hughes when you need him most?

Both the male and the female owl are there, the male sometimes sharing his mouse with the female and she flying right to the top of the tree to feed her young. We could see the two youngsters way above us, sticking their heads out of their nest.

Spotted Owls are easy to film and easy to study. Researchers attach little radios to them to track their movements. They have no real enemies. Even their rather dodo-like trust in human beings has not been abused by hunters. The one risk to their survival is their dependence upon a natural habitat which has been steadily eroded and now requires elaborate protection to keep it in existence.

• Trouble at Mill City •

The Lesser Spotted Owl may have found its salvation in the Endangered Species Act. But is the genuinely endangered species now the lesser employed lumber worker? For the last part of the film we headed up to Mill City, whose very name celebrates its link with logging.

On the way there it was striking to see what a remote part of the world this is. Backwoods, in fact. It is a long way from Washington where vital decisions are taken; and it seems light years away from New York or Los Angeles.

Everything around Mill City is built on wood. And it is built from wood. Its public lavatories are wood-panelled. Everyone has wooden houses, so they have a rather temporary air. You feel that, in the event of an Indian uprising, they could be formed into a circle to resist attack.

In the town's Trio Tavern the locals gather for a beer and to crack jokes about Spotted Owls and interfering middle-class hippie activists who cannot see the wood for the trees. The tree-huggers have ruined trade. And taken over the White House. The drinkers in the tavern were loggers and drivers and mill workers, all worried about losing their jobs. An Englishman, very popular in the bar and who now sells garden furniture, tells me he was the original drummer with Status Quo. He got out of rock music after the group's first hit, as he did not think they would last. I wonder if he keeps in touch with Pete Best? Naturally, he is in favour of leaving things the way they are. Surprisingly few of the regulars were actually born in Oregon. Until a few years ago Oregon was still attracting people from elsewhere in America. But not any more. Nobody comes here looking for work now.

Everyone wishes things could return to the way they were. Good old boys remembering the good old days. The problem for Oregon is that people cannot go any further west in search of a living. It is a worry for those who want to work in the forests and for those who want to save them. For everybody, this is the final frontier.

• Opal Creek, made to make your mouth water •

One way to stir things up in the Trio Tavern is to mention George Atiyeh. As a boy he spent a great deal of his time in Opal Creek, a virtually unspoiled piece of ancient woodland a few miles from Mill City. His cousin's grandfather owned the mining rights to the area and for many years prevented the Forest Service moving in and cutting down the trees. On the old man's death, George took up the cause and, through a friend's company, has acquired the mining rights which, under nineteenth-century laws designed to encourage the extraction of natural resources, allowed him to fight and win many legal battles to preserve rather than destroy the environment. George has been a student, a playboy, a logger and a pilot. He is a bit of a sixties hippie, but very well-connected. Quite apart from his rich college friends, his uncle used to be Governor of the state.

To get to Opal Creek we drove along the road built by the Forest Service years ago when it was trying to get access to its trees. Once we reached the gateway we rode the rest of the way on horseback.

The mountain track takes you through trees which are hundreds of years old. One is said to be one thousand years old: a Douglas fir which was growing before the Norman Conquest of England. In the valley flow the crystal clear waters of the mountain streams. Here and there are the boarded-up entrances of old copper, zinc and gold mines. And at the centre of the reserve is Jawbone Flats, a collection of old miners' wooden houses occupied now by George, his friends and employees and therefore equipped with TVs, CDs and PCs, but from the outside looking just like the set of a Wild West film.

Opal Creek is available to scientists and students who want to come and understand the workings of a more or less virgin forest. There is a modern (wooden) building with reception rooms and bedrooms for visitors. During the winter the whole place gets snowed in but in the summer months it is a pure delight. Hydro-electric power provided by the fast-running river lights and heats the place: an environmentalist's heaven.

The only blot on the landscape is waste matter from some of the mine workings, but plans are in hand to clear that up. Ironically, although it is George's intention to keep the whole area in as pristine state as possible, he does have to continue mining activities so he can maintain his claim to keep the Forest Service off the land.

George may be a hero to the environmental movement, but in his own local community he is a pariah. One man's saved tree is a lot of other men's lost jobs. As George himself points out, they are decent folk around these parts but they are not above uttering death threats when they are riled. It happened to him so often that he even changed his answerphone message to encourage anyone making a threat to speak up if they were nervous about doing it for the first time. 'Leave your name and number, I *will* get back to you.'

People have refused to drink with him, or talk to him – he is the Salman Rushdie of Timberland. In the noble tradition of the Wild West he has come through it all to earn grudging respect from the local community, mixed with absolutely unbridled hatred.

It is a shame that it takes so much effort to preserve such a delightful place. North America is so huge that it is extraordinary to think there might not be enough room for places like Opal Creek. And room to cut and grow trees for fun and profit.

It may well be that the hatred of the environmentalists is simply a focus for the loggers' frustrations. Whatever happened, they would run out of ancient forest eventually. Unemployment, so it is said, would have hit the logging industry because of mechanization and competition from other parts of the world. So possibly the loggers are barking up the wrong tree.

Ingeniously, the logging industry argues that it is much better for the global environment if they are allowed to cut timber in Oregon, where replanting always occurs after trees are chopped down. If logging is stopped here, demand for wood products will not suddenly cease in America. That demand will be met with trees in other parts of the world where replanting practices are likely to be much less strict. Ironically, logging will probably have to continue if only to supply paper for the mountains of reports, studies, legal case papers and books which the issue generates.

My last act before leaving was to plant a tree on some clear-cut ground. Everybody wants trees around here, be they logger, environmentalist or owl. For comic effect I accidentally drove over my sapling as I headed home. But have no fear. I planted another tree alongside it. In fact, no tree suffered in the making of the film: even the one I drove over bounced back immediately.

Maybe there is some hope for the future of trees in Oregon after all.

OUR
MAN
IN... HAWAII

O F all the places I visited in this series, Hawaii must be the one which most closely conforms to the notion of paradise. It consists of a group of sun-drenched, tropical islands, lost in the warm waters of the world's largest ocean. In your dreams, you may or may not have visited Hawaii, but you have certainly been there while listening to *Desert Island Discs.*

As it happens, I was not anticipating perfection. High-minded visitors usually report that Hawaii's indigenous beauty has been overwhelmed by the United States of America, into which it has been incorporated. Hawaii's native charm, they say, has been destroyed by the large numbers of non-Hawaiians who either settle or holiday there, while its remoteness ensures that, nonetheless, it is still an expensive place in which to live. Overwhelmed, over-populated and over-priced, it has long acquired the reputation of a paradise lost to all but the rich and tasteless.

It is certainly lost to Native Hawaiians. Two hundred and fifty years ago they had never met anyone from beyond the seas. One hundred years ago they were still a sovereign nation ruled by their own royal family. Now firmly under American control, pure-bred Hawaiians account for somewhere between 1 and 4 per cent of the total population. Even so, there is a political movement which seeks independence for Hawaii, possibly by way of reinstating the old monarchy. Hawaii for Hawaiians. Why not? It was certainly worth a trip to paradise, however tarnished, to find out if it could be done.

• End of the Earth •

The Hawaiian Islands are in the middle of the Pacific Ocean, a long way from anywhere. They are 2000 miles from the American mainland, 3000 miles from Japan and 4000 miles from Australia.

Human occupation was a recent innovation to Hawaii. It was first populated in about AD 500 when Polynesians finally found their way there during their steady migration through the islands of the Pacific. The very first settlers were supplanted five hundred years later by migrants who arrived from Tahiti. And there was a further wave of

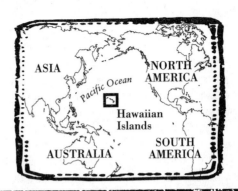

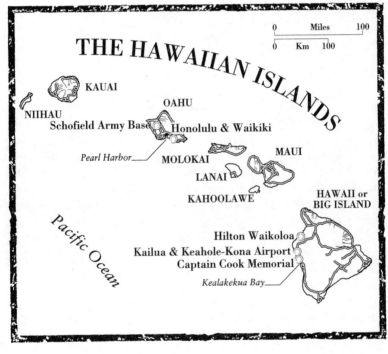

THE HAWAIIAN ISLANDS

KAUAI

NIIHAU

OAHU

Schofield Army Base

Honolulu & Waikiki

Pearl Harbor

MOLOKAI

MAUI

LANAI

KAHOOLAWE

HAWAII or
BIG ISLAND

Hilton Waikoloa

Kailua & Keahole-Kona Airport
Captain Cook Memorial

Kealakekua Bay

Pacific Ocean

0   Miles   100
0   Km   100

migration, again from Tahiti, in the twelfth century. But after that, humans on Hawaii appear to have been pretty much on their own.

Life may well have been idyllic. There were wars between the six main inhabited islands, fearsome punishments handed out to enforce a rigid caste system, and human sacrifice performed as part of religious observance, none of which is to everyone's taste. But the benign climate, fertile land, abundant ocean and freedom from outside influence made for a simple and overwhelmingly pleasant life. Or so it seems, looking back.

What is undoubtedly the case is that, when it eventually came, contact with the outside world was a catastrophe for the Hawaiian people and their way of life.

• Over-cooked •

The great British explorer Captain James Cook discovered one or two of the Hawaiian islands in 1778 and received an extremely friendly reception. He returned in 1779 and landed for the first time on the largest of the islands. This island is the one called Hawaii but, since that is the name of the whole archipelago as well, it is generally known as the Big Island.

As every schoolboy knows, Captain Cook met his death in Hawaii, but I do not think that even as a schoolboy I had understood the extraordinary details of the events surrounding his demise.

On 17 January 1779 the Hawaiians were in the middle of a celebration of *makahiki,* a festival dedicated to their god of fertility, Lono. Legend had it that Lono, whose symbol was a white banner held high on a crossbow, would one day return, possibly to the bay known as Kealakekua, the pathway of the god. The legend said that he would arrive travelling clockwise round the island.

On that day in January Cook and his men – almost certainly the first outsiders these Hawaiians had ever seen – arrived in their two sailing ships, *Discovery* and *Resolution*. They dropped anchor in Kealakekua Bay, having first sailed clockwise round the island. The Hawaiians believed that Captain Cook was surely Lono made flesh. If there was any doubt about it, the white sails of his ships looked, to the Hawaiians, exactly like Lono's symbolic banners.

So, not surprisingly, Cook was hailed as a god. He was greeted by hundreds of canoes and thousands of people. The people bowed before him. He and his men were offered every comfort and entertainment.

The beautiful Hawaiian women were eager to enjoy the sexual favours of these divine visitors and, after months at sea, Cook's sailors really would have been super-human to have resisted them. They must have thought they had died and gone to heaven. As the song put it just under two centuries later, 'If paradise was half as nice as heaven that you take me to ...'

After two weeks, it was time to go. Cook had arrived as a god and was leaving with honour. But having set sail, things took a turn for the worse. A storm which broke the *Resolution's* mast forced Cook to return to the bay. This time there was no festival in progress, and his ships sailed the wrong way round the island. Gone were the crowds of adoring disciples. The natives were still friendly, but the broken mast had indicated a suspicious lack of godlike omnipotence. The Hawaiians started helping themselves to interesting artefacts on the ships, eventually making off with the *Discovery's* cutter.

Captain Cook knew what to do in these circumstances – he set off to take an important chief hostage in order to secure the cutter's return. Unfortunately, while he was doing this, there was a further altercation in which another, lesser, chief was killed.

This poisoned the atmosphere and, abandoning his hostage, Cook had to fight his way back towards his ship. The sailors fired at the Hawaiians, thinking that this would intimidate them in the same way that it had unnerved other Pacific islanders.

But it enraged them instead and, when Cook was struck on the head by a rock in the shallow waters of the bay, he was then stabbed to death in a frenzied attack, with many Hawaiian warriors passing the weapons between themselves to share in the kill. Cook's body was hacked to bits and taken away for some dreadful purpose. Most of it was returned, however, after Cook's distraught men took equally ferocious revenge on the Hawaiian people.

This violent end to Cook's glorious career marked the beginning of disaster for Hawaii. It was not, however, the violence which was Hawaii's doom. Friendly relations were restored more or less immediately once the remaining portions of Cook's body were handed back.

It was these friendly relations which caused the trouble. Cook had done his best to minimize intimate contact between his sailors and the alluring locals. Hawaiian women were not supposed to come onboard ship. Any of Cook's men known to be suffering from syphilis were to be thrashed if they slept with the local women. But in the way of these things, sexually transmitted diseases were transmitted sexually and they spread rapidly amongst the promiscuous islanders. Killing was done here, but with kindness.

For so long an isolated population, the Hawaiians had little resistance to venereal disease and the various other infections, plagues and pestilences that every group of visitors brought with them from civilization.

In eighty years, their numbers fell from about 300 000 to fewer than 60 000. In 1823, King Kamehameha II (Liholiho to his friends) and his favourite wife decided to go to Britain to visit King George IV. But before they could meet the King of England, both the King of Hawaii and his consort died of measles.

There were corresponding disasters to the fabric of the islands. At the time of Cook's discovery, Hawaii had extensive forests of sandalwood trees. The trees were bought by American shippers and sold to China where the wood was highly prized. But in fifty years the sandalwood was all gone and the profits mostly in the hands of the shippers. Kings and chiefs had been paid for the wood, but largely in expensive foreign imports. The ordinary Hawaiian had done back-breaking work hauling the wood to the coast, but a combination of *naïveté* and greed meant that very little was gained from what might have been a long-term money-spinner. Similarly, Hawaii came and went as a whaling centre as the whales came and went in the Pacific. Finally, sugar and then pineapples were developed as cash crops, with more and more labourers brought in from China and Japan to work in the fields.

Along the way, the Native Hawaiian population continued to decline and the number of incomers soared. The old Hawaiian religion of gods and taboos died away, and Christianity took its place. The ways of money, business and land-ownership so familiar in Europe and America supplanted the old feudal system and communal way of living which had applied before. The Hawaiian way of life withered away.

The Hawaii that Cook discovered was divided into its separate islands, but they were soon to be united under King Kamehameha the Great, who succeeded in imposing his rule on the other islands partially with the assistance of weaponry which he had acquired from Cook and later visitors.

The kings and queens who succeeded King Kamehameha were sometimes not so great but the Hawaiian monarchy lasted until 1894, when a consortium of *haole* (white) business people forced the establishment of a republic which four years later was annexed by the United States.

Hawaii had not been conquered by military action. The closest it had come to that had been in 1843 when Captain Lord George Paulet decided to claim Hawaii on behalf of Great Britain. He reckoned it was the sort of thing you were supposed to do in those days. Coming back from the South Seas without another piece of territory for the Empire would be like coming back from Torremolinos nowadays without a bullfight poster. But Queen Victoria was not amused to have a fellow royal family stripped of its domain and after six months Hawaii had to be given back to the Hawaiians.

Interestingly enough, the Union Jack forms part of the Hawaiian state flag, but not for any reasons connected with this very brief period as a British possession. In fact, the Union Jack had already been included in Hawaii's flag some time before 1816, possibly because a British sea captain had given the nation one of his flags, perhaps in recognition of British protection at that time. There is also a fanciful story that the Hawaiian flag was deliberately made to look like a combination of the British Union Jack and the American Stars and Stripes in order to deter pirates from attacking Hawaiian shipping. If true, this could not have said much for the intelligence of the pirates.

There is the usual list of suspects for the bringing down of Hawaii as a nation state: plantation-owners, missionaries and the military.

The military were interested in Hawaii as a coaling station and strategic base. They anticipated that Pearl Harbor, the large natural haven just up the coast from Honolulu on the island of Oahu, would have an important part to play in some future war. The missionaries did their work in establishing the Christian faith in these far-off islands. And their descendants became important land-owners as the years went by. But it was the plantation-owners, businessmen and traders who did the most harm. They feared that Hawaii's last monarch, Queen Liliuokalani, was too keen to reassert the royal powers which they had prised from her predecessors. They wanted free access to American markets for their sugar. And so, despite a certain amount of discouragement from the American government of the day, Queen Liliuokalani was dethroned and she was replaced by a republic dominated by whites. The Queen was eventually convicted of treason, for daring to countenance resistance to the various land-owners and carpet-baggers who had assumed control of her kingdom. By 1959 Hawaii's Hawaiian history was all but forgotten and 90 per cent of its citizens voted in favour of it becoming an American state.

Fewer than 4 per cent of the population is of pure Hawaiian descent, and no more than 30 per cent claim to have any Hawaiian blood at all. Hawaii has become a true melting pot of Japanese, Caucasian, Chinese, Filipino, Puerto Rican and Polynesian ingredients. In the main it is an advertisement for inter-racial harmony but it does suggest that any idea of restoring a king of the Hawaiians would be difficult.

• Aloha Athletic •

Well, that was just the background. When I flew into the city of Honolulu which, together with Pearl Harbor and 80 per cent of the Hawaiian Islands' population is on the island of Oahu, I was wondering how we were going to capture the complex history and politics of Hawaii's situation. But the director had the problem well in hand – we were going to make a spoof of the TV series *Hawaii Five-O*.

I arrived in Honolulu on the evening of the day I had left Heathrow. Or it might have been the day before. Or possibly the day after. Hawaii is on the other side of the world from London, a few miles from the International Date Line as the Jumbo flies. By the time you get there you literally do not know what day of the week it is. All I did know was that I had to get up the next morning, very early, to be filmed rowing in a Hawaiian canoe because a canoe sequence is featured in the end credits of *Hawaii Five-0*.

A Hawaiian canoe is a long hollowed-out tree trunk, or nowadays an equivalent structure made from modern materials. It has an outrigger attached to one side to keep it from rolling over. The rowers sit in a line facing forwards. The oars are like large misshapen shovels which are used to propel the boat through the water. In my boat there were to be six oarsmen. Or, rather, five oarsmen and me.

The eclectic racial mix in Hawaii has produced some very beautiful people. Their coffee-coloured skin is enhanced by a life spent in the sun, and their muscles are toned by the outdoor life and healthy exercise.

On the other hand, my personal racial mixture is very British: Scots and English, with maybe a dash of Viking. My peelie-wally skin encases a body grown slack from a sedentary indoor life spent mainly under the grey skies of London. As a group we were not so much east meets west, as east meets etiolated.

But off I set to make as big an idiot of myself as was absolutely necessary. The camera crew followed in a rather more comfortable, well-equipped, motor boat.

A strange thing happened just before we started. From nowhere a group of beautiful girls arrived. Possibly they were friends of the oarsmen, or of the captain of the motor boat. Maybe they just wanted a ride. More likely they were conforming to the ancient customary law of all nations which requires that all motor boats, pleasure craft and yachts sailing in or near fashionable resorts have to be decorated with an appropriate number of glamorous women. The next time you are in Monte Carlo, or the Caribbean, or Hawaii, check it out. Better still, get a boat.

The basics of rowing Hawaiian-style were reasonably easy to pick up. I do not think the technique is as efficient as the method used at Henley Regatta or in the Oxford and Cambridge Boat Race, but at least you can see where you are going and the novice has less chance of capsizing the whole boat by fouling his oar. You just toil away, pulling your shovel through the water, trying not to splash the guys sitting in front and behind. Alternate oarsmen row on opposite sides of the canoe: every ten or so strokes, on a signal from the lead man, you swap sides. We spent an hour or two rowing up and down in front of famous Honolulu landmarks. Sometimes putting on speed to catch a wave to surge towards the beach, sometimes stopping to rest or fool around jumping in and out of the clear, warm water. I did my best to keep paddle in time with the others, knowing that one false move would (a) slow us down and (b) inevitably be the only moment shown in the film.

Well, it was a small price to pay for being in such a glorious location. What is everyone on about? Hawaii seemed pretty good to me.

• On the waterfront •

You can see from the water, from the air and, for that matter, from any episode of *Hawaii Five-O*, that Honolulu has developed into a fully-fledged American city. It has high-rises and highways just like Miami or Los Angeles. So many Americans have come here to get away from it all that they have brought it all with them. Waikiki is a particular sadness to those who knew it in the old days. Waikiki is a narrow strip of land bordering the ocean, separated from the rest of Honolulu by a waterway called the Ala Wai Canal. More or less everything about it now is artificial. The canal is not a natural waterway, it is not even a canal for carrying barges. It was built in 1922, to drain the land that most of Waikiki is built on so that it could be developed as a resort. Waikiki does have a beautiful, if usually crowded, beach of white sand. But even that is not genuine any more – what with one thing and another, the original beach has been washed away so they have to go round the other islands digging up remote beaches to replace it. Now, that is obviously a sensible idea, because all Waikiki's hotels and souvenir shops have already been built so there would be no point in making the tourists traipse off to find these other beaches. Nowadays the mountain can be brought to Muhammad.

But for all that, Waikiki is good fun. Americans like shops and shopping, so there is a full range of expensive stores to keep them happy. And lots of cheap ones as well, which for some reason are all called ABC. Plus restaurants and bars and swimming pools. And it is just as well that there are things to do on land because there are so many hotel rooms in this tiny area that if everyone did go to the beach at the same time they would be rationed to one grain of sand each. As it is you can only get a tan if the person next to you has had their ears pierced.

There is a strong Japanese presence. They make up approximately 22 per cent of the population. Waikiki is also a popular Japanese tourist destination. Especially, it would seem, for weddings. Against a background of holiday-makers in bikinis and T-shirts, elaborately dressed Japanese couples pose for their wedding photographs in the grounds of the beach-front hotels. On the lawn of the Sheraton Moana Hotel I saw one wedding party, which included the bride in a perfect white dress and the groom sporting a matching white tail coat. In the shimmering heat they looked like figures from the top of a wedding cake designed by Liberace. This is all phoney. The couple will have got married already in some mundane ceremony in Japan, but then have flown to Hawaii for their honeymoon, during the course of which they stage a fantasy wedding for the photo album.

The Moana Surfrider hotel is a survivor from a golden and more elitist age of Waikiki holiday-making. A time when the Moana was one of only two or three hotels by the beach, and not part of an uninterrupted line of ocean-view balconies. It has been recently restored to what is known in the trade as its former glory. And in fact it is pretty glorious. In an elegant courtyard in the afternoon a group of Hawaiian musicians play steel guitars and sing their high-pitched whining songs which are strangely similar to Swiss yodels. This sort of stuff is played all over the place in Hawaii. On the radio, in the lifts, in restaurants and, in theory, it should get on your nerves. Yet, rather like bagpipes, it has such an emotional haunting quality that you can listen to it for days on end before screaming for it to stop.

The group in this high-class hotel are very good and they are accompanied by two beautiful girls waving their hips in sensuous hula dances. Hawaiian girls look almost too beautiful. A perfection of tan-coloured skin, curvaceous figures, long black hair and permanently smiling lips. Perhaps they are not real either. But if you can think of no better accompaniment to a full afternoon tea (choice of various Twinings teas made at your table, scones and cakes), I suggest you go there.

• We will fight them on the beaches •

We started our serious filming on a less artificial beach at Makapuu, a few miles east of Honolulu. For a year or so this was the site of a beach occupation. Native Hawaiians had built a veritable shanty town of tents and shelters around what is a holy place in Hawaiian tradition, but which in the modern world is supposed to be a public beach where you are not allowed to stay overnight.

On the beach I spoke to A'O Pohaku. She is a leader of one of the many organizations pressing for Hawaiian sovereignty. She believes that it is necessary for the spirituality of the Hawaiian people to be retained, spirituality being the element which is most notably lacking in the American consumer society which currently holds sway here as in so much of the rest of the world. Even after all the shacks had been removed, A'O and her supporters had been coming back to the beach to water the plants they had put around a stone cairn marking a spot significant to their ancient beliefs.

For all the spiritual aspects of the movement, and an aspiration for sovereignty, there was also a more immediate, practical aim to the beach protest.

Native Hawaiians have felt themselves marginalized by Hawaiian society as it has developed over the last hundred years. Rather like Aborigines in Australia, they have become strangers in their own land. They claim to feature higher in levels of unemployment and homelessness than all other racial groups. Their culture was deliberately suppressed. The Japanese and the Chinese and, of course, the Americans were allowed to have schools which taught in their own language, but not the Hawaiians who were living here before anyone else.

They are now fighting back and using the law to do it. Again like the Aborigines in Australia, and Indian tribes in America, they are using ancient treaties and statutes to support their claim for title to land. In 1848 there was a fundamental distribution of land in Hawaii under King Kamehameha III. Roughly one-third of Hawaiian land was to be kept by the king, one-third was to go to chiefs and one-third was to be government land for the Native Hawaiian people who, even then, were already heavily outnumbered by newcomers.

Most of the Crown land and the government land was later ceded to the United States government, but Native Hawaiians have insisted that it was done without their consent and some of this land has been returned to Hawaiians so they can establish homesteads for the homeless. The beach occupation was intended to force the relevant government department to allocate some of this land to the occupiers. In that it has succeeded, and a chunk of land has been handed over. You can see this either as squatters jumping the (long) queue for the allocation of homestead land, or the first step towards the reassertion of Hawaiian rights.

On the newly allocated land up in the hills I met the leader of the occupation, Dennis 'Bumpy' Kanahele. Pure Hawaiians tend to be large people, and Bumpy looks every inch, or rather every cubic inch, a Hawaiian leader. He had been described to me as a bit of a bully, liable to intimidate his opponents with his sheer physical presence. But with me he was all smiles and amiability. When I jokingly offered to arm-wrestle with him as we sat chatting at a table he kindly refrained from snapping my hand off at the wrist. He and his people were busy building an encampment to live in. There was a communal dining area under a tent and any number of subsidiary shacks and vehicles around which people were sawing wood and chopping down trees in what I assume was an organized way. The trees they were felling were eucalyptus trees which, not being native to Hawaii, they regarded as something that should be removed.

Bumpy makes an obviously charismatic rebel leader. Apart from anything else, the thing which hampers him and the rest of the sovereignty movement is the low numbers of Native Hawaiians and the high number of sovereignty groups. Like all radical movements, there is much scope for arguments about to what extent one should co-operate with the powers-that-be, and even more scope for personality clashes. Bumpy scores highly on personality and on the fact that he dares to confront the authorities, but he is condemned by some for negotiating the grant of the land. But on the homestead, Bumpy was king and monarch of all the ground they were surveying.

Yet it seemed to me that the whole movement was at least one hundred years too late. It is unlikely that the majority of the population now resident on Hawaii would want to break links with America and, even if they did, would the 70 per cent of the population who have no Hawaiian blood be prepared to hand over any more power to those who do? To the modern way of thinking, the very notion of determining a person's rights by reference to his racial origin looks weird, if not positively immoral. But the law in Hawaii has already adopted that approach. Positive discrimination is exercised in favour of people who can prove they have 50 per cent or more Native Hawaiian blood.

• Pay paradise •

Hawaiian life of a sort is preserved every night at Paradise Cove along the coast. This is beach-side entertainment purporting to provide a genuine Hawaiian evening. Coach parties are bussed there for a bit of a knees-up. Drop-dead gorgeous girls in grass skirts and coconut-shell bras pose with you for photographs. Later they dance and cheer as their male counterparts shin up trees or organize the punters into Hawaiian activities. Old Hawaiian sports on the sand are played by old American sports in the crowd. The accent is on family fun. There is plenty to eat and drink and songs and laughter as night falls. The whole evening might not be to your taste, however, especially if you have any taste. It is a shame to see a native culture reduced to a series of catchpenny attractions, but who can doubt that this sort of thing would be here whether Hawaii was part of the United States or was an independent nation trying to attract American dollars for its balance of trade?

• Sorry seems to be the hardest word •

In 1993 the United States actually apologized to Native Hawaiians for the overthrowing of their kingdom. Public Law 103-150 is a resolution of the Senate and House of Representatives which in three or four pages sets out the history of America's illegal take-over and then apologizes for it.

It is quite an abject admission of wrong-doing. Its only concession to *realpolitik* is to add a one-line disclaimer which says that nothing in the Resolution 'is intended as a settlement of any claims against the United States'.

As Bumpy was keen to point out, it is all very well for America to apologize for illegally taking the country. But surely they must give it back? A thief who says sorry for taking your car does not usually get to keep it.

Well, deciding the sovereignty of a country is not as straightforward as determining the ownership of personal property. But America's apology, which was probably put through in fulfilment of a presidential election promise, certainly opens up a can of worms. And the man to use the worms to full advantage is Hayden Burgess.

Hayden Burgess lives about 30 or 40 miles out of Honolulu in a pleasant, if slightly run-down suburb which he said was occupied in large part by Native Hawaiians. It looks very American for all that, with quiet streets of green grass verges and neat houses. At the side of Hayden's house are a couple of wooden prefabs, one of which he has converted into his office. From here he runs his legal practice which is focused on arguing in favour of the rights of Native Hawaiians.

Once upon a time Hayden served in the American military but he got booted out when, after becoming conscious of his Hawaiian identity, he refused to salute the Stars and Stripes. He continues with what is basically a conscientious objection to everything to do with the American presence in Hawaii with all the zeal of an obsessive combined with all the tenacity of a lawyer. Plus, it should be noted, an enormous amount of charm.

He refuses to accept American citizenship, which means he declines to have a Social Security number. This makes many aspects of life rather difficult. He cannot, of course, pay taxes or apply for a driving licence, or comply with a hundred and one other requirements of the state and its bureaucracy.

In a more intolerant age or place Hayden would have been thrown into jail years ago but the way things are in America he is free to practise at the Honolulu Bar and argue cases in front of judges whose legitimacy he utterly denies. His logic is faultless. The American take-over was illegal. Congress has admitted that, in Public Law 103-150. Therefore everything which flows from that take-over is illegal. All title to land granted under American laws, all state structures, all agencies. Everything.

If the whole issue is ever decided in the courtroom you feel Hayden could get a result for Hawaii. He is convinced that he has right on his side and that it will see him through to victory, even though his land has been taken from him. Possession may be nine parts of the law, but self-possession is nine parts of the lawyer.

To say the least, there are a few problems with this approach. Most territory around the world has at some time in the past been won by right of conquest, the usual term for trespass and larceny on a grand scale. Should all conquests be subject to legal analysis, generations after they were committed? And what about immigrants who have arrived since the unlawful events that are being complained of? And anyway, was the manoeuvring for power in Hawaii really as bad as armed conquest?

There are a number of different ways forward for Hawaiian nationalists. The restoration of the sovereign state of Hawaii, coupled with the return of its monarchy, is the most extreme possibility. There could be independence without the monarchy, or the setting up of a sovereign nation with the United States, based on the model of several mainland Native American peoples. Some people would settle for little more than the setting aside of sort of Hawaiian reservations in the islands to reflect their historic demands. Only the future will tell if history can be rewritten in some way.

For the present, Hayden lives his life in as Hawaiian a way as possible. He prefers to be known by his Hawaiian name of Poka Laenui. He grows only native species of plants in his garden, and raises edible freshwater fish in a tank in his backyard. The tank is a high-tech structure with pumps and filters, but it follows the Hawaiian tradition of growing fish for the table in fish ponds. He will be demanding road signs in Welsh next.

• American pie •

On the way back to downtown Honolulu we visited a more up-market suburb to hear the views of two other Hawaiians. The suburb of Makiki is a part of town built on a hill overlooking the skyscrapers of Honolulu central. Dr Esau Masunga has a house there. He is a second-generation Hawaiian, a dentist of Japanese extraction. He sees no prospect of Hawaii breaking away from America. Nor can his friend Lloyd Jones, also a Hawaiian citizen but originally from Australia. They point out that people like them have as much right to a say in Hawaiian affairs as anybody of the original Hawaiian race. And their life here is based on Hawaii as an American state. As it is they can travel to and from the other forty-nine states, their children can attend the American university of their choice. They do not need a visa to visit, or live in, California. And they are not about to vote any of that away.

Even more forthright in his criticism of the Hawaiian cause was Bob Parkinson who we visited later in his apartment overlooking the Ala Wai Canal. He is in real estate and thinks the Hawaiians should join the real world. He is impatient with Native Hawaiians sitting around demanding compensation or hand-outs because of injustices that may have been suffered by their grandfathers. It is all in the past. It is tough luck they lost their kingdom. Sure, it may have been wrong then, but now they should just knuckle down, get a job, get a life and stop living off welfare. He thinks it is only the dead hand of political correctness which prevents people speaking out in praise of all the benefits which flow from the connection with America and against all this Native Hawaiian nonsense.

I tried to persuade him that an independent Hawaii could turn itself into great offshore tax haven. I think he was interested, but it was not quite enough to bring him round.

We were off to another apartment. In the opening sequence of *Hawaii Five-0*, Jack Lord (who played Steve McGarrett) stands on a balcony overlooking the city of Honolulu, a rose-white city half as old as Los Angeles. So we were going to re-create that sequence with me in the Jack Lord role. In fact, in an unusual and somewhat pointless piece of honesty in film-making, I was to stand on the balcony they had actually used. Apparently the flat really had been owned by the actor Jack Lord.

It is a penthouse and the balcony consists of a large flat roof. Luckily for us the flat was for sale and so we were able to get permission to film there. To re-create the shot we had to hire a helicopter to hover above the rooftops so the camera could catch me executing a dynamic turn and resembling the lantern-jawed crime fighter. I stood on the roof as the Swiss pilot drifted towards me. (I don't know what a Swiss was doing in Hawaii. Perhaps he had been attracted there by the yodelling music.) I had to make my move only when the helicopter got as close as possible, my cue coming from a shout relayed on a walkie-talkie by my feet. In the event, I could not hear anything but the noise of the chopper's engine so I had to guess when to go. I did not want to move too soon but, if I went too late, instead of *Hawaii Five-O* we would have re-created a bit of *Catch 22*. You know, the scene when the helicopter cuts someone's body in half.

Once we had finished, the real estate agent tried to interest me in buying the apartment. Apparently, $2 000 000 gets you an attractive service flat with three bedrooms. In addition to the $2 000 000, you have to pay $700 a month for maintenance charges and $515 a month property tax. An ideal holiday home for a TV star, the agent thought. Something tells me that TV pays better in the US than it does in the UK.

• Cook's tour •

It was time to pay a visit to the Big Island of Hawaii. For this we flew the 200 miles or so to land at the pleasant outdoor airport of Keahole-Kona while our all luggage flew in the opposite direction to Kauai, the island at the opposite end of the chain of islands. It really boosts your faith in airline security to know that twenty metal boxes of camera equipment can fly unaccompanied in a small plane.

Would we be forced to take some time off while we waited in a luxury hotel for our camera to catch up with us? No such luck – it turned up early next morning.

The country of Hawaii is rather bigger than I thought. It had been possible to spend hours driving on the freeways leading out of Honolulu without running out of road. The total land area of the islands is something like 6400 square miles, which is eight times the size of Wales. The Big Island, 96 miles long and 76 miles wide, is much bigger than all of the other islands put together. But as if concerned to maintain its largest island status, the Big Island continues to grow, its shoreline pushed outwards by lava flows which leak from its periodically active volcanoes.

• Paradise in paradise •

The luxury hotel complex we were visiting was the Hilton Waikoloa. And I do mean luxury, and I do mean complex. This awesome hotel development, which in its brief history was once a Hyatt Regency, has more than 1200 rooms and covers 62 acres of land. To get there, the road from the airport goes through barren countryside which is a moonscape of black volcanic rocks only slowly being colonized here and there by the hardiest of plants.

Once you get to the hotel you can forget barren. The approach roads are bordered by strips of verdant grass verges and a neat row of trees watered by automatic sprinklers. To the horizon there is a view of bleak, black rocks which will take years, centuries maybe, to turn into fertile ground. But the foreground is a green and pleasant band put there for your delight. Herbaceous window-dressing, it prepares you for the pleasures inside the resort. For, once inside, there is everything that your heart, stomach and most other parts of your body could desire. There are seven restaurants serving food from Italy, Japan, America, France, and even Polynesia. There are shops, swimming pools, salt-water lagoons, golf courses, bars and $4 million worth of art.

To get around the resort you can use the train service. The trains stop in the enormous open-air lobby and take you to the tower which houses your bedroom or away to whichever restaurant happens to take your fancy. If you think that travelling on this American equivalent of the Docklands Light Railway lacks romance, there is an alternative canal service featuring little boats captained by smart young things in jaunty yachting outfits.

In the sea-water lagoon you can swim and interact with dolphins. I was rather keen to do this but all three female dolphins were pregnant at the time and so not up to appearing on-camera. And the male, I assume, was too exhausted.

Waikiki may be artificial but it has nothing on this place. Hawaii is famous for its waterfalls, but there is no need to go looking for them around the islands because a few of them have been created within this resort. Just like the real thing, if you ignore the sound of the water being pumped back up to the top of the rock. There are trees aplenty, all of which were shipped here at vast expense. A million cubic yards of top-soil was delivered in lorry-loads from the mountains; the canal boats, designed by Disney, were flown in from Florida; the trains came from Switzerland.

This is excess taken to excess, comfort at a level which is quite dis-comforting. Don't get me wrong. It is all highly enjoyable, but a bit weird, soulless and definitely lacking in the spirituality that A'O had been talking about. You can sit on a beach here, but not only is the sand imported, it is enclosed in a man-made lagoon and faces away from the sea. The sea does wash up against the nearby shore, but the coastline is made up of hard, scratchy rocks. And you do not come here for anything hard or scratchy. There is no awe to be experienced at the wonders of nature, only wonder at the power of money.

Perhaps this is the true meaning of paradise? Although we generally use the word to mean the Garden of Eden before the Fall or as a syn-onym for Heaven, originally in Persia a paradise was simply a pleasure garden, a place set apart to be enjoyed by those escaping from the awfulness of life. And this is a pleasure garden where there are no poor people, no muggers, beggars or street entertainers. Only employees of Hilton International. A true paradise, in fact. Either that, or a re-cre-ation of *The Prisoner.*

Just one thing. In paradise, however you define it, do you really want to find yourself dashing from the lift to catch the train on your way to dinner?

We filmed an interview with Moani Akaka as she and I sailed on one of the boats on the canal. She is another Hawaiian activist, but one who has agreed to become a trustee of the state-sponsored Office of Hawaiian Affairs. She had never been to the resort before and rather disapproved of it. She had specific complaints about the alteration to the coastline which had been made when the complex was built and about the resources that the resort consumes. She was also concerned about the wages structure and the distance that employees have to travel to work there.

Anything so new and so luxurious does look rather tasteless built amidst the poverty of its surroundings, but the land that the resort is built on is barren rock. Its only assets are sun and sea, both of which are effectively exploited by what is essentially a giant tourist farm. OK, so the tourists are not free-range but, if they like being penned up in this pleasure factory, what harm is being done?

Moani Akaka retained her doubts as we sailed along in the heat of the day. As we went up and down the canal we realized that the boats are attached to a mono-rail under the water. The guys in nautical uniforms are not really sailing them from landing stage to landing stage – they only control the speed as they go along their fixed course. The whole thing is a train with the right kind of water on the line. Even the canal boats are not really real.

• Once more on to the beach •

Back in what we assumed was the real world, we went to see Maloni Pai who was at the centre of another beach protest. Pai and his family live on a beach which actually comes under the jurisdiction of the National Park Service. They do not hold formal title to the place, but claim that because Pai's family have lived there for generations they have an ancient right to remain.

The family live in a series of lightweight structures and shacks right by the water's edge. This is the traditional Hawaiian way, though they do have generators for electricity and large pick-up trucks for transport. Pai's own house is on a little island, a tiny circle of sand like the ones that cartoonists put shipwrecked sailors on. Except that this is not surrounded by miles of ocean, it is only a few yards from the shore.

Pai is a rather intense man, anxious to preserve or recapture the ways of his ancestors. Before we begin the interview he insists on saying a prayer to his gods at a special shrine. This resembles a bamboo scaffolding tower, but its various parts have a significance in the worship of the various ancient Hawaiian deities. It is sited on a particular piece of rocky shoreline. Pai warned us not approach too close to the shrine unless our intentions were good. 'Harm awaits anyone who goes beyond this rock, unless his heart is pure', he solemnly informed us. Superstitious nonsense, of course, but on going beyond the rock, the director stumbled clumsily and cut his leg open on the sharp coral.

Pai wants to stay here to look after the beach. The Park Service want him to go because this is a heritage site, and he and his structures are messy and his dogs are dangerous. Pai argues that he is the heritage and belongs here. He reckons enough damage has been done to this area already. In one direction there is a yachting marina, and further up the beach *haole* nudists come and display their bodies in a way the white man used to preach was sinful. Pai has set up a school here to teach the Hawaiian language and customs. We were going to film it, but the only pupils that day were his uncle and aunt.

How genuine is this slice of Old Hawaii? When I interviewed him Pai was dressed in a loin cloth and ochre robes. This is what a Hawaiian should look like and how he wished to appear on-camera. But before and afterwards he was in a T-shirt and shorts like any other American citizen.

• In memoriam •

There is a memorial to Captain Cook right by the spot where he was hacked to death in Kealakekua Bay over 200 years ago. It is quite easy to reach it by boat. The film was to start with me arriving there by helicopter, but we actually got to it by going overland. And to do that you have to be ready for a rough journey and to know where you are going. There is no sign pointing the way to the memorial at the point where you have to turn off the main road. There is only the roughest of tracks leading first through brush and woodland and then over volcanic rock. You can drive part of the way but eventually you have to get out of your vehicle and walk the last mile or so. When you finally get there the memorial is a simple white obelisk surrounded by a chain fence. It is decorated with badges and symbols of ships whose sailors have made the pilgrimage to the site. Its closeness to the place where Cook was actually put to death, and its remoteness from pretty well everything else, gives it the poignance of a grave accidentally discovered on a lonely hillside.

The lack of exploitation of the place as a tourist attraction suggests that Hawaiians are not that interested in the British explorer who literally put them on the map. There is something positively un-American about the lack of refreshment facilities of any sort. Perhaps this is a corner of a foreign field which does remain forever England.

• Independence days •

We did not remain on the Big Island much longer. We had to get back to Oahu for the 100th anniversary of Hawaii's last day as an independent kingdom on 3 July. There was to be a march through Waikiki in commemoration, and as part of the continuing campaign for Hawaiian rights.

Most of the sovereignty campaigners I had met in Hawaii were taking part. Hayden Burgess made a speech to the crowd at the start of the march. As ever, he was sticking to his principles. Permission to stage this march had not been sought from the occupying powers-that-be, because they had no right to be in power. Not even the City of Honolulu Traffic Department.

But having got wind of it all, the police had asked them to march on the pavement and not the roadway itself. A request that Hayden was going to ignore. A Hawaiian should always be able to walk down a Hawaiian road if he wanted to do. Certainly that was what Hayden himself was going to do, and he suggested everyone else followed suit. So off went the march, with everyone daring to stay off the sidewalk and remain in the gutter. There were about 1500 marchers from a variety of independence groups, plus a bishop in a flowery shirt, gay rights activists, environmentalists, anarchists and royalists. The rainbow alliance of the sort of people who like to go on demos. They walked along the road but the police did not seem to mind. They marched past loitering tourists out taking the evening air but the tourists did not seem to care. None of the tourists I spoke to opposed the idea of Hawaiian independence, and that cannot just have been because Bumpy was somewhere looking on. It was a pleasant evening's stroll the length of central Waikiki, drawing the attention of anyone who wanted to listen to the grievances of the Hawaiians. It was all very peaceful and unthreatening. At the end everyone got into cars or buses and went home.

The next day was 4 July and at Schofield Military Base there were celebrations for America's Independence Day. I thought this might feature an awesome display of America's military presence and power. But in fact it was more of a family day out for the soldiers and their families. Between 40 000 and 50 000 people were scattered over a large field eating and drinking and enjoying the all-American fun. There were hamburgers and hot dogs and a parachute display team. A brass band played the 1812 Overture. At nightfall there were fireworks on a grand scale. Before that a famous singer called Wayne Newton had flown in from Las Vegas with his orchestra to belt out a selection of hits, standards and patriotic songs to entertain the troops.

Even here I could find almost nobody in the crowds of GIs to say that America should hang on to Hawaii at all costs or even hang on to it at all, though I must admit I was not able to speak to Wayne Newton about it. So, unlikely as it first seemed, maybe Hawaii will be the last star on, first star off the American flag, as somebody's T-shirt had said on the march through Waikiki.

• Take me to your leader •

Before leaving Hawaii I met the State Governor, John D. Waihee III. He saw me in a proper American press-call room. There were rows of chairs for the media, a lectern with insignia on it and a desk for the Governor. He was happy to talk about the sovereignty issue. He is part-Hawaiian himself and reckons that there will be some sort of autonomy for Hawaiians in the near future. He expressed, in very ambiguous terms, his support for the independence movement, though he came across as a very American-style politician.

But if Hawaii were to become a monarchy again, who would be king? Not John D. Waihee III. King Kamehameha VI is the answer, but where is he to be found? Sadly, the answer is in a Federal prison in Colorado.

King Kamehameha, or Windy Lorenzo, was sentenced to thirty-three months in prison for an attempted tax fraud. It was a rather complicated crime. Windy had been elected king by a council of chiefs which had considered his genealogy, fitness to rule and so on. He had then laid claim to large tracts of Crown lands and billed the present occupiers for rent of $750 000. When that was not paid he applied for a refund on the tax he would have paid on that money, had he received it. As an assertion of royal power it seems rather confused. As a crime it was bound to be detected as he was asking the Inland Revenue to repay money he had not paid out in the first place. So he was rather easily caught. Colorado is a long way from Hawaii, but apparently there is a no Federal gaol in Hawaii.

So on the way home to London we stopped off at Denver and went over to interview King Windy. It looks as though Colorado has been selected as the prison which is about as far away in miles and spirit as you could get from Hawaii to incarcerate the pretender to the Hawaiian throne. I assumed it was a deliberate policy, but the truth may be more mundane.

Los Angeles and San Francisco have Federal prisons but they are full of drug dealers and the like. The inland state of Colorado actually built a new prison and donated it to the Federal authorities, not to deal with local crime but to provide local employment opportunities for prison guards and so on. And prisoners from all over the country are transferred there to use the available prison cells.

It is a smart high-tech clean-cut kind of place set on a bleak Colorado hillside. A maximum-security institution is being built alongside it, but the prison Windy is in has fairly low-key security. For most of the prisoners, it would be a long way home from here, and most of them are not the type to try to make it. We received every co-operation from the authorities to film in and around the prison, including filming an interview with Windy himself.

Whatever the reason for his being there, and however up-to-date the facilities, Windy is not enjoying his time in custody. He claims he was set up by the IRS in the first place and does not see why he should be punished. He has lost a lot of weight, the food is not to his taste and he fears the whole institution may be polluted with radioactivity. He is filled with a sense of injustice at the overthrow of what should now be his kingdom and will continue to work towards the restoration of the monarchy when he gets out of gaol. Like all the activists I spoke to back in Hawaii, he fails to explain how the monarchy could be restored if the majority of the people now living in the islands do not want it.

He is a long way from home and a long way from being in power. For Windy to become king of a fully independent nation of Hawaii he would need the support of the majority of all the people of Hawaii and the acquiescence of the American government. The last time anybody attempted to cede from the Union it lead to civil war. And the only good thing to come from that was *Gone with the Wind*. Perhaps Windy will have better luck. I think he is going to need it.

OUR
MAN
IN... BEIRUT

FOR more than fifteen years, images of war-torn Beirut appeared on television sets all around the world. The world got used to the sight of a city blowing itself apart: rocket attacks on blocks of flats, mortars bringing down holiday hotels, suicide bombs, kidnaps and endless bloody massacres.

We also got used to hearing the relevant terms: Maronite Christian, Phalangists, Druze Militia, Hezbollah, Mainly Muslim West Beirut, Walid Jumblatt – terms which seemed to lose rather than gain meaning by repetition. Mantras recited by foreign correspondents in times of stress.

By 1992 the fighting had stopped or, at any rate, had stopped appearing on the news. Had the war ended? Or had the attention of the world's media merely shifted to the former Yugoslavia, Rwanda and troubled, but hitherto unremarked, republics which had once been part of the USSR?

Well, no news is good news – or good news is not news, as I think Martyn Lewis put it. Either way, I went to Beirut to discover if they really had found a lasting peace after so many years of war. And, if so, what they were doing to rebuild their shattered city.

• Airport Insecurity •

As a sign of better times in Lebanon you can now fly direct from London to Beirut with a new company called British Mediterranean Airlines. Its Chairman is Lord Hesketh, who has previously financed a Grand Prix racing team and the manufacture of British motorcycles. So flying planes in and out of Beirut must seem like a stress-free operation to him.

The arrival of British Mediterranean represents good news for everyone in the area, except possibly the long-established Middle Eastern Airlines which weathered the storm of the war years only to find a competitor moving in now that things are calmer.

It is still quite a thrill to arrive at Beirut airport. My plane was greeted by soldiers armed with AK40s or M16s, or some such heavy-duty weaponry. This was simply routine, you understand. No particular trou-

ble was expected just at that moment. But it was unsettling, nonetheless. One soldier got his weapon tangled up trying to get through a revolving door to the terminal building, and we just had to hope he had got his safety catch on. Perhaps he should have used the semi-automatic doors.

The first surprise at the airport was to see so many pictures of the President. Of course, a lot of countries make something of a fetish of leaders, displaying an inspiring portrait in every shop and public place. But the pictures at Beirut airport are of Hafiz al-Asad, President of Syria. I knew Syria was in military and political control of Lebanon, but I had not expected them to be quite so blatant about it. Obviously, I had a lot to learn.

• The Story So Far •

There is quite a lot to learn about Lebanon, which has a lot of history for a small country. The modern state of Lebanon occupies just over 4000 square miles, or half the size of Wales. It has a population of about three million – roughly the same as Wales.

Beirut is the capital of Lebanon, and by far its largest city (something like 1¼ million people live there). It is an important port, and before the fighting it was the major banking and entertainment centre of the Middle East. There has been a city or, at any rate, a human settlement there since about the fifteenth century BC.

Making up (or, perhaps I should say, dividing) the three million people who live in Lebanon are more than fifteen ethnic or religious communities: there are Sunnis and Shi'ites from either side of the great division that has split the Muslim world since a few years after the death of the Prophet Muhammad, plus the Druze, an Islamic sect more or less unique to Lebanon.

On the Christian side there are Maronite Christians, who are also distinctively Lebanese; communities of Greek (or Eastern) Orthodox; Greek Catholic; Armenian Orthodox; Armenian Catholic; Armenian Protestant; Syrian Catholics; Jacobites (or Syrian Orthodox); and virtually every other church and denomination you can think of apart from the Wee Frees.

Lebanon's geographical position has put it at the centre of the civilizations, the fighting and the empires which have come and gone in the Middle East throughout recorded history. And its geographical features – notably the rugged slopes of Mount Lebanon and other highland terrain – have, over the centuries, made it a place of refuge for persecuted religious and ethnic minorities. This partly accounts for the extraordinary diversity of its people.

In the seventh century, the Maronites (named after an early leader) were a Christianized Arab tribe who settled on Mount Lebanon to avoid forcible conversion to Islam by the Arabs who by then were in command of the whole region. At the same time, Shi'ite Muslims were also settling in Lebanon to escape the influence of the dominant Sunni Muslims.

The Druze are an exotic offshoot of Shi'ism. They first emerged in Cairo in the eleventh century but in due course they also found Lebanon to be a more secure place in which to develop and defend a community life. They are somewhat secretive about their beliefs. Even Druze themselves are not fully initiated into the tenets of their region until they are forty. But apparently they have incorporated pre-Islamic beliefs and customs into their faith, including some notion of reincarnation and a certain reverence for the goat. There have been communities of Druze elsewhere in the world but, elsewhere in the world, they have not survived.

The Crusaders, on their way to the Holy Land, built forts in Lebanon in the twelfth century, expanding eventually to take control of the whole country. They were given support by the Maronite Christians who were eventually slaughtered by the Muslims once the Crusaders had been driven away at the end of the thirteenth century.

Coming more up to date, for 400 years Lebanon was part of the Ottoman Empire, although Turkish rule was sufficiently relaxed to allow the various peoples to enjoy autonomous control of their different mountain valleys and villages, and Lebanese life continued in its fragmented Lebanese way.

The tensions between the religious groups were always there and always subject to outside influence. In the nineteenth century, Maronite Christians grew in importance, benefiting from links with France. The political rivalries between France, Britain and Russia found expression within the different Lebanese factions. (Britain tended to support the Druze.) At its worst this produced a twenty-year-long civil war, leading to a massacre of the Maronites by the Druze in 1860. *Plus ça change ...* as a Maronite might have put it.

Between the First and Second World Wars, Lebanon was ruled by France under a League of Nations mandate. The borders of Lebanon were expanded to include areas occupied in the main by Shi'ite and Sunni Muslims, and a constitutional basis for power-sharing between the communities, known as confessionalism, was further developed. Lebanon formally became an independent state in 1943 but might have stayed under the influence of French military power at the end of the Second World War had Britain not insisted that the French withdraw its forces and stop playing the imperialist power in the region.

According to a census taken in 1932, Maronite Christians made up 28.8 per cent of the population; Sunni Muslims 22.4 per cent; Shi'ite Muslims 19.6 per cent; and Druze 6.8 per cent. With the addition of all the non-Maronite denominations, the Christians were just in the majority. (Maronites had encouraged Christian Armenians, themselves riven by religious and political differences, to settle in the Lebanon to keep up the Christian numbers.)

On independence, a compromise was reached under which parliamentary representatives and government appointments, including the judiciary and the military, would reflect a six–five balance in favour of the Christians. It was settled that the President was to be a Maronite, as was the Commander-in-Chief of the armed forces, but the Prime Minister had to be a Sunni Muslim and the Speaker of the Chamber of Deputies had to be Shi'ite. This was never written down, but was an understanding known as the National Pact.

There were some Muslims, Sunni and Shi'ite, who favoured union with Syria, of which historically Lebanon had often been considered a part. But for them the National Pact made it at least possible to get rid of the French. And for those Muslims engaged in the growing areas of trade and commerce in and around Beirut, reaching an accommodation with the Maronites made good business sense.

The carefully balanced constitutional structure was inherently unstable. In the modern world, populations of people do not remain static in any sense of the word. In Lebanon, the richer Christians tended to have smaller families than the poorer Muslims. They dared not have another census for fear of what it would reveal. Economic changes drew more and more people away from their traditional homelands in the hills to the suburbs and slums of Beirut.

But the settlement held together reasonably well until about 1975. Well, there was a civil war in the 1950s sparked by reactions to the Suez crisis, but in general the National Pact lasted longer even than its architects had expected. In fact, many Lebanese now look back on the 1950s and 1960s as the good old days, at any rate for those in the money. Playboys and playgirls were attracted to Beirut and it was known, in the guide books at least, as the Paris of the Middle East. A golden age – as long as you had the gold.

• So Far, So Complicated •

Civil war broke out again in 1975. Even though it ended with a ceasefire of sorts in 1976, it turned out to be the beginning of more than fifteen years of fighting.

In addition to the country's own internal tensions, the various groups within Lebanon had all responded differently to the Arab-Israeli conflict which exploded into warfare on Lebanon's doorstep in 1948, 1967 and 1973. Complicating all these issues were the Palestinians living in Lebanon. There had been an influx of Palestinian refugees who were displaced from their homes by the setting up of the State of Israel in 1948. They were augmented by Palestine Liberation Organization (PLO) fighters expelled from Jordan in 1970. In the main, the Palestinians were Muslim and their arrival therefore disturbed the delicate religious balance within Lebanon.

Even more importantly, after the 1967 Arab-Israeli war the PLO began launching guerrilla raids on Israel from its bases within Lebanon which, together with the Israeli military responses to these attacks, brought heavy-duty fighting on to Lebanese soil. The Palestinians were largely confined to refugee camps which operated virtually as a state-within-a-state from 1969 onwards.

Meanwhile, radical Palestinians and leftist Muslims had formed the Lebanese National Movement, under the leadership of the Druze leader Kamal Jumblatt, which pressed for the secularization of the Lebanese state. The civil war saw fighting between this National Movement and the Lebanese Front which was largely made up of the Maronite Phalange Party. This party was founded by Pierre Gemayal who was inspired by a visit to the 1936 Berlin Olympic Games. (That is, by the rise of right wing politicians rather than the running of Jesse Owen.) The Phalangists' attachment to military ways and uniforms might have rendered them joke figures in more settled times. As it was, they became the main focus for Maronite action. In 1982 Pierre Gemayal's son Bashir was elected President of the country, but assassinated before he could take office which went instead to his elder brother Amin, who mysteriously stayed alive right to the end of his elected term.

This civil war was ended by intervention from Syria to prevent the Christians being defeated, presumably to stop chaos breaking out so close to home. By then, virtually every religious and ethnic group in Lebanon had formed its own militia, recruiting from the unemployed and dispossessed to form units to defend and fight on the streets. In 1976, Israel used the Syrian intervention as a pretext to extend its operations in South Lebanon and in 1978 set up the South Lebanese Army of Christian Lebanese, to aid its own border security.

In 1982, Israel mounted a full-scale invasion of Lebanon, in particular bombarding Muslim West Beirut, with the aim of crushing the PLO. As many as 19 000 people were killed in the fighting, but the PLO leadership was able to withdraw, weirdly triumphant in defeat, to Tunis. While the Israelis were in command of the city, thousands of unarmed Palestinians were massacred by Christian Lebanese Forces in the Sabra and Shatila refugee camps. An American-led multinational force was dispatched to Beirut to protect Muslim civilians, although they were eventually forced to withdraw after American and French barracks were hit by suicide raids and other attacks from Muslim activists.

After a year, the Israelis withdrew to South Lebanon and fierce fighting broke out in the Chouf Mountains between the Druze militia and Christian forces who had established a stronghold there under Israeli protection. What followed was chaos, with rival factions on every side fighting for territory, for influence, for the hell of it. Attempted peace deals failed for want of agreement from one or other group within the country or one or other states outside it: Israel ruthlessly pursued its own interests, as did Syria, as did America and the USSR, as did Iran and Iraq.

From the mid 1980s onwards there was a rise in Muslim fundamentalism, and Iranian-backed Hezbollah and Amal groups resorted to kidnapping foreigners to gain support for their cause. These included John McCarthy, Brian Keenan, Frank Reed, Joseph Cicippio and David Jacobsen. Terry Waite, the Archbishop of Canterbury's special envoy, was kidnapped on 20 January 1987.

In 1987, Syrian troops were invited back to Beirut to suppress fighting between rival Muslim militias; the following year, a war of liberation was fought in an attempt to drive the Syrian troops out again.

In 1989, Lebanese MPs went to Ta'if in Saudi Arabia and elected a new president, René Moawad, but seventeen days later he was assassinated. (Not an uncommon event in Lebanese politics.) He was succeeded by the current (at the time of writing) President Elias Hrawi, a Maronite Christian who enjoyed good relations with Syria.

General Michel Aoun had nominally been Prime Minister since 1988, although his appointment broke precedent as he too was a Christian (see the National Pact above). He had disbanded the rival Christian militias and led the fierce fight against Syrian troops, during which many of the inhabitants of Beirut attempted to flee the city and the economy was all but destroyed. Aoun decided he ought to be President; there was bitter fighting between his forces and those loyal to Hrawi who was supported by Syrian troops. General Aoun eventually lost out and fled to France in 1991.

Essentially, what finished him off was the Gulf War. He had received weapons from Iraq but once the Iraqis invaded Kuwait in 1990 and were confronted by the United Nations and the United States, they were not in a position to export anything anymore.

Almost certainly as part of a deal to gain support in the Gulf War, the Americans let Syria have its way in Lebanon. By the end of 1991, with the assistance of Syrian forces, the Lebanese government had reasserted its authority over the various Muslim and Christian enclaves into which the country had fragmented.

By 1992, all the foreign hostages, including Terry Waite, had been released. The new constitutional deal provided for equality (rather than a six–five split) between Christians and Muslims in parliament and government jobs. Peace, albeit one enforced by Syria, had been restored

Rafik al-Hariri, a Lebanese multimillionaire property developer with no previous political experience, was appointed Prime Minister. Elections were held for the first time in twenty years. The Maronites attempted a boycott of the election because of the continued presence of 35 000 Syrian troops, but they only managed to dent their own vote. Hezbollah did rather better than expected, gaining 8 of the 128 seats. But the bitter fighting flared down as quickly as it had flared up and Lebanon looked forward to a period of calm.

I have tried to explain all this in simple terms. In reality, it was very much more complicated.

Maps of the region show that Lebanon is almost completely surrounded by Syria. In fact, as I have already mentioned, Syrian forces are in control of the whole country except for a strip of land in the south which is still controlled by Israel in what it calls a security zone. Not that it is shown as a security zone on locally produced maps. Indeed, maps produced in the Arab world do not show Israel at all. The state of Israel was established in 1948 and has been a major factor in Middle Eastern politics ever since, but here the maps still label it Palestine.

• Paintballs •

As an opening to the documentary, the director decided to show me taking part in a game of paintball. In case you are not familiar with it, paintball is a kind of war game for grown-ups. You divide into teams, each armed with air rifles which fire balls of paint. You run around shooting at your opponents who have to retire from the action when splattered with paint. Although they are not lethal, the paint balls do hit quite hard so you have to wear masks to protect your eyes.

It is the sort of game you might expect to find being played by overweight yuppies in Epping Forest, not by recently retired militia men who have survived a decade and a half of actual warfare. But in the hills just outside Beirut, Georges Abboud, a rakish, twinkly-eyed veteran of the troubles, has a country club where Beirutis ride horses, shoot clay pigeons (clay pigeons are a bit of a pest round here), and enjoy themselves generally in outdoor pursuits, including paintball. Only a few years ago, these men were firing real bullets. It was kill or be killed. Now it is just red paint. Dye or be dyed.

There is nothing, I imagine, to make you better at avoiding gunfire than the prospect of actually getting killed, and it certainly made these men very good at avoiding paint marks. So we were able to film soldiers in action, without any actual blood. Although in the end there was some real blood spilt. Mine.

It was arranged that I should scramble down the hillside with a line of 'soldiers' and arrive at the waiting camera to provide an explanation of what was going on, before charging into the fray. So, I scrambled, I did my piece to camera – and charged into a tree. In fact, I gouged a piece off the top of my head with the sharp branch of a tree growing in an inconvenient place. I had not noticed it because I had tipped the mask up off my face, thereby slightly obscuring my vision; because I was looking at the camera and not where I was going; and because I was pathetically clumsy, not having had years of practice in the field. The wound to my head caused a little concern and a great deal of amusement to the battle-hardened veterans but it did pose some problems for the film.

The top of my head is something of a battleground itself, where the forces of baldness and hairiness have been waging war for at least as long as the Lebanese crisis. Most respected observers predict that, without outside intervention, baldness will surely prevail. But some follicles – the so-called hairy enclaves – refuse to give in. Damage to this sparsely covered area is particularly obvious. On someone with a full head of hair, a cut scalp would not be visible at all. Someone with a completely smooth pate could cover it with make-up, or even a sticking plaster. But my head is an unhappy halfway house of wispy strands and low-growing scrub where camouflage is next to impossible. Even careful combing is liable to disruption in the slightest wind – a problem known to make-up artists as the Bobby Charlton factor.

What made it particularly troublesome was that we had already filmed the next sequence. We could not, therefore, make a big thing out of my injury without explaining how all traces of it would disappear when I am next seen, only for the cut to reappear miraculously again once we get to the scene after that. I considered dealing with this by pretending to bump my head every now and then throughout the filming, but we rejected that plan in favour of doing nothing and hoping no one would notice.

The ex-fighters enjoyed showing off their skills to the camera but the idea of a non-combatant enjoying himself in sham fighting on the outskirts of Beirut bordered on the tasteless so I left them to their post-battle cigarette and headed into the centre of town to see the effects of real warfare.

• Taxi Driver •

I had several guides to show me around Beirut. The first was an extremely animated and engaging taxi driver called Mohammed el Bitri.

Mohammed is one of those larger than life characters you find yourself spending a lot of time with abroad, especially if you are filming a documentary. In the past he made a pile of money and then lost it in a business deal caught up in some way with the Gulf War. He lived for a while in London and was away from Beirut during some of the fighting. But in the end, he had returned. However bad Lebanon got, it was his homeland. And he missed all the excitement of the bombing.

At one point he had been taken hostage by some gunmen. They caught him at home, at a vulnerable time – his wife was about to give birth. So they were able to extort from him his taxi and a valuable collection of vintage cars. Fearing for the safety of his family, he had no choice but to give in to their demands. Adding audacity to injury, the kidnappers phoned him a few days later to offer to sell him back the vintage cars. He declined, reckoning there would be nothing to stop them holding him up again.

He tells this and other war stories without any apparent bitterness. They have assumed the status of tall tale and anecdote. All the same, he did not reckon it was yet safe enough to give any clue as to who his kidnappers had been.

Mohammed explained that he and other taxi drivers had earned a precarious, but exciting, living driving their cars around the city and across the Green Line which divided Mainly Muslim West Beirut from Mainly Christian East Beirut. By a mixture of good luck and good judgement he missed being blown up by bombs and being killed by sniper fire. At night the drivers went to clubs and drank together with bodyguards, militia men and others determined to come through the whole experience alive.

Mohammed tried to take me to one of his favourite clubs, a sadly diminished place now the fighting is over, he confessed. But even more sadly the club had gone up in flames that very day. A mundane peace-time fire, but we could not get in.

The city is an extraordinary sight. I have never been to Belfast, but I understand that you can go there and find most of it completely unaffected by the troubles. It is not like that in Beirut. There is scarcely a building without chunks taken out of it, or bullet marks at every level.

There are blocks of flats with the whole of one side blown out yet still providing a home to families clinging to the wreckage. Well, on the Christian side of the line there are quite a lot of properties in pristine condition but, when I pointed them out, they turned out to have been built since the fighting ended.

The Green Line – a notional boundary between East and West Beirut which runs from the appropriately named Martyrs Square to the airport – is unremarkable now. There are no more road-blocks. You can cross it with impunity. The streets and the underpasses are open again. It is noticeable now only because it is where the damage is greatest.

Road surfaces are rough. The most popular car on the road is the Mercedes, closely followed by the Range Rover. The Prime Minister drives around in a Mercedes closely followed by several Range Rovers. (We seemed to keep coming across his motorcade.) In fact, the Range Rover is so suited to conditions in Beirut – a flashy 4 x 4 capable of being a status symbol in a city where status is important but built to cope with a disintegrated road system – that you wonder if Rover have not financed the troubles for their own ends. (I am only joking, but there are more unlikely conspiracy theories that people do believe in. Some turn out to be true.)

Try as I might, I could not quite establish with Mohammed (nor anyone else) how life of any sort carried on in Beirut during such upheaval. Life in London breaks down if there is a strike by a few key workers, a lorry sheds its load on the North Circular, or half an inch of snow surprises everyone in mid-January. The whole British economy collapses through lack of confidence if the Chancellor of the Exchequer has a mild disagreement with the Governor of the Bank of England. So how was it possible for Lebanon, which imports all its oil and a lot of its food, which earned its living through banking, trading and tourism, to carry on anything approaching a normal life when there was fighting on every street and buildings blown up here, there and everywhere? They cannot have had a feel-good factor, or even a feel-safe factor.

Mohammed just shrugged his shoulders in response to questions like that and said that everything was obtainable on the black market. Nor did he quite get to the bottom of the Great Bank Robbery. *The Guinness Book of Records* cites the raid on the Beirut branch of the British Bank of the Middle East in January 1976 as the biggest ever. The raiders are supposed to have got away with between 20 and 50 million US dollars, largely from safe-deposit boxes. Others have doubted whether anything like that sum was taken (the initial estimate of the loss was 2.2 million pounds). Since safe-deposit boxes contain undeclared sums and valuables known only to their owners, it is a little difficult to prove one way or the other.

In the most satisfying version of the story, two warring militias are supposed to have called a cease-fire in Beirut's banking district while between them they blasted their way into the bank and then shared out the enormous proceeds before resuming the battle. A modern, greedy version of the story of the break for a game of football on Christmas Day during the First World War. Some say rival Christian militias were involved, the Phalangists and Tigers, others say it was Palestinians, but everybody agrees it is a good story which, however inaccurate, captures the essence of the Lebanese war. Mrs Alexis Cheeseman, Public Relations Manger of the Hong Kong & Shanghai Bank, owners of the British Bank of the Middle East (BBME), was kind enough to help with my researches into this story. But the bank's official history is very discreet about the matter. Phlegmatically it records: 'During the 1975–6 Civil War the BBME's Beirut main office building was looted and badly damaged. The robbing of the bank's safe-deposit boxes earned it the doubtful honour of an unsubstantiated entry in *The Guinness Book of Records*, under the heading "the world's biggest bank robbery". BBME's Area Manager, J.C. Kelly, kept the bank in operation during the crisis.'

In any event, Mohammed was an excellent companion, tolerating my attempt at a joke about his name and the religious divide – I asked him 'So, are you a Muslim, Mohammed?' – by ignoring it every time I tried it. He dismissed all the fighting as something induced by the international situation, which degenerated rapidly into a gangster war. Beirut was a rich city but had plenty of poor people ready to be recruited into the militias and gangs of the warring factions. Mohammed was markedly free from the bigotry on which the fighting fed.

'I'm a Moslem, my wife's a Christian. Where's the problem?' he asked with another shrug of his shoulders.

'Your children are Buddhists?' I asked.

'No, not Buddhists.... I believe in God. Don't steal, don't harm, don't, don't, don't ... Why should I kill my brother? Why should I kill a human being?'

If everyone thought like Mohammed, perhaps there would never have been any fighting. But in the Lebanon people do not think alike. The existence of the fifteen different ethnic and religious groups is evidence of that.

• All Fall Down •

To demonstrate some of the damage to the fabric of the city, we wandered into a building near the city centre. There are several well laid out streets which were built during the French Mandate. They betray their French origins in their grand style and their street names: Rue de la Marseillaise, Rue Foch, Rue Allenby. (Actually, Viscount Allenby is one of ours. He was the brilliant British commander who delivered Jerusalem to the British in time for Christmas 1917 and went on to be High Commissioner in Egypt.)

Through an open door, which must once have been served by a flight of stone steps, we hopped up into the entrance hall of a block perhaps five storeys high. Each floor could have accommodated a very grand apartment or sumptuous business premises. You cannot see exactly what was once here because all the fixtures and fittings have been blown away.

All the way up the crumbling staircase, at any rate until the staircase itself crumbles away, are bullet holes and pockmarks. The balconies to the front have been shattered. From the remains of a balcony on to which we ventured at our peril, the cameraman playfully trying to push me over the edge, you can just get a view of the blue Mediterranean between the rows of similarly deserted properties.

Around and about are earth-movers moving earth, air-compressors compressing air and bulldozers dozing bulls. Teams of men are now employed knocking down the worst of the buildings and shoring up the rest. Perhaps they were part of the fighting which destroyed the buildings in the first place, unless they are some of the large numbers of Syrian workers who are now to be found all over Beirut, employed at wages lower than the Lebanese are prepared to accept. The whole area, like so much of Beirut, is full of dust and noise, although the sight of so much destruction stuns us to silence.

On nearby sites archaeologists were having a field day. Pretty French and Italian girls in T-shirts and floppy hats worked alongside earnest men in beards picking over the remains of earlier civilizations revealed by the bombing and destruction of today's civilization. How pleasant it looked in the sunshine, rummaging around in the dust of history for the artefacts of the Ottoman Empire. Distance lending enchantment to the travails of previous times.

I tried quoting Agatha Christie to the diggers. She was married to an archaeologist, which she recommended on the basis that the older you get, the more your husband is interested in you. I think it lost something in translation.

As we wandered around the dusty bombsites and flattened streets we were trailed by a young kid selling postcards. He was selling the only postcards of Beirut available which show the sights as they were a decade or more before he was born.

• The Wrong Place at this Time •

Rebuilding the city is not easy. The first problem is that almost every-where, however badly damaged the buildings, there are people living in them.

The years of fighting forced many people to leave their homes, either because their homes were physically destroyed or they felt threatened where they were and so retreated into 'safe' areas with their own people. The home of a Muslim abandoned in what was a predominantly Christian area will now be occupied by a Christian who has fled perse-cution in another part of the country. The Muslim cannot go back with-out displacing the Christian. Then there are Lebanese from the southern part of the country who have fled the Israeli security zone and have found homes further north, mainly in the abandoned areas of Beirut. In central Beirut, the government's solution is to pay these internal refugees to move on, to make way for the luxurious new city centre. The problem for the people is that they have nowhere much to go.

To see how this works on the ground we went to Wadi Abou Jml. Lit-erally translated, this means the Valley of the Father of the Beautiful, although truth to tell there is nothing very much of beauty here at the moment. Here, hundreds of families are living amid the ruins of the city, waiting to be moved on by the bulldozers of Solidere, a company com-missioned by the government to rebuild the city centre. I went there in the company of Giles Trendle, a British journalist who lived through the fighting in Beirut, and a local shopkeeper called Monzer Safwan.

Monzer explained that this had been one of the most fashionable parts of Beirut until the war drove the fashionable people away and unfashionable people came to squat in the half-destroyed buildings. He has a shop selling fridges from which he tries to make a living, although the shop does not have an electricity supply, which cannot help.

Nor, unfortunately, does it have a generator. Supplying little diesel generators is the business to be in at the moment in Beirut as almost everybody else does have one. Generators whirr and moan away in every alley and driveway all over the city, adding to the noise and the pollution. To avoid having to use a generator too much, though, a lot of people just sling up a wire, plug into the main supply and help them-selves to some buckshee wattage. The streets are criss-crossed by untidy spiders' webs of wiring put up with goodness only knows what cost in shocks and accidents and short circuits. Naturally, all this extraction of current puts additional strain on the system, which increases the num-bers of power cuts. And the need for generators.

Monzer's shop is at a busy crossroads. Cars and lorries skirt a rubbish dump to pass along a road axle-deep in stagnant water. Pedestrians – including me, walking for the benefit of the camera – use a half-submerged tramline to help them across this particularly squelchy bit of city street. On the other side of the road is a shop selling joints of meat hung out to take the air.

The area is under development and things are being made worse before they get any better. Monzer wryly noted that it was going to become the best bit of Beirut again as we stood surveying the shambles and squalor. It might take twenty-five years, and twenty-five years are a long time in Lebanese politics.

Blocks are being picked off one by one. Presumably, clearing the whole area at once would be impractical. Apart from anything else, the residents might riot. So softly, softly the forces of the government and Solidere approach the occupants of a block, pay them their money to leave, then knock their block down. For the ones who still remain, added to their problems are the dust and noise of demolition.

Giles had arranged for us to meet a family who were due to be evicted from their home in this area. Their block must once have been rather elegant, its doorways and balconies decorated with delicate wrought-iron work. The balconies, however, are now home to little lean-tos trailing pipes from which drip water and heaven knows what else. The staircases are unlit owing to a lack of bulbs and electricity, and of course the lift is long since out of use.

Five or six members of the family welcomed us in. Like everyone else in Beirut they were automatically very hospitable to visiting strangers, offering us all cups of coffee and sweets. A young man incongruously dressed in a New York Rangers Ice Hockey shirt did a great deal of the talking, although his mother's sad face and the pictures on the wall of other sons killed in the fighting also spoke volumes.

With Giles translating, I asked them to state the obvious for the cameras – that their position is pitiable. They had been living in the apartment for nine years but they would have to go in a few days' time. There would be a knock at the door and they would be sent away. As we were speaking, we could see and hear through the window the next block being pulled down. Their world, not for the first time, was crashing around their ears.

They said they cannot go back to where they were living before. The war changed things, they lost their right to return to the house they used to rent. They were going to get the equivalent of 6000–9000 US dollars in compensation – even at this late stage they were not absolutely sure of the exact amount. They were absolutely sure, though, that it was not going to be enough. A few thousand would not be enough to buy anywhere, nor pay the rent for very long. As far as they knew, houses for poor people were not being built.

In the short term, they will have to split up and will have to squeeze into the already overcrowded homes of other members of their family. In the long term, they depend upon the success of the government's economic policies. The Prime Minister, Rafik Hariri, made a fortune from property development in Saudi Arabia and his masterplan is to entrust the regeneration of Beirut's city centre to Solidere, a specially created property development company.

In an attempt to understand the new model Beirut, I went to see Solidere's chief architect, Harvard-educated Oussama Kabbani.

• And Solidere's the Only Game In Town •

Solidere – the Lebanese Company for the Development and Reconstruction of Beirut Central District – is a joint stock corporation which was set up in 1994 to rebuild the shattered central area of Beirut. The plan is to redevelop 2.2 million square yards of the very centre of the city. This is apparently five times the size of the Canary Wharf development. The area includes not only the Wadi Abou Jml I had visited, but also Martyrs Square, Place de l'Etoile, and the traditional souks and banking district of Beirut.

In addition, an enormous rubbish dump called the Normandy (named after one of the many hotels lost in the so-called Battle of the Hotels which started around Christmas 1975 and continued into 1976) is to be reclaimed. During the war all sorts of rubbish was dumped at this waterside site. There were fears that some of the rubbish included toxic waste imported from Italy by Christian militias in order to pay for their war effort. Solidere think that those fears were exaggerated, and in any event have arranged for Greenpeace to monitor their reclamation work.

As I understand it, the Normandy dump is crucial to the plan. The profit generated by its redevelopment will finance the rest of the project. Solidere is funded by investors interested in making a return on their money. But owners of properties within the designated area have also been required to participate, in the sense that they have to accept shares in the enterprise in return for Solidere incorporating their buildings into the scheme. Oussama denies that this amounts to compulsory purchase, preferring the term 'compulsory partnership'.

To say the least, the scheme has its critics. Opponents say it could only be dreamed up by a property developer coming late to politics – it is a grandiose capitalist enterprise supported by government powers. There has been an outcry about the number of buildings being demolished rather than restored. Others complain that the building of a futuristic city – office blocks and hotels and luxury accommodation – before building homes for the people is an obscenity.

Then there is the question of a conflict of interest. The Prime Minister is fabulously wealthy and scarcely needs to line his own pocket but he does have a financial interest in the company to which he has granted quango-like powers.

Oussama was having none of this as he showed me the model of the city at Solidere's headquarters. At first sight the model is very pretty: a whole cityscape re-created on a vast display table in its own air-conditioned showroom. It is only on closer inspection that you realize it shows you practically nothing of what the new Beirut is going to look like. All the models are of buildings which are already there. New buildings have yet to be agreed.

Even so, it does show some of the interesting pieces of infrastructure which have been agreed already: a walkway to follow the original Phoenician harbour wall (the Phoenicians were here before the Romans, the Christians and the Arabs); a public park; some boulevards; and improved roads. All charmingly empty of traffic and, of course, people. It is all very pretty. What great places architects and planners design before they are mucked up by human beings.

The model gives a rough idea of the solution to another problem. If Beirut did not have troubles enough, the east end of the Mediterranean is due to have an earthquake which will create a tidal wave, so plans for this futuristic city have to include a way of coping with this threat as well. The model shows sea defences and marinas strategically placed to protect the city, although they have not yet fixed upon a way of achieving what will be a massive engineering task.

Oussama is very slick. He is used to selling this idea, as much as designing it. He has returned from America to get involved with this scheme and is bowled along by the excitement of it all. He accepts there have been criticisms of the plans, but the plans have been adjusted to take them on board. He refutes suggestions that, left to themselves, the owners of the various properties would have been able to save more of the original buildings. A patchwork of owners would have taken years to recover the confidence to renovate or rebuild anything, he says. And they would have had difficulty co-ordinating the infrastructure. Nor could they have got rid of the squatters. So statutory powers were necessary to get things to happen.

On the other hand it was also necessary to involve private finance as the government would not have had the money to do all the rebuilding. So the government makes the law, capitalists provide the money, and everybody wins in the end. There is no alternative.

Hang on, what about the squatters, and the poor people generally? Are they not being forgotten in all this? The problem of where illegal occupiers go, Oussama insists, is not Solidere's responsibility, that is for the government. And of course you cannot complain to the government if the rebuilding does not go well because that is the responsibility of Solidere who they have appointed to do the rebuilding. You know when you've been quango-ed.

I suggested to Oussama it will take decades to know whether any of this really works, but he cheerily suggested we could come back in three years' time to see what has happened. Something has to be done about Beirut and they are doing something. Apart from anything else, the scale of the work they are engaged in will regenerate the economy.

Well, it might take longer than three years to see any positive results. At some point I suspect there will be an impressive centre, lacking the charm of old Beirut but providing up-to-date business-class facilities for the modern world. But what is the betting it will be surrounded by over-crowded suburbs and shanty towns?

• For Richer, For Poorer •

It is not only the poor and homeless who are put out by the government and Solidere's reconstruction of the city. It is also of great concern to the rich and well-connected.

I was invited to lunch at the house of Raya Daouk to mix in Lebanese high society. For many years a glamorous Druze society hostess, Raya is married to Omar, a Sunni Muslim from one of the oldest and richest families in the country. Their house is a generously proportioned mansion in central Beirut. That it survived the years of fighting may be a result of good fortune or it could be a result of having a good fortune. It was, apparently, possible to bribe the militia to leave specific buildings alone.

The house and well-tended garden would not look out of place in a smart part of Hampstead, but they are beginning to look out of place in Beirut. The views of the sea are being gradually obscured by new buildings. The current style of architecture in the Lebanon is perpendicular concrete, condemned by sensitive souls as 'Saudi' but tolerated everywhere as buildings are thrown up in the absence of planning controls.

Raya herself was not a disappointment, nor was her lunch. Gathered in the garden were business and professional people; a husband and wife, the former managers of the glittering Casino de Liban; a former MP; the son of a former Prime Minister; and Lady Cochrane, once married to an Irish peer, now passionately concerned about the destruction of Beirut buildings.

This class of person is rich enough to have survived the war with their lifestyle more or less intact. The rich, like the poor, are always with us. Having said that, they have lost a great deal. Money tied up in properties which have been bombed, squatted in or now acquired for redevelopment by Solidere is gone, possibly forever, possibly just for their lifetimes. More than that they have lost their glorious, sophisticated city and their positions of influence. The former manager of the Casino de Liban recalled the days when a glamorous St Tropez set of people came to play roulette at her most fashionable establishment. You had to prove you had money to get in, but those days are gone. These people were, or had been, the great and the good, a veritable *Who Was Who*. But now they feel as dispossessed as the squatters in the bombed-out buildings.

Everyone was eager to explain Lebanon's problems. A politician sighed over the difficulties of maintaining a democracy in a country so divided in a region so undemocratic. A psychiatrist – imagine the workload for a psychiatrist in Lebanon – explained that many of the militia men took drugs to get themselves through the fighting. The fighting is now over, but many are left with the addiction.

Ultimately, the country is in the control of the Syrians, and it is being rebuilt by Solidere and a government over whom the dispossessed rich exert no influence. They lost out in the war, and now they are losing out in the peace.

One guest was kind enough to give me an enormous book of photographs of Lebanon in its heyday, when life was good. She wanted me to have some idea of how good life had been. But, moving from the sunlit garden to the elegant dining room for the lunch for about thirty, served by Sudanese servants, it seemed that something of the luxury lifestyle had survived the bombing. I wondered if all the magnificent Lebanese cuisine was laid on for the benefit of our cameras but I was assured that hospitality at this level is the norm.

I liked the food and the wine at Raya's table. Hummus had pomegranate seeds stirred into it, giving a standard Middle Eastern dish little bursts of flavour in the mouth. There were succulent meats, beans, salads. And, for our benefit, a cake in the shape of Lebanon which we cut up and consumed. Funny, eh? Magnificent though the whole lunch was, the director could not include it in the final version of the documentary. So we ate the cake, but did not have it in the film.

• Eat, Drink and Be Merry •

There was more eating to come. Lebanese cuisine is famously good. It is something to do with the country's position between the Mediterranean and mountains, having eastern and western influences, Arab and

Christian traditions. Or it could just be that they like their food. Being ruled by France for a while will not have done any harm either. Who knows what the Syrian influence will produce now, not to mention the Israeli-occupied zone in the south.

For a sequence in the film to illustrate the point that there is fun to be had in Beirut even before it is rebuilt, we headed up into the hills to an extraordinary restaurant built into a cave. Here, traditional Lebanese food is served to fun-loving Beirutis and, when there are any, tourists wanting a good night out.

Our destination was the Al-Siwau Restaurant and Cave in Mayrouba. You need to know exactly where it is to find it. In fact, that appears to be true of most of the Lebanon. Outside Beirut there are no addresses, street names or numbers as such. You just have to remember where something is and hope the area does not change too much between visits.

There is a pleasing anarchy about a great deal of Lebanese streetlife. You know that feeling you get when you are driving around a tire-somely regulated city. There are no-entry signs, one-way streets and traffic lights, all supposed to make things easier, but which often make life more difficult. And, you think, what if none of this were here? What if motorists had to work it out for themselves? Would that not do just as well? Well, that is how it happens in Lebanon. They have got as far as stopping people sniping from the rooftops; they have not got around to give-way signs and traffic-calming measures. (Who needs sleeping policemen when the roads are already full of pot-holes?)

At junctions you decide for yourself whether to give way or not. You give way if it is obviously a main road, or if the car going across you is going too fast, especially if it is a BMW. The BMW is the preferred means of transport for the ex-militia man. Starved of the excitement of warfare he gets his kicks from reckless driving.

And, do you know, it works all right. Beirut is choked with traffic most of the day, and routes going out of town in rush hours are dread-fully congested, but no worse than any other city. In the main it is possible to work out a way of accommodating other motorists without recourse to yellow lines, contra-flow systems, road signs, traffic wardens, parking meters and all that kind of stuff.

Anyway, we drove up into the hills for a banquet. Accompanying me on this part of the trip was Mouna Mounayer, a better companion for a night out than Giles. Mouna worked with us for most of our time in Beirut as a guide to the intricacies of life there. She is part Lebanese, part British. Knowing the delights of the Orient but familiar with the weakness of the British constitution, she had cautioned us against eating salads (dodgy water supply), anything made from mince (uncertain refrigeration), anything sold on the street (uncertain hygiene), but now on camera she insisted I tuck into anything and everything.

I have found that being on television is a splendid way to expand my diet. It has led me into eating locusts, wasps, sea slugs, chickens' feet, and all manner of things animal, vegetable and inedible. Inevitably, I found myself eating a sparrow which apparently they hunt around here for fun and profit. I will have to apologize to the RSPB although it was not my fault, I was only eating the order. I drew the line at raw, still warm liver. I do not even like liver and bacon. Live and let liver is my motto.

While we ate, an open fire raged next to us through which we could see an oriental dancer. This gave the whole thing an old-fashioned, cinematic air. An early James Bond, perhaps. In international spy thrillers the hero often goes to a night spot in Cairo, Tangier or indeed Beirut. And, once there, there is always an oriental dancer somewhere just in case you forget where you are. Actually, we were doing the same thing. We had brought our own oriental dancer with us.

Have you noticed I have called her an oriental dancer three times? For the benefit of this scene we had the services of one of the top dancers in the Lebanon – and woe betide you if you call her a belly dancer. She is Dany Boustros, and comes from a distinguished Lebanese family who were rather shocked to find her taking up this activity. As it turns out, though, she is extremely good at it and dances all over the Middle East. Even to an inexperienced eye, the dances consist of elaborate, highly controlled waggling of the hips, breasts and, er, tummy. The difference between proper oriental dancing and the cheap-jack belly dancing you might get in an Egyptian night club would, I was assured, be immediately obvious and I made a mental note to give the subject some careful study.

As part of the full Lebanese experience, Mouna attempted to predict my future from the grounds in my coffee cup but, having elaborately swilled the coffee in and out, it turned out there were no grounds in my cup at all. Mouna declared that this must mean I had no future to look forward to.

'Ho, ho … No future in television, do you mean?' I asked her nervously.

'No,' she said firmly. 'No future at all.'

• And That's Why they Call them the Druze •

Having done so badly in coffee futures, next morning I set off for the Chouf Mountains to interview Walid Jumblatt, the charismatic leader and hereditary warlord of the Druze. The Druze have always exerted an influence in Lebanon beyond their numbers – there are only about a quarter of a million of them – and engaged in some of the most ferocious fighting in the years of war.

Walid inherited his role in Druze and Lebanese life from his father, Kamal Jumblatt. Kamal was an even greater leader with even more charisma and more warlike qualities than his son. Although widely respected as a philosopher and thoughtful politician, he led the Druze with blood-curdling threats against the Christians. Almost certainly it was the Syrians who gunned him down in 1977, but the Druze slaughtered some Christians in revenge anyway. At the time of his father's death, Walid was only twenty-seven, a rather wild young man more into large motor bikes and having a good time than politics; all in all something of a disappointment to his father. But some people are born warlords, some become warlords and some have warlording thrust upon them. And once he became leader of his people, Walid rapidly grew into the role.

Walid is now in the Lebanese cabinet as the minister responsible for rehousing displaced persons. He also has a paramilitary approach to environmental work: he has encircled some ancient cedars of Lebanon with land-mines to prevent their destruction.

The Chouf Mountains are beautiful and a welcome break from the rather claustrophobic feel of Beirut. It is about a 40-mile drive to Walid's palace at Moukhtara through a landscape of high-sided mountains studded with trees, scrub and rocks and beautiful, stone-built villages. Even going by road you can get a flavour of how this rugged terrain might have been home to the various Lebanese factions. As you get closer to Walid's country home the view across the deep valleys becomes ever more spectacular. There is a pretend palace, known locally as the House of Moses, a sort of mini Disneyland tourist attraction, but further on you get to the real thing.

Walid's home looks out over a lush valley. It is a fabulous place, more of a castle from *A Thousand and One Nights* than a palace, surrounded by courtyards, steps, streams, springs and shady trees. I was warned in advance that Walid was very unpredictable and might or might not be in the mood for giving an interview.

When we arrived, Walid did worry us at first. He claimed not to be aware of an arrangement that had been made for him to drive me around the area while discussing and demonstrating that Christians were coming back to live in the Chouf. In the 'War of the Mountains' there had been some grim fighting, and the Christians who had traditionally shared the area with the Druze had been driven away. He suggested that instead we go and film a funeral which was taking place nearby. Both Druze and Christians would be attending; it would show how things are improving and people are drawing together again. We could come back for lunch.

I was somewhat dubious about this. Was he giving us the brush off? In any event, can you turn up uninvited to a funeral with a camera crew and start filming? Well, I know you can, but is it right? Is not this the behaviour of tabloid journalism? Would the mourners be upset or stone us?

As it happened, I need not have worried. The funeral was just ending when we arrived, so we were not able to be intrusive anyway, and the mourners – the whole village – were picking their way down stone steps from where the service had taken place. The Druze were in mourning versions of their traditional clothes (they are the only community in the Lebanon to retain 'ethnic' dress), the men in black trousers baggy to the knees, the women also in black. But Christians were there too, also dressed in black to show solidarity and friendship with their neighbours.

Far from being unwelcome, we were pressed to come into several houses for more Lebanese hospitality. We had to limit it to two houses, one ancient, one modern, to have coffee and almond-flavoured cakes and biscuits. In the second house, a very voluble lady explained how dreadful it had been to have fighting in the past. The Druze really loved their Christian neighbours and welcomed them back now. The fact that there had been slaughter was the fault of outsiders and nothing to do with the Druze or the Christians themselves. On further enquiry, I discovered that, around here, 'outsiders' generally means 'Israelis'.

Back at the palace, Walid was now in a much more expansive mood. Pre-lunch drinks were served in his study/sitting room, decorated with a collection of ancient maps and probably working weapons, as possibly befits a warlord. The maps were fascinating, if only because the names of the countries and areas of the Middle East come and go as frequently as the maps are redrawn. The Holy Land, Palestine, Israel, Trans Jordan and Jordan are all names that come and go. Lebanon is part of Greater Syria, the Ottoman Empire, the French Mandate. Who now speaks of Asia Minor? There was a time when this area was known as the Near East; China and Japan were the Far East; India somewhere in the middle. But who now speaks of the Near East?

Lunch was another magnificent Lebanese feast of meze, kebabs, breads, fruits and wines. During lunch (when we were not filming) Walid was magnificent, funny, teasing and extremely entertaining, making outrageous remarks about Americans and the Oklahoma bombing, denouncing another member of the cabinet of which he is a member as a crook, and merrily recalling a recent visit to Eurodisney with his children, claiming he had been too scared to go on the Magic Mountain.

This fits in with his unconventional image. Even in government, he arrives at cabinet meetings in jeans and on a Harley Davidson. All right, it is not that unconventional, but you cannot imagine John Gummer doing it.

Lunch over, Walid was looking forward to an afternoon siesta but instead we insisted on getting an interview underway. Naturally, he was much less outrageous on camera. He confined himself to some very French expressions of scepticism. With shrugs of his shoulders and exasperated looks to the skies he doubted whether there is such a thing as a Lebanese identity at all.

'There is a so-called Lebanon as a geographical entity created by the French and the British in 1920,' he said. 'There is something called Lebanese entity, but I don't believe in it. Lebanese nationalism does not exist for me.'

Indeed, from time to time in the conversation he seemed resigned to the foreign influence in his country.

'Israel and the Syrians are here. At one time we had the Soviets and the Americans fighting here. So what? Now we have the Iranians, tomorrow I don't know.'

But he was a passionate defender of his community during the fighting. I asked him if he accepted the title of warlord.

'Warlord, yeah. And then what? Clinton is a warlord and Bush was a warlord. So what? And Churchill was a warlord … I have to defend myself and my community. Mount Lebanon was peaceful before the arrival of the Phalangists. They disrupted the whole harmony between Druze and Christian. I had to go on fighting. I am for separating the state from religion. We have been able to do that. We should do it one day so as to be able to avoid civil wars.'

'And do you think there is any prospect of that?' I asked.

'Not now.'

'When?'

'Not in my lifetime.'

Naturally, Walid regrets the damage which was done to Beirut during the war but complains also about the further damage done in the reconstruction by Hariri and Solidere.

'We are close friends with Mr Hariri, political allies, but this does not mean I always share his political opinions. But he's a good man and among the Sunni class the only man.'

'But you speak as though you are not part of the government,' I said, puzzled.

'I am part, and not part.'

'It's a strange constitution in Lebanon.'

'Everything is strange in Lebanon,' he said.

He was at his most forceful on the subject of the Palestinians.

'They are treated like dogs, and if I were to say something, I would like to take care of the Palestinian refugees ... They should be given adequate treatment until one day there should be a Palestinian state.'

'But what about the Israelis?' I asked.

'We have nothing in common with the Jews coming from Russia or Poland or Germany or somewhere else. We have everything in common with the Jews who were living in the Moslem world.'

'I understand what you are saying and no doubt people said that in 1948. But it is now roughly fifty years on from there. Those Jews coming from Russia or Germany have put down roots. They've had children and grandchildren. How long before you can say they do have something in common with you?'

'I think we should read the history of the Crusaders,' he told me. 'They stayed for 250 years and they went back.'

'Do you really think the Israelis are going to go back?'

'I think and I hope so. We've been here for a thousand years; it's our land. They came yesterday and will leave one day. We're not in a hurry.'

All of Walid's views were delivered in a world-weary way, like a cynical French diplomat stating the facts of political life to a table of innocents at a Parisian dinner party. On a personal level, he seemed very much the agreeable companion you would be happy to go into the jungle with, if only to avoid meeting him coming in the other direction. To paraphrase Mrs Thatcher's verdict on Mr Gorbachev, he is someone you could do business with.

Back at my hotel I mentioned to a French journalist that I had been to see Walid that afternoon. He had seen something of the fighting between Druze and Christians and gave his opinion of Walid Jumblatt – 'He is a murdering bastard. He ought to be shot.' (Something of the venom, though, may have got lost in translation.)

• Taking Refuge •

But what of the people Walid said were treated like dogs? There are said to be 300 000 Palestinians now living in Lebanon. If that figure is correct, they constitute roughly one-tenth of Lebanon's total population, comfortably outnumbering the Druze. For the most part, the Palestinians live in camps surrounded nowadays by Lebanese and Syrian checkpoints. Displaced by the Israelis in 1948 from what they still regard as their homeland, they have ultimately been treated no better by the Lebanese.

Shatila refugee camp is a woeful place. Given the state of other areas of Beirut, its physical condition does not come as too much of a shock, nor does it look much like a camp, but it is woeful nonetheless. The way into the camp leads from a rather pungent market along a road which on the day we visited was flooded with what appeared to be the run-off from the drains of the rest of the city.

A young man called Sammy was to take me past the checkpoints into the camp. Sammy spent some of his childhood in America, sounds like an American, and indeed has an American passport. But he dislikes America and has decided to come back to live among his people, the Palestinians. He was too young to participate in the fighting here in the 1980s but acted as a messenger supporting the troops.

Shatila was originally a camp with tents, but in the years since 1948 the Palestinians have built themselves a township of narrow streets and houses two and three storeys high. This is in the face of legal restrictions which basically forbid the construction of anything permanent by the Palestinians. They have rebuilt their houses despite the bombardment by Israeli and Lebanese forces which razed them to the ground. They have hung on after the massacres in the camp; they continue despite internal disputes; they remain defiant despite the departure of Yasser Arafat and the PLO leadership.

It is impossible not to sympathize with their plight, although they have attracted little sympathy from either the Christian Lebanese or the Israelis, both of whom seem to regard them as sub-human. This is a profoundly un-Christian attitude and a profoundly depressing attitude in the Israelis given the persecuted history of the Jewish people.

Men who came here as children in 1948 are now the leaders of this desperate community; not wanted here, not wanted in their homeland, not knowing which way to turn. They are not even supposed to have jobs. By law they are allowed to take up only the most menial types of employment, the categories being ever more restricted, though you cannot help wondering if such rules are ever enforced.

Sammy's tour took me to the underground shelter which did service as an operating theatre for doctors trying to treat the injured. He showed me the mosque which had been turned into a burial ground for the dead. We bumped into an old woman looking desolate in a single room. She has no children, she has no property, she has no country. Is she to blame for the trouble she has seen?

After the tour I settled down in a street to interview the community leaders, men who hold sway over this or that corner of this pitiful place. Everywhere there was the hub of life. A machine involved in some cooking process bubbled away behind us. A group of men pulled and pushed at a lorry stuck in a hole in the road. The camp is not far from the airport, so every few minutes or so a plane goes overhead. A damned nuisance if you are recording sound; a dreadful reminder if your camp was not that long ago repeatedly fired on and flattened by incoming planes and missiles.

What do you think about your lot if you are a Palestinian leader? Were they foolish to have left Palestine in the first place? Or would it have been worse if they had insisted upon staying? Should the Arabs have attacked Israel in 1948? 1967? 1973? Can any settlement now be negotiated? Is there any solution to two peoples claiming the same territory?

Still these leaders demand the right to return to Palestine. There is talk of a peace treaty between Syria and Israel, but they know that is not going to help them. They are contemptuous of the treatment they have received at the hands of the Lebanese. Contemptuous, too, of Yasser Arafat who ran out in 1982 and who they say is selling out now.

They say they will continue to fight, so I asked if that means politically or on a battlefield. They replied that they will continue to fight as best they can. Because they are so desperate they have resorted to suicide bombs. Highly illogical, but what else can they do? Where else can they go now?

• Hezbollah •

In truth, the Lebanese Palestinians are a spent force. But Islamic fundamentalist militia do continue to fight the Israelis in the south under the banner of Hezbollah.

Hezbollah has its own clutch of oft-repeated terms to describe itself. An Iranian-backed umbrella organization of fundamentalist Muslims, you can call them freedom-fighters or terrorists depending on where you stand and what they have been up to recently. But apparently they have moved into the mainstream. In Beirut not only have they managed to secure a number of members of parliament, they also have their own TV station.

The idea of Hezbollah having its own TV channel seemed rather odd at first, but the more I thought about it, the less surprising it seemed. Political groups have always published their own newsletters and magazines, so why not use the modern medium of broadcasting? Their station is said to be the fourth most popular in Lebanon, although just how impressive that really is, it is difficult to say.

We went to Hezbollah's broadcasting centre headquarters of Al Manar TV, which is housed in a rabbit-warren of utilitarian offices, corridors, studios and editing suites, short on space and lacking in a great deal of aesthetic charm, i.e., just like every television studio in Britain. The security guards were as ferocious as those at the BBC's Television Centre in Shepherd's Bush. Just as watchful about possible attack on their premises, but more accommodating about parking.

Female members of our party, with many mutterings about interference with civil liberties and women's rights, agreed to cover their heads, ankles, wrists and other forbidden bits of their bodies and we made our way to see Mohammed Afif, the station director. We were all gratified to notice on the way that the station does employ a demurely dressed woman newsreader.

Waiting to get an interview started, to break the ice, I began chatting to the director about football. The night before, Arsenal had won an epic semi-final in the European Cup Winners' Cup against the Italian club Sampdoria. I had been pleasantly surprised to find that it was transmitted live on another of Beirut's TV stations. ('Arsenal', by the way, sounds great in Arabic.) Mr Afif is a big football fan, and in particular he favours Italian football. We thus lapsed into one of those pointless arguments familiar to football fans the world over about the merits of various players and styles. This was bad news. Was I going to be the first member of the British media to come to blows with Hezbollah over football?

No. The actual interview was much more inflammatory. Before getting on to the television side of things I thought I would establish to what extent Hezbollah is or was involved with fighting in Southern Lebanon, car bombs in Beirut, kidnapping in the past, that sort of thing, if only to point up the change of policy in going into television.

For some reason, Mr Afif was reluctant to deal with this sort of enquiry and things got a little heated. His use of English, although generally pretty good, was not conducive to a discussion of the subtleties involved. Anyway, according to the director, our conversation shed more heat than light and in the event we illustrated the trip to Hezbollah's TV station with film of a guided tour of their premises, during which I was taken round by Mohammed's brother Hassan.

He was a very cheery and informative guide. When the camera crew hung back to get a shot of us disappearing round a corner he even quipped that he thought they must have been kidnapped. Great joke – especially when we were in an underground corridor controlled by Hezbollah.

Actually, the trip round did have its problems. When we were taken to his door, the man in charge of censorship did not want to be shown on film. (A perfect example of self-censorship.) In another department there was a chap editing American films. Hezbollah are happy to show

Hollywood blockbusters, but cut out anything which is too sexy or violent. Where Arab-looking characters are being portrayed as baddies (as they often are in American movies), they will add a voice-over to explain what is going on and how the audience is manipulated. This seems an excellent idea. A similar thing should be done in Britain to Walt Disney films. All evil characters, unless they are black, have British accents. Children in America are being taught to fear anyone who sounds like Jeremy Irons. Keep it in mind the next time you watch *The Jungle Book* or *The Lion King*.

I had been told that they even censored films which showed women in dominant or important roles, but they denied this. It is just sex and violence which they are concerned about, plus a determination to plug their party line. It is like a TV station run by a combination of Mary Whitehouse and Norman Tebbit. Whatever else they are a threat to, they are not likely to challenge Rupert Murdoch.

In another suite, a technician was working on some footage of a military campaign in which Hezbollah had achieved a small victory against Israel. A cameraman had gone on the mission and returned with newsreel footage which is shown again and again as propaganda for the cause.

On a whim, I asked Hassan if they would ever interview an Israeli spokesman. You know, just to hear the other side of the question. Hassan thought my suggestion was ridiculous and quite incredible, as though I had suggested he jump off a tall building. In fact, he would have thought more of jumping off a tall building. I asked if he preferred working on the television side rather than fighting in Southern Lebanon where Hezbollah fighters are still risking their lives.

He acknowledged he was playing his part in television but he explained that nobody minded being killed on behalf of Islam. In fact, they all *wanted* to be martyrs. He, too, wanted the Israelis out of what he called his Islamic land. Actually, when he was saying this to me I was not quite sure if he was referring to the bit of Southern Lebanon which Israel occupies or all of Israel itself, though I suspect it would not matter which area he was thinking about.

So not much hope for a peaceful settlement here.

• The Sound of the Suburbs •

Whoever or whatever Hezbollah actually is, it still holds sway in Beirut. On another trip to the southern suburbs we stopped to film my car going down a street. Armed though we were with an official permit from the government, we were on Hezbollah territory. (A large picture of the Ayatollah Khomeini decorated the turning into the street, so there had been a clue.) A Hezbollah representative wanted to know what we were up to and made his decision as to what we could or could not film, government permit notwithstanding.

We were in the area to film a club held in a school in which older teenagers teach dances, songs and games to youngsters. A good time is had by all and it keeps alive some of the happier traditions of village life in inner city Beirut. The director thought this might show the way to a happier future for the Lebanon: the teenagers regaining the childhood they had lost in the fighting, the young children innocent of the blood feuds which have so long racked this troubled land, that sort of thing.

Well, the children playing games were quite fun. The youth leaders were an amiable and mixed group. Some in jeans and T-shirts would have looked at home in an American high school or, dare I say it, on an Israeli kibbutz (no, I did not dare say it). Others were dressed in more traditional Arab clothing. One girl teamed a headscarf and full Arab dress with bright red lipstick, which seemed gloriously to miss the point.

In talking to the youth leaders, like everybody else, they complained about foreigners invading their country – by which, like everyone else, they mean Israel – and had no complaints about Syria being there. (Still less about Iran funding Hezbollah.) The fighting is over but they did not look forward to reaching any sort of accommodation with Israel. There can be no negotiating with the enemy. No great hope for a peaceful future here, either.

• Model City •

The growth in religious fundamentalism in the southern suburbs mirrors its growth throughout the Islamic countries in the Middle East and beyond. Half an hour away from the headquarters of Hezbollah television, you are in mainly Christian East Beirut. I cannot say I detected any uprising in Christian fundamentalism, but it is extremely Western in its orientation, so to speak.

We filmed a Christian service here. We were in Beirut for Easter Sunday. At any rate, it was Easter Sunday for the Orthodox churches; the Western Easter had been the week before. Early morning mass is preceded on Easter Sunday with a special ceremony called Hajme. We were expecting something quite rumbustious. What happens is that the congregation throw the priest out of the church. The congregation then follow him out and he has to hammer on the doors until they are all let in again. Like so many Christian traditions it is supposed to be based on some ancient pagan ceremony, but it is taken to symbolize Christ's decent into hell before His resurrection, or possibly His time in the wilderness.

We went to film at St Dimitri's Church. Perhaps because the Bishop was conducting the service and the congregation included government ministers and other VIPs, it was all conducted with great decorum. The church is very white and beautiful inside, like a wedding cake. From the high ceiling hang spectacular chandeliers which are pulled to and fro, to give the impression of the church shaking and quaking, while the priest knocks on the door.

Beirutis are very smart dressers and even at this early hour they were done up in their very best – Sunday best. Fashionable dresses or skirts for women, well-pressed suits and ties for men, plenty of gold jewellery. The children were itching to get out of the formal outfits their parents had forced them into before daybreak.

My film crew observed their own ancient custom and practice of wearing T-shirts and jeans. No power on earth, or above it, can make a film crew wear anything else. As it happened, we were not the only TV team there. The service was being broadcast live on Lebanese television. Their cameramen were in T-shirts and jeans as well.

• Commercial Break •

Adverts on hoardings in East Beirut use nearly-naked women to promote any and all kinds of products in the normal way of liberal democracies in the modern world. But posters which are too near the knuckle and are put up too near the Muslim side of the city are routinely spray-painted over by offended Muslims who will not tolerate the public display of bare buttocks, tiny bikinis or even pictures of men and women kissing. Even in peace this is a divided city.

The outbreak of this peace has seen the return of some of the Beirutis who were rich enough to escape the fighting by going abroad, and the resumption of such capitalist activities as advertising which struggled to keep going during the war.

Ellie Khoury is head of the Saatchi & Saatchi agency in Beirut whose business, like everything else, had to adapt during the fighting to survive. I asked what they had advertised during the fighting and he glibly told me whisky for the fighters and chocolates for the pot smokers.

I met him at the end of a photo-shoot. A beautiful model, Julie, was pictured dancing down the Jemyzeh Steps, in a quaint corner that has survived the destruction, and he took me (and Julie) for a drive.

The world of advertising is sometimes perceived as sham and false, reflecting only ephemeral values, but Ellie is the genuine article. He wears black clothes, dark glasses and a ponytail: John Travolta in his *Pulp Fiction* reincarnation. He drives an open-top Mercedes and knows all the switched-on people in Beirut.

Naturally, he is pretty cynical about the whole conflict although, I dare say, realistic. He pointed out that, even after all the years of fighting, nobody won the war. It is not simply that everyone lost friends and family in the fighting and now suffers the economic loss of the destruction. Nobody achieved their war aims. The Christians' desire was to rid the country of foreign interference, but it now has Syrian troops in residence. Muslim Lebanese wanted more political power. The Christians do share their political power, but they share it with the Syrians. The Palestinians are still living in their wretched refugee camps, no nearer returning to Palestine. Even the Israelis, who always seem to win the wars in the Middle East, are still fighting in South Lebanon. Nobody feels any more secure than before the fighting started all those years ago.

I asked Ellie if he is an optimist.

'Let me tell you, in my opinion, if it doesn't work in Lebanon, east and west, it'll never work between them.'

'Islam and the West, you mean?' I asked.

'Exactly. If it won't work in Lebanon, then it'll never work. And prepare yourself for the Third World War.'

We prepared for the Third World War by going to Ellie's party.

Ellie invited me round to meet the beautiful people of Beirut, drawn from the worlds of advertising, publishing, the media and the arts. We stood in the sunshine around a swimming pool. The men were all in black, the girls were all beautiful. They partied as though there was no tomorrow. It could have been a pool-side party in Los Angeles, New York, London or Paris. But everyone here knows how fragile is the peace. They are living life to the full, but living it on the edge.

No matter how much the people of Beirut want to return to a normal life, the reality is that the war has left the population even more fragmented than before. Fundamentalist religious groups have grown in strength while the central government has grown weaker, and only able to govern with the consent of the Syrians. Displaced persons eke out an existence in temporary homes while the rich plan to make money from a property boom. And nobody can forget the fighting which pitched Muslim against Christian, Christian against Christian, Lebanese against Lebanese. And which leaves everyone still looking over their shoulders, just in case.

I ended the film recalling a courtroom tale about F.E. Smith, the British lawyer and politician who was made 1st Earl of Birkenhead. He was explaining a complicated case at some length to a judge who, after hearing him out, said 'Well, having listened to you for some time, Mr Smith, I am afraid I am none the wiser.'

And F.E. is supposed to have rejoined: 'Perhaps not, your lordship, but at least you're better informed.'

And that is how I feel about Beirut after my stay there: much better informed but not really any the wiser.

How is it that the Lebanese, so free and easy with their hospitality towards strangers, find it so difficult to get on with each other? How is it that the various religious and ethnic groups have remained so separate, anyway? How can a country which has seen such violence see a way forward?

Well, perhaps they will find a settlement to satisfy everyone within the country, and even a way of removing themselves from Syrian control. Perhaps the Arab world as a whole can reach an accommodation with the Israelis while at the same time meeting the aspirations of the Palestinians, and a lasting peace will finally come to Lebanon. If not, I fear that one day we will see war-torn Beirut back in the news again.

OUR
MAN
IN... LAGOS

• Day 1: The Worst City in the World? •

FOR some reason or another, probably connected with cost, we went to Lagos via Zurich. In particular, we had to hang around for a couple of hours in Zurich airport, which seems to be constructed entirely out of stainless steel. You drink coffee sitting in a building bearing a close resemblance to a 1970s coffee percolator. It was an odd route to take, but it did provide a hygienic Swiss contrast to the more robust conditions we found in West Africa.

We were allowed to film on the plane and I was shown anticipating my arrival in Lagos by looking it up in a number of guide books. They are not encouraging.

The Lonely Planet Guide to West Africa says: 'Most travellers detest Lagos.'

The Rough Guide to West Africa is no better. Its section on Nigeria begins with these dispiriting words: 'Why build your hopes up? Nigeria is a country many people feel needs no introduction: corruption, military dictatorships and urban violence seem to be its very definition.' On the subject of Nigeria's largest city, it is equally gloomy: 'Lagos is no more of a hell hole than any other gigantic, seething, impoverished city with a military administration and an intolerable climate.'

The Lonely Planet Guide to Africa (as a whole) caps them all: 'A recent survey of Third World cities confirmed what travellers have known for years. Lagos is the worst city in the world.'

The plane was eventually going on to Accra in Ghana, and most of the passengers offered me their profound sympathy at having to get off at Lagos. But one man, a Scot who had worked in Africa for many years, said that he had always coped with Lagos just fine. His American company traded very happily there. They made sure they had nothing to do with the payment of bribes and corruption, which is supposed to be endemic, and still did good business. On the other hand, his company had been unable to trade in Kenya because of the demands for substantial backhanders at the very highest level.

Yet, in the public mind, Kenya is a paradise and Nigeria is regarded as a hell on earth. (Which is why we included Kenya in the first *Our Man*

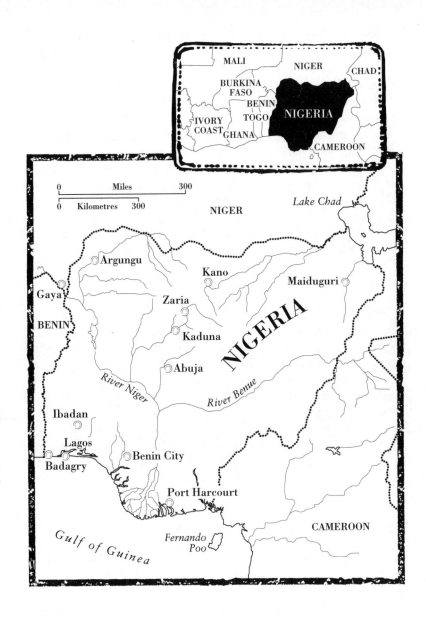

In … series on fantastic places and Lagos in this second series on not-so-fantastic places.) Would I be revealing a better side to Lagos, or adding to the stereotyping?

Lagos airport certainly has an unenviable reputation. Stories abound of travellers being asked for a *dash* – an ambiguous local word for either a bribe or a tip – just to get into the country. In addition there are criminals who pose as officials to ask for a bribe and con men who pretend to be taxi drivers or the drivers of cars sent to meet you, who take you off and rob you before you can even check into your hotel. There is an often repeated tale of a team of Scotland Yard detectives, sent to Lagos to investigate international fraud, who were met at the airport by what they thought were their colleagues in the Lagos Flying Squad. They found themselves taken to an out-of-the-way building where they were strip-searched and eventually sent back to the airport, their tails, as it were, between their legs. In fact, to look on the positive side, the guide books suggest that it is *only* the activities at Lagos airport which give the city – and the whole country – a bad name.

To look on an even brighter side, we had no trouble whatsoever at the airport. We were only allowed to come to the country to film with the express permission of the Ministry of Information and they arranged for an official to greet us and to pilot our way past passport and customs controls. This was probably essential as the amount of equipment necessary for filming makes you liable to hold-ups and delays in even the best-run airport (wherever that is).

Once into the country we were met by a driver, but there was no sign of the director of the film nor the researcher who had arrived before the rest of us to set things up. Assuming they had better things to do than meet us, we got into the car. Many porters, volunteers and hangers on had pressed forward to help load our heavy tin boxes into our vehicle, and many more had presented themselves for payment afterwards. Some backed up their requests for cash with claims that they were in charge of this part of the airport forecourt, but in the main there was no more hassle than you get arriving in any strange city. The driver was our driver and not a con man, the weather was hot and sticky but, so far, so not too bad.

The airport is on the mainland, on to which the city has expanded from its origins on Lagos Island. A magnificent causeway – a motorway, really – built along the coast and several miles long, prosaically called the Third Mainland Bridge, nowadays connects the mainland and Lagos Island.

The bridges, skyscrapers and even a whole new capital city 400 miles away at Abuja, are tangible results of an oil boom which, by the end of the 1970s, was earning Nigeria 25 billion US dollars a year. But, since then, the oil price has slumped and a succession of more or less corrupt, usually military, governments – the latest is led by General Sani Abacha – has grabbed the oil revenues for themselves but left the income of the average Nigerian as low as it was before the oil boom started, the country more in debt than it was than at the end of the Biafran War, and the economy on the point of breakdown.

At the time of independence from Britain in 1960, Nigeria was divided into three very different regions. The Muslim north of the Hausas; the south-west, including Lagos, of the Yorubas; and the south-east of the Ibo. One of the many criticisms of the British administration was that it created this vast country (today with a population of over 100 million people) without doing anything to resolve the regional differences between areas of very different traditions. Once independence had been achieved the three-way split proved to be a recipe for political infighting, violence and massacres. A government led by General Aguiyi-Ironsi attempted to abolish Nigeria's federal structure which, as it happened, would have benefited his Ibo people. This led to a revolt by northerners and a coup which installed General Gowan in power. It also led to the slaughter of Ibos in riots in the north of the country. In 1967 the military governor of the south-eastern region, Lt-Col. Ojuku, withdrew it from the Federation to form the Republic of Biafra and a ghastly civil war was fought for two and a half years. Biafra received support from France and other countries interested in securing influence over the oil reserves which are located in the south-eastern area. Britain and America broadly supported the federal government which eventually triumphed, but not before one million or more people had died in the fighting and famine. Reducing the risk of breakaway areas, Nigeria is now divided into twenty-one federated states.

Lagos Island is still the centre of the city. We were staying in a hotel called the Eko on the neighbouring Victoria Island, which has some of the smartest residential neighbourhoods. Eko was the original name for Lagos – the story goes that it was changed to Lagos because it reminded the Portuguese of the Lagos in their own country. The Hotel Eko, though, is not old. It is rather grand in a modern kind of way. The reception area is open on two sides to allow cooling winds to blow through it from the sea. Steps lead down from the reception area to a large swimming pool and to a couple of restaurants and a bar. The bedrooms are housed in the modern way in a tower block, and we were on the tenth floor.

We checked in and made contact with our missing colleagues who had, it turned out, been waiting for us in the wrong part of the airport.

This did not seem important at the time – we had found our way to the right place and they had got back from the airport – and we wandered into the bar for a quiet drink.

Having a quiet drink is not that easy. The bar is agreeable enough but late at night it becomes the haunt of prostitutes of a very direct and persistent kind. Giving them the brush off is not easy.

'I know we look like sad businessmen in need of company, but we are in fact doing some work,'

'I am feeling horny. Take me to your room, my clitoris is dancing.'

'You will have to excuse me. I have had a long flight and I want to get my head down.' An unfortunate choice of words but I was trying to be polite.

'Come on, I will swallow your cock.'

Given even the slightest encouragement, these rather forward local girls will follow you to your room and bang on the door, demanding to come in. Or so I was told. To avoid involvement and embarrassment, I adopted the demeanour of a diffident, repressed Englishman abroad. You know, like Hugh Grant. (This was written before Mr Grant's slight mishap in America.)

• Day 2: Information, Security and a Dash of Police •

Early morning started with a tropical rainstorm. Rain is obviously bad news for filming, but we had to go to the Ministry of Information anyway for our accreditation.

You do not have to be George Orwell to know that the main task of a Ministry of Information is to prevent too much information becoming available, but we needed to receive a press pass and to meet the Ministry of Information officer – a minder – who was going to be attached to us. This, we hoped, would be a straightforward procedure: providing passport-sized photographs of ourselves, mother's maiden name, father's occupation. Dull, dry facts to some people but meat and drink to government bureaucrats the world over.

The Ministry of Information occupies a row of single-storey buildings just off a compound and car park where, over the next week or so, we seemed to start every day. There we met our minder, a quietly spoken and generally very charming man called Olu, but first we had to be spoken to by a colleague of his called Irene.

Irene had received a report, she told us, that my director and researcher had gone to Badagry, which was not on the schedule of places to be filmed. Furthermore, instead of meeting the rest of us the previous day they had been filming in another part of the airport. This made Irene very cross and she was determined to make this clear, while Olu shook his head at the stupidity of their behaviour.

At this stage I had not heard of Badagry, so I could not work out why my colleagues should or should not go there. I was pretty confident they would not have filmed at the airport. Anybody knows you cannot film at airports in an even halfway sensitive country. Thousands of people pass through airports every day, but paranoid governments think they can keep them secret from their enemies (other paranoid governments) just by keeping out cameras. And, apart from that, my colleagues did not have a camera to film with as we had brought them with us.

After three-quarters of an hour or so it seemed to be all right and we were shown into another office, which was full to bursting with a three-piece suite. We were given a cup of tea and some Rich Tea biscuits. Then we were taken to another office and told we would be issued with our press cards later that day. This came as a minor blow as we had intended to start filming before lunch and thought we had been kept waiting while our documentation was being prepared. No, we were told, come back this afternoon.

In the afternoon we were finally issued with the vital cards which we had to sign. This indicated our acceptance of the law that we could not film without permission; we had to get permission from the relevant department of government at any location or, failing that, the Ministry of Information. Something like that. I cannot quote directly as Olu took the cards away from us on the very last day of shooting. For security reasons. Broadly speaking, the cards appeared to convey no rights, merely to remind us of our duties under Nigerian law. But, anyway, we were now in a position to get going.

The film is supposed to show my arrival in Nigeria, starting with me being picked up at the airport car park. We could not actually show that happening because you cannot film at the airport. (We now knew this only too well.) So I was filmed being met by a driver in the car park of a hotel instead. If enemies of Nigeria should watch the film to get clues as to where and how to attack, they may well be fooled into going for the parking lot at the Sheraton International.

Then we reconstructed what should have been my first night. We could not film on the actual first night because, of course, we had not yet received our accreditation.

For the reconstructed first night I decided to stay in a flat in a protected compound to avoid travelling too far after dark. Many expats live in well-guarded apartments and take trouble not to get caught outdoors late at night because the crime rate, including car-jacking, is reported to be very high.

My flat was loaned to us for the night by Guinness, which is a company long established in Nigeria and successful all over Africa. Passing through a security gate resembling Checkpoint Charlie, I arrived at the door to my overnight apartment. A rather jolly doorman with a torch led me up the two or three flights of stairs to the flat. For some reason, the lights did not work on the staircase, but they worked well enough in the flat itself.

The flat was well appointed but had that bleak feel of any place that is occupied only on a temporary basis. Lonelier than a hotel room, scruffier than a show flat, emptier than a real home. The three or four locks on the front door caught my eye at first. But you might get that level of security in any city in the world. However, there was a security door of iron bars to be clanged shut as well. 'Lock yourself in,' the doorman said. He was not kidding.

'Stone walls do not a prison make, nor iron bars a cage,' wrote Richard Lovelace, unless it was Ronnie Biggs. But iron bars certainly make you feel as if you are in a prison, especially as there was another cage door which had to be shut in order to lock the corridor to the bedroom. So if burglars happened to break in through the sitting room window while you slept, they could help themselves but they could not get at you. Sweet dreams.

In the film, the whole point of the Guinness flat was that it was a safe refuge from the dangers of travelling at night. Nonetheless, at around midnight we decided to go back to our hotel on the opposite side of town. We were not robbed but we did run into one of the other inconveniences of travelling after hours: a police patrol.

We had been already been warned about this. Groups of policemen set up a road block, pull you over and demand a *dash* to let you proceed. There are plenty of rich people in Lagos, but lots more who are desperately poor. In the natural order of things, the wages of public employees such as policemen have not kept pace with inflation. So underpaid policemen have taken to augmenting their wages by drifting into private enterprise.

On first hearing, this seems dreadful. It does not take much to imagine the corrosive effects of policemen pocketing bribes on a regular basis and the discomfort this causes to honest citizens and visitors. But then you start to think that it might work, in a crazy sort of way. To collect their tips, the police have to be out there on the streets. Stopping vehicles means that they will bump into criminals from time to time, if only by accident. The bribes paid by ordinary folk merely correspond to the sums they would otherwise have to pay in higher taxes to pay the police a proper wage in the first place. But, no, I cannot support privatizing police pay in this way. That way madness lies. Either that or a seat in the next Conservative cabinet.

The police who stopped us were a lively bunch, fascinated by the collection of foreigners they had trapped. Their polite enquiries about where we were from, however, were cut short by a chap from a local TV company who was with us, as it turned out, just for one day. He barked at the officers that they should not talk to us; they should only talk to him. This aggressive attitude did not appear to work in our favour and we were required to produce our ID cards and so forth. In due course the happy atmosphere was restored and we were allowed on our way. I harboured the thought that our man had made things worse, but it turned out that he had paid the police on our behalf, so perhaps he knew what he was doing all along.

• Day 3: Overview •

A good day for filming. We managed to get some aerial shots from the top of an office block on Lagos Island. Lagos is a substantial city (7 million plus) with a full complement of high-rise buildings. To get access to the roof we had to call on the office of an obscure trading company whose premises were on, I think, the seventeenth floor. Well, it was out of the way wherever it was because it was one floor above the highest storey reached by the lifts. We had got permission in advance but the woman at the front desk demanded rather forcibly to see an official letter. Does everyone bark at each other as a matter of course in this country?

Most of the rest of the day was spent with me being driven up and down the Third Mainland Bridge. This was in the luxury of an air-conditioned Mercedes, although in fact the temperature, and especially the humidity, were too much for the air-conditioning to cope with.

In the evening we found a restaurant serving Nigerian food. (There are restaurants of every nationality and type to be found in Lagos.) This one was a wooden room overlooking a stretch of mosquito-friendly water. A couple of cheery waitresses encouraged us in our choices but seemed to misunderstand whatever we said. The goat was off, so instead we had, I think, pepper soup and pounded yams.

• Day 4: Black Gold •

The first substantial interview was with Chief Franklin Adedeji Akinti-ilo. He publishes *Nigeria Oil and Gas* and other magazines connected with the oil business. He has had plenty of experience in the oil business generally and came highly recommended as someone able to describe the industrial and commercial problems facing Nigeria.

I think he would have preferred to have been interviewed in his office, but offices are rather dull backgrounds to films and so he was persuaded to take us to the house he is having built on Victoria Island. On land reclaimed from the sea, what amounts to an estate of rich people's homes is under construction. It all looks a bit bleak at the moment – the land is very flat and the houses are rather grey – but this is where anybody with money is seeking to build. I would be rather worried about the sea claiming the land back again. Near our hotel, a great long stretch of sand called Bar Beach has been almost washed away, undermining half of the coast road. The beach is being restored by pumping sand back into position. And nothing much more by way of sea defences protects these prime acres of real estate.

Chief Akintiilo says all that is under control, and the water and electricity supply will be in place by the time the house is completed. His villa is nearly finished. While it is clearly costing quite a lot, it is not ostentatious. Like all rich people's houses in Lagos, it is surrounded by a large wall. Perhaps the garden wall will be topped by razor wire, the almost ubiquitous sign of a crime problem in the city.

Our idea of showing an interesting house under construction was thwarted by the rain which arrived at the same time as us, and we ended up doing the interview with a backdrop of an unfinished concrete wall. About the dullest, dreariest view you could hope not to see, and much worse than we could have got at the office.

Even so, Chief Akintiilo was good value. With an ironic sense of humour, he sketched out some of Nigeria's problems. The country has gained and suffered from the oil boom which sucked the life out of other industries and agriculture: farms were abandoned as farmers were drawn to Lagos to earn easier money. The slump in oil prices has left the country without the agriculture and without a great deal of the oil revenue.

Even with a drop in the price of oil, it remains overwhelmingly important. Oil accounts for something like 85 per cent of the whole economy (and 95 per cent of exports). But only 1 per cent of the population actually derive an income directly from the oil business. This represents a huge concentration of wealth in the hands of those who are in the business, or who are responsible for taxing it. Given the fact that there was a government representative sitting listening to the interview, Chief Akintiilo was prepared to be quite critical of the military government and the lack of good leadership in the country.

He was rather disappointed that the international oil companies have carried on trading with Nigeria without apparently exerting any pressure to encourage democracy. This, although a fair point, seemed to put the oil companies in a difficult position. Trading with a military dictator-ship does sustain it in power; but refusing to do so, or insisting upon constitutional changes, would amount to industrial imperialism.

Chief Akintiilo clearly doubted the military's capacity to run the gov-ernment, although he blunted his criticism by suggesting that their civil-ian politicians had been just as bad when they had been in power.

This all sounded rather dispiriting but he insisted that he has to remain optimistic. Having recently been in South Africa, he said he rather wished someone like Nelson Mandela would come along in Nige-ria. The best I could suggest was that, with their oil wealth, the Nigerians should put in a transfer bid for him. Either him or Jack Charlton.

In the evening we went back to the north of the city to interview Brian Farrell, the Deputy Managing Director of Guinness, Nigeria. The interesting location for this was a bar, an outdoor beer garden which at night is lit up with what we confidently expected to be a fantastic dis-play of lights.

Bars like this are relatively rare in Lagos, Mr Farrell told me. Drink is sold mainly in the take-home trade, small drinking rooms and for par-ties. Parties are a big thing in Nigeria. Guinness are big in Nigeria as well. Guinness, Mr Farrell assured me, do not get involved in politics. Like any large company, they prefer stability to instability. He was trying to indicate that Guinness and politics do not mix, but in practice it means they are happy enough to trade in a country run by a military government.

I quizzed him about corruption, but he stoutly maintained that Guinness was an ethical company which did not get involved in dodgy practices. (Most businessmen tell you this: however corrupt the country, their company is able to prosper without getting soiled.) Of course, I reminded Mr Farrell of the scandal which surrounded the Guinness take over of the Distillers company, but he cheerfully dismissed that as a hiccup in its usual probity.

Anyway, although Nigeria is very different from his native Ireland, he enjoys himself here. (The happy expat, I called him.) He reckons that with a little care you can avoid getting mugged and that he has met, got to know and got on with many Nigerians. Expats who fail to do this, and keep themselves apart, are the ones who get the least out of the country. This was all rather encouraging, although we had difficulty filming it. The rain poured down as we sheltered under the bar's large metal umbrellas at the tables. There was no light because of a power cut (a rather localized one – the bar had not paid its bill) and there was no generator. Nor did they have any candles until we sent someone out to buy some.

By the time we got back to our hotel we were wet through and I had consumed large quantities of the locally produced Guinness which I had been required to drink for the benefit of the camera. At our hotel, all the waiters were in Viking helmets to celebrate Danish week at the Eko. It was a weird way to end the day.

• Day 5: Sex, Drugs and Rock and Roll •

The next day, though, was even weirder. We spent it in and around the home of Fela Kuti, otherwise known as the Kalakuta Republic. Fela Kuti is almost certainly Nigeria's best-known rock singer, musician, folk hero and protester. In the 1960s he went to America and came under the influence of Malcolm X politically and James Brown musically. He brought together American soul music and West African traditional music to form what was called Afro-Beat. He has spent some time in political exile, some time in prison on trumped up smuggling charges, and had his house burned down by the government.

He is now in his late fifties and lives in his extraordinary house together with a selection of wives, girlfriends, groupies, minders, fans and hangers on. It is a largish, three-storey building in a residential district. In the front yard sit maybe a couple of dozen people chopping up huge loads of marijuana, smoking, selling beers and listening to music.

Cannabis is illegal in Nigeria but the smell of it is noticeable in the street and the smoke visible from the moment you reach the front gate. But Fela has acquired an immunity for his little community. For some reason the authorities tolerate what goes on, and there was no objection from our minders to us filming there.

The longer we stayed in Nigeria, the more incongruities about the controls that are exercised emerged. Newspapers have been closed down in Nigeria, journalists arrested, magazines seized, and yet others offering trenchant criticisms of the authorities are still sold everywhere. Our minders were full of worries about our filming what seemed to be quite innocent street scenes, but made no objection to us filming Fela's house.

Anyway, as soon as we got to the front yard we were offered deals on all the various bits of merchandise. I said I did not take drugs while filming, which I thought preserved both respectability and street cred.

It was not all dope. An earnest young man came straight up to me and told me he had millions of dollars that he wished to get out of the country. He had worked in the pipe-laying side of things and by unspecified means had managed to siphon off a fortune which he had hidden away somewhere. What he needed was someone to smuggle it to England for him.

I pointed out that I was with a film crew with huge amounts of suspicious-looking equipment which was liable to be searched. I would not be a good bet as a smuggler ...

No, no, he said. I was being naive. He did not need to move the money physically. All he required was someone with a bank account in London into which he could transfer these millions of dollars. It would have to be done secretly, of course. Even his wife must not be told ...

I may be naive, but I was not born yesterday, I reminded him. This scam is exactly what Lagos is famous for. Lured by the thought of millions of dollars I am supposed to set up an account for this man, who further down the line will ask me to put up some money to get the vast sums released. And when he disappears, who will I complain to? Since ripping money off greedy foreigners is such an established part of the Nigerian criminal scene, I was not surprised to be approached. I was only surprised that anyone should attempt it when I was so very obviously trying to film a TV programme. I was even more surprised that he expected me to believe his story when it was the very first contact he had had with me. I am not that easily duped. I want the equivalent of a gin and tonic and a candlelit dinner before parting with my assets.

Inside the house there were more relaxed people. Sleepy-looking guys, pretty-looking girls, sitting around in a smoky atmosphere on more comfortable Nigerian sofas and chairs. Soft furnishings and soft drugs.

Fela himself was asleep somewhere in the house, but did not wish to be filmed. He has done too much television and has gone off it. But he has not gone off women. It is claimed that he has fifty women on the go at any one time. He claims not to be able to sleep without a woman beside him. He did not emerge while we were there – probably too tired.

I tried to sit down in an empty chair to talk to one of the girls, but it turned out that it was for Fela's exclusive use. The girl explained that some of the people in the house were singers and dancers, but she herself is his girlfriend. (The girlfriend? A girlfriend? I did not establish this.) Fela can get away with the drug-taking and the rest of the bohemian lifestyle, she told me, because he is so powerful, but beyond that she could not explain how he has immunity from interference by the authorities these days.

For someone held in such awe by his followers, it is appropriate that Fela has his own performing space called the Shrine, and that is where we went that afternoon. The Shrine is a long, shed-like structure with a stage at one end and a bar at the other. The walls are open at the top on most sides to provide some sort of ventilation. Even before you get inside you realize it is an extension of the Fela Empire. Guys looking slightly spaced out were hanging around the entrance. They might be doorkeepers, bouncers, drug salesmen or anything. Inside, there were long benches at which were sitting a few dozen devotees, there to listen to a rehearsal, roll joints and drink beer.

The rehearsal involved not Fela Kuti but his son, Femi Kuti, and his band. Femi Kuti is an athletic-looking man, who could be a young version of Courtney Walsh, the West Indian cricketer. But he is, of course, a young version of his father. Like Fela, Femi sings and plays saxophone (although not at the same time). Also like his father, he fronts a band which mixes African music with what were long considered to be American jazz rhythms.

In fact, his band is a twelve-piece, featuring keyboards, sax, trumpets, guitars, drums and bongos. And there are three gorgeous girls (two of them his sisters) providing an erotic display of dancing. Like his father, Femi is a musician and singer with uncompromising views about the state of his country. But, unlike his father, he is not a womanizer, nor does he use cannabis, unless he happens to breathe while he is in the Shrine. The atmosphere is heavy with smoke from joints, some of which are the largest any of us have ever seen: joints with the dimensions of medium-sized bonfires wrapped in a roll of wallpaper. The drug squad turns a blind eye to all this, but surely the authorities could get them under the Clean Air Act.

It was a long afternoon while the musicians prepared to play and we prepared to film them. It seemed to get even longer for me as I found myself in immediate need of a lavatory. You know, foreign travel, change of water, unusual food, hot temperature. Suddenly the lower body goes on red alert. And being a man in a pale suit about to be filmed for television, warning signals like that are not to be ignored.

A simple enough requirement in a concert hall, you may think, but the door to the gents was locked. So, as it was an emergency, I had to venture into the ladies, which fortunately was empty. There I found two cubicles, one with its door hanging from its hinges, the other with no door at all. There was no light, but as far as I could see both lavatories were blocked.

On these occasions you have to follow your head or your heart, and my heart and all points south were not to be denied. I held the door shut against another man who tried to come in. He was quite understanding but then through the door I heard a tremendous argument between him and a woman, who claimed it was quite intolerable of him to be in the wrong lavatory. She was still there when I emerged from my cubicle, shamefaced but feeling better inside. I did not stay to hear her views on my presence there.

Thus refreshed, I went to be filmed tapping my toe to the rehearsal before interviewing Femi and his sister Yeni. Femi gives an energetic performance. Stripped to the waist, he moves from dancing to singing to saxophone playing, dominating the stage. Alongside him the girls dance and the musicians do a well controlled two-step shuffle in the background.

All of them are about to go on a tour of America, having been signed by Motown Records. They are big fish here in the Shrine (although still overshadowed by Fela). They are big fish in Nigeria. I hope they do not get lost in the teeming waters of the American music industry.

In any event, Femi would not want to stay in America. He gets his inspiration from Lagos, his home. In political terms he is radical beyond the dreams of Vanessa Redgrave. He opposes the military government but, like Chief Akintiilo, he is dismissive of politicians. In addition he reckons Africans should get rid of the boundaries between countries which were imposed by European imperialists and find an African identity. Furthermore, he is scornful of the hold Christianity has over many Nigerians, and Islam over many others.

To get rid of two world religions, politicians and the military is quite an ambition. But he aims to put all this into his music. And it has quite a beat, as well. Despite this, he feels that he lacks charisma, compared to his father and his sister. We agreed that his sister Yeni should stand for President, or perhaps be made Queen.

We had arranged to go back to film at Fela's house in the evening. The Kalakuta Republic is somewhat less comfortable after dark. The number of cool-looking dudes claiming to be in charge of events in and around the house seemed to have expanded. One man told us we could come in, then someone else immediately said we could not. Eventually an instruction was issued that we could come in once the girls were ready. Ready for what? What girls?

We were shown back up to the room we had visited earlier in the day, where there were lots of people bustling around. And just as we got inside there was a power cut.

Fela was expected at any moment, we were told. He was out of bed.... He was having a bath.... It was like being at the court of a medieval king. And finally he arrived. Not medieval, perhaps, but middle-aged.

Fela did not speak to us or acknowledge us in any way. He sat in his accustomed chair and seven girls lined up in front of him. Fela was dressed only in his underpants. What was going on? Were the girls there to prevent us filming him? Were they an honour guard which precede him all day? Were they a selection of new girlfriends? Why just underpants?

The answer is they were dancers, here to be taught to dance. There is a dancing master but Fela was here to take over the lesson. He took them through the steps, first showing them, in a rather confusing way, what to do and then berating them for not being able to follow.

He has a lithe body, well preserved for a man of his age, but wearing just underpants was a mistake, especially as they kept slipping off his rather wasted-looking backside.

For some reason I presumed that a rock legend would be very kindly in his teaching methods – a smile here, a word of encouragement there, a little touch of Fela in the night. But he was much more the cruel sergeant major, reducing raw recruits to a state of panic and fear. A fat girl was criticized for being too fat, another was told she was only capable of doing white men's disco dancing, not the simple steps familiar to ordinary Nigerian girls in country villages. He humiliated each girl in turn, inducing a mixture of scornful and nervous laughter from everyone else in the room.

While this was going on, an underling handed us candles to hold. Then Fela turned on the dancing master and ordered him to remove his shirt and to demonstrate the steps. The dancing master was not bad at the movements but was castigated nonetheless for failing to produce better results with his class.

Who would be next? Would he demand that I have a go? No, the great man was done. He was departing, leaving the demoralized dancing master in charge. We could film now, he said as he left the room. And so we filmed a little of what was going on, a hand-held camera illuminated by a hand-held candle.

Fela came back into the room to demonstrate some more dance steps. The position about filming was ambiguous. He had said he did not want to be filmed; and then said we could film once he left the room. Now he had returned. Should we stop filming? Surely if he wanted us to stop, he would say so.

The cameraman decided to carry on filming. And everything was fine, but after five minutes Fela noticed what we were doing. It was difficult to see why it had taken him so long. The light was so poor that the camera had been in closer contact with his buttocks than most of his underpants. But once he had noticed, our lighting problems were over because Fela was incandescent with rage. He ranted about our treachery, we proffered apologies and claimed it was a misunderstanding, which indeed it was. The room, the whole house, the street outside was full of people who hang on his every word and we were the objects of his rage. Was this just a display of his famed power, or could the situation turn really nasty?

We decided it would be a good idea to leave and we made our exit with as much dignity as we could muster. (In my case, this very nearly featured me falling down a storm drain, a trench 3 or 4 feet deep full of dark water and all kinds of rubbish, just outside the gate. That would have capped a perfect evening.)

Were we ever in any danger at this crazy place? The most reliable person we worked with in Lagos was the driver of the Mercedes, Schweib. He always arrived on time, drove well and was friendly, uncomplaining and was never on the make. Even he was affected by the events at Fela's. His voice rose by several octaves as he tried to convey how uncomfortable he thought our – and his – situation had become.

• Day 7: Breakdown, Polo, Beach, Storm •

We thought it was about time to show something of downtown Lagos. It was a hot day and we set off to drive down Broad Street, and into Tinubu Square.

We made slow progress. Lagos is famous for its dreadful traffic jams. They are not as bad as they were – the economic recession has reduced the number of cars on the road far more effectively than rules to keep even-numbered registration plates off the roads on alternate days ever did. In addition, completion of the causeways, bridges and flyovers has relieved some of the worst bottlenecks.

But Broad Street still operates at a slow crawl and it seemed to take all morning to get along it. At Tinubu Square there were some road-works and our Mercedes conked out. This was all a stroke of luck, as in between the road workings we found somewhere we could rest the car while it was sorted out. (Overuse of air-conditioning straining an already weak battery. Or it might have been the big end. I am not very good on cars.) Also, the breakdown provided me with a perfect excuse, in the film, to get out and look around.

By this time we were being accompanied by two minders, Olu and Florence. They seemed to come from two different departments and had slightly different approaches. They were not sure whether showing our car breaking down was good for the country's image. We assured them that no one would think any the worse of Nigeria because a Mercedes had gone wrong in Lagos. Germany might have grounds for complaint, but not Nigeria.

All right, we were allowed to film the car at a standstill, but we must on no account show the Bank of Nigeria building which, though possibly I should not tell you this, is just by Tinubu Square. Actually, we wanted to show that Lagos has an impressive number of skyscrapers: it is a built up city on a world scale. This was acceptable. We also wanted to show that there was a bustling street scene with little shops, stalls selling strange medical cures, crowded buses. This was all right, within reason.

Having managed to commit something of the street scene to film, we headed off to the Polo Club. This was to attempt to illustrate the power structure within Nigeria. The Hausa people, from the north of Nigeria, have always occupied a powerful position in the country's hierarchy. They are also great horsemen and liable to be found playing polo. And someone on a horse cannot fail to look superior.

There was no polo being played that day, nor in the end did we ever manage to arrange a time when we could be there to film a horse being ridden in anger. So nothing was achieved, although one of Lagos's top bankers (Charterhouse and LSE) stood us a beer at the very agreeable bar.

We had been in Lagos for a week now and progress had been very slow. Each morning seemed to start with a delay, a trip to the Ministry of Information to find our minders without whom we were not allowed to film at all, and power cuts and traffic hold-ups. So we decided to go to the beach.

About an hour and a half's drive out of Lagos is Elecko Beach. It is a pleasant drive through fields and stretches of woods and forests and the odd banana plantation. Midweek, the beach is more or less deserted, apart from a line of fishing shacks and boats. There are no signs of tourist development but a few kids ran excitedly after our car as we arrived. They were even happy to do it again for the cameras, for a fee. A dash for a dash.

Going to the beach was going to be the last scene, and we should have been filming it at the end of my stay in Lagos. It was a suitable location to sum up the good and bad side of the place. Even though we had only been there a week, and had loads more people to meet and interview, I did my best to sum up my reactions.

Strolling along the sand, I said that Lagos was nothing like as bad as it was painted, and with beaches like these it might even be considered as a holiday destination. I noted, however, that you always have to look out for the sting in the tail (something expat businessmen call Wawa: West Africa Wins Again). You cannot swim from these beaches as there is a vicious undertow which would sweep you out to sea, where the sharks would get you.

And that might have been the reasonably upbeat ending to the documentary. I even threw in an impromptu leap in the air to express a certain *joie de vivre*. (This was captured by Victor Agunbiade who was with us some of the time to take photographs. He was unlike any other stills photographer I have worked with in that he appeared to take so few photos. Most photographers fire off shots the whole time in the hope that some will be all right. Victor was cool, calm and laid-back, and seemed to wait only for the great moment. It must save on film. Anyway, he was a very reassuring presence to have around, and he did grab this moment which he had no way of anticipating.) But from this point on, everything seemed to go wrong.

That evening we set up our cameras on the balcony of the restaurant at the top of our hotel. With the night sky of Lagos winking in the background, I was going to have dinner with Makin Soyinka, who has a great affection for the city even though his father, Wole Soyinka, the Nobel Prize winning author, has been forced into exile by the Nigerian government.

It never happened because, just as we were setting up, a storm of epic proportions broke out over the city. Thunder and lightning cracked and fizzed in the blackening sky and rain cascaded down relentlessly. The waste of an evening's filming, but worse than the weather was to follow the next morning.

• Days 8 and 9: Anything You Say •

By day eight, there was a rhythm to my days in Lagos. After a night kept reasonably cool by the noisy air-conditioning in my room, I would dress in a freshly laundered shirt and a clean pair of trousers. There was a short walk to get to the lift and a long wait for the lift to get to me.

The lifts were a constant puzzle. You could more or less always get them to reception on the ground floor, and they would take you to any floor you wanted on the way down. But when summoned to a higher floor they would arrive only after a sullen and resentful delay. In the hot, airless landing I could feel myself starting to sweat after a few seconds. After a few minutes my linen shirt and cotton trousers were clinging to me. After ten minutes I really needed another shower and another change of clothes. There was an alternative, and often I would trot down ten flights of the service stairs, arriving quicker but even sweatier.

Anyway, on this morning when I arrived in reception I bumped into Emma, the producer, Clive Maltby, the director, and Arlen, the researcher, in earnest conversation with what I took to be the hotel staff. I greeted them with a cheery hello and expressions of surprise that they were up so early. (On most days I was the first one down to breakfast.)

Emma was in no mood for light-hearted banter.

'Clive,' she hissed, 'these men are from the SSS, and they have come here to take us away.'

The SSS is the sinister-sounding name of the State Security Service. A couple of SSS men had arrived at Emma's bedroom door at seven in the morning and demanded that she go with them to reception immediately. She had persuaded them to let her dress first and in due course Maltby (as I shall call him to avoid confusion) and Arlen had been assembled in reception as well, to be taken to SSS headquarters to be questioned.

I was rather surprised not to be included in all this. The SSS must, I imagined, have a pretty sophisticated view of television programmes not to assume, like most viewers, that absolutely everything on a film is done by the presenter. Anyway, if I was not being carted off myself, I decided to offer my advice as a lawyer. They should remain polite while firmly making the point that they were only prepared to be taken anywhere for questioning because the SSS insisted. (This, incidentally, I think is good advice if you are subject to random arrest in Britain or America, say, preserving as it should your right to sue for illegal detention in due course. Probably of no great use the way things are at the moment in Nigeria.)

By this time the lead SSS man had noticed me and soon discovered who I was. He suggested they would be delighted to take me along as well. Emma tried to argue him out of taking me with them, but I felt rather more ambivalent. Nobody wants to be questioned by a secret policeman, but shouldn't I be there if my producer and director were being given the third degree? So, in the end, I did not really take my own advice and let myself be carted off.

I was by no means certain I had made the right decision. Apart from anything else, we only had the word of the men taking us away that they were from the SSS at all. They wore no uniforms, they drove unmarked cars, they showed us no identification cards. They did not even tell us their names. Given the number of scams and frauds operating in Lagos, they could have been con men out to rob us. The only thing that convinced us they were the genuine article was the terror they induced in the hotel staff.

We sped through the Nigerian streets, on this Saturday morning free from the clogging traffic of the working week. How annoying – we were already missing out on a day when we could have got around to get some filming done rather more quickly than we had so far managed.

I wondered if I had done the right thing to have with me a bag full of research notes, newspaper articles critical of Nigeria and other 'incriminating material'. I had it all with me to read over breakfast and to refer to in the course of the day, but when I was being included in the routine questioning party I reckoned it would draw more attention to insist upon leaving it at the hotel.

As we drove along the sunny roads, keeping a mental note exactly where we were going just in case, I told myself the whole thing could not be too sinister. Could anything too dreadful be happening in a place decorated with advertisements for Schweppes, Marlboro and Coca Cola? How frightening a place can a country be whose Premier League football is sponsored by Bournvita?

Eventually we turned off the Lagos-Ibadan Expressway on to a side road and into an unmarked compound surrounded by walls topped with rolls of barbed wire. It was about nine o'clock in the morning when we were shown into a large, bare waiting room with a lumpy brown carpet. Cliché though it is, the only word for the whole business is Kafkaesque.

For a start, we had no idea why we were being questioned or which offence we had committed. We were filming with the permission of the Ministry of Information. In *Our Man In ... Havana* we had done some secret filming with dissidents and had expected trouble from the authorities (which never came). But here we had done nothing like that, we had always had our minders with us. Was it another misunderstanding like the one about the alleged filming at the airport and Badagry?

Or had this been sparked by some undiplomatic communication from London? The publishers of this book had sent an open fax referring to the TV series as *A Hope In Hell* (the original sub-title) which might not have been the best of ideas when contacting someone visiting a military dictatorship. The TV production company had also been more than frank in a fax dealing with our arrangements for our video tape, oblivious to the fact that security services might be informed about the fax's contents by one of the hotel staff.

Or had someone said something in an interview? Had I said something in an interview that the powers that be disapproved of? After about an hour, John Momah, a Nigerian television producer who had been helping with technical and other arrangements, arrived but he was unable to enlighten us much further.

The main SSS man came to thank us for having been so co-operative and not causing any trouble when we were taken from our hotel, and to warn us not to use any recording equipment because we were going through to a secure area.

Oh, no! Had we been too acquiescent when we were being taken away? Since we needed government permission to continue with our filming we had not liked to cause a fuss. Should we have summoned the British High Commissioner, or made a run for the airport? You read about the Highland Clearances – hundreds of people being shipped out of their own country. In Nazi Germany, concentration camp victims going calmly to their deaths ...

STOP IT! This was just routine questioning by the entirely polite officials of a Commonwealth country. There was nothing to fear whatsoever. The worst they could do was stop us ever showing our film which, let us face it, could happen anyway given enough bad reviews or an important golf match which has to be screened on BBC2.

We were shown into a larger, better furnished room and invited to sit at a large boardroom table. In due course, Arlen, Emma and I were left there guarded by a sleepy underling while Clive Maltby and John Momah were taken off elsewhere. We had to fill in a form, a 'Record of Interrogation'. On this we were required to reveal our name, tribe and address. And the address of our brothers and sisters.

Another hour or two went by. Our room looked out on an open courtyard, passing through which were various people going about their quiet, bureaucratic business. Heading roughly in the same direction as our colleagues had been taken went a man carrying some electric cables. Not electrodes, surely? Eventually, we were shown into another office where we rejoined Maltby and Arlen, together with Olu, our Ministry of Information minder, who had arrived as well by now.

Everyone was being very polite, but the SSS had demanded to see what we had already filmed. And Maltby and Arlen had already agreed to let them see it. I cannot say I was happy about this but it was a condition, apparently, of our being able to continue with our film at all. It was annoying, nonetheless. The first series of *Our Man In ...* had been shot on film, and it would not have been possible for anyone to watch it before it was processed. But for this series we were using videotape and so it was not difficult to replay it, even though it was going to take some time because we had already shot hours of material.

It was also going to take some time for us to be allowed to do anything at all. Apparently someone superior to the man we were talking to had to take a decision about us, and we had to wait until this superior arrived. Maltby and Arlen carried on ingratiating themselves with the SSS man, engaging in small talk designed, I suppose, to demonstrate how fundamentally decent we really were. I maintained a sulky silence. Emma fell asleep.

The room was decorated with a couple of signs. One was an exhortation to remain loyal to the organization for which you work and not to go around moaning about it. If you want to criticize, it said, resign your position and criticize from the outside. This seemed odd advice for anyone working for a secret police force. The other was simpler and more apposite: 'I distrust my friends, even you.'

Time drifted by. We had already missed out on a morning's filming. How much more were we going to lose?

There happened to be a newspaper in the room, so I read it to while away the time. (It seemed better than rummaging about in my bag.) The newspaper contained a report of the FA Cup Final, claiming that Everton's Nigerian player Daniel Amokachi had been the key figure in winning the semi-final but had been deliberately dropped from the Final line up (he only came on as a substitute) because of Everton's racism, which is of course typical of Britain's racism. Everton was once famous for not having any black players long after every other club had signed several. But would they exclude a player who was an important match-winner from such an important match? Is this how the British are perceived in Nigeria?

Meanwhile, for some reason Clive Maltby had started to explain the rules of rugby to our official captor. Surely he would have to let us go if only to save himself from death by boredom. Eventually our captor left the room and returned to say that the all-important superior had now visited this building and ruled that we were to be released, but we could not resume filming until Monday at the earliest, and even then only after our existing footage had been inspected.

Breaking off from the rules about line-outs, Maltby pointed out that it would be highly inconvenient not to be able to film for two days. Surely if our videotape was to be looked at anyway we could carry on as normal, otherwise we might miss two days' filming for no good reason.

No, this was the decision of the superior. No, we could not discuss it with him, he was no longer in the building. Although we had been waiting for him to arrive, he had now left again and it was now impossible to contact him. In any event, it had been someone even more superior to him who had made the decision. This was getting beyond Kafka.

But finally, in the early afternoon, we were released.

Back at the hotel we were reunited with our camera crew. John (camera) and Adam (sound) had woken up to find the rest of the team had been taken away by the mysterious SSS. They had decided to record their thoughts while they worried about us, contacted the British High Commission, and so on. These little scenes were so good they were included in the final documentary. For me, this was the most depressing aspect of the day's events. The camera crew could make a film very well without me. Could I have carried on filming without the camera crew?

For the rest of Saturday (when we were supposed to be filming an event at the Lagos Yacht Club) and Sunday (when we were supposed to be going to a church and back to the Shrine) we could do nothing but hang around waiting to hear the reaction of these authorities to our film. We were hoping they might let us resume filming sooner rather than later, fearing that they might be sending us home immediately.

We became paranoid, imagining that every eye which watched us in the swimming pool belonged to secret agents checking up on us. We went out in the evening and thought we were being followed by spies driving beige Peugeots. By that time we were so fed up we decided to have a traditional British meal that would remind us of home, so we went to a Tandoori restaurant.

• Day 10: Money, Football and Introduction •

On Monday morning we resumed filming. The authorities had decided that whatever remarks I or my interviewees had made on camera, whatever nasty bits of Lagos we had shown, we could continue filming.

I was to be filmed changing pounds sterling into the Nigerian currency, the naira. I could have gone to a bank, but everyone says you can get a better rate on the black market, or rather in a craft market. At craft stalls you can exchange almost any currency. If you insist you can even buy a piece of craft. In fact, to be within the law you probably do have to buy something. You get a better exchange than you would at a bank's official rate, but you probably lose it by being overcharged on the craft work.

Just a short, but hot, walk across the hotel's front garden is a large shop housing a dozen or more dealers in wood carving, beads, trinkets and the sorts of thing you feel compelled to buy to prove you have been to an exotic country. Nigeria is not over-blessed with tourists but our hotel was well stocked with businessmen in a hurry who need to grab something to take back to show the wife and kids how much they missed them, so the dealers probably do all right; almost as well as the prostitutes do with the same businessmen during the night.

There are items which are apparently carved in ivory. In the old days the salesmen would have asserted this was the real thing, not some bit of old bone made to look like ivory. Nowadays, they have to decide quickly whether you are seeking genuine elephant tusk or whether your concern for the environment means you will only buy it if it is old bones.

In the event I bought a necklace from one of the more engaging salesmen and changed some money. He gave me 130 naira to the pound, which I imagined was a good rate. The naira has steadily been going down in value thanks to the oil price and all the other difficulties. For some reason the government have not adjusted the denominations of their banknotes to take this into account. The very largest banknote they have is fifty naira. Since credit cards and cheques are largely distrusted, payments of large amounts in cash are quite common. With fifty naira being worth less than fifty pence, this means you have to carry around huge bundles of money to pay for things. The end of a meal in a restaurant is an endless procedure of counting and recounting grubby notes. I made the point to the craft market dealer, by suggesting you must need a suitcase to carry your money around. He agreed, and offered to sell me a suitcase.

Things seemed to be getting on a bit better. Florence was quicker than absolutely necessary to find reasons why we could not film things, but she was in a good mood over lunch. She joined a couple of waiters in teaching us the rudiments of Yoruba, one of Nigeria's languages.

The afternoon was spent investigating a football theme. Football in Nigeria is pretty big. Not only did the national team qualify for the World Cup Finals in America in 1994 (which is more than England, Scotland, Wales, Northern Ireland and France managed), there is a lively football scene which engages the interest of many Nigerians. Increasingly, Nigerian footballers are finding careers abroad. Clive Maltby was keen to show football in Lagos as an escape route from Nigeria's economic woes. To this end, at different times we filmed kids playing in a public park, a full professional game and, on this afternoon, an interview with Joseph Dosuh, captain and goalkeeper of the Julius Berger Club, but nothing particularly relevant to the story of Lagos emerged from these pieces.

In the evening we managed to do the interview with Makin Soyinka. It was another stormy night, but the storm restricted itself to a few flashes of lightning while we were talking on the balcony. Makin is in his early twenties but very self-possessed. He was apparently unfazed at being interviewed while a representative of the government which has exiled his father listened in.

He eloquently defended Lagos from its detractors. He comes originally from Ibadan, which was once Nigeria's largest city but has long since been eclipsed by Lagos. Makin reckons he switches to a higher gear when he comes to Lagos. Even London has little to compare with Lagos for dynamism and excitement. In addition, Lagos has a music and club scene second to none. Because everyone has a struggle to survive, they tend to have more than one job. A lawyer or a doctor will get involved with importing shirts when he travels abroad. All sorts of people sell things on the street to make ends meet. Power cuts and traffic jams are a pain but they are also all part of the fun.

More obviously part of the fun are the parties. Getting married, being made a Chief or getting buried all call for vast gatherings. Makin had been surprised to hear of Whitney Houston's wedding celebrations in America which had attracted one hundred people. A party with only one hundred guests in Lagos would be a disaster. Makin would expect more than that from just his immediate family members.

Makin reckoned the problems with crime are over-rated and it is possible to go through many years without being robbed. He was, however, attacked three times in the past year, which made him not such a good advertisement for the city's safety. All in all, he painted a picture of Lagos as a fun, if tough, place to be. Fun if you are young, fit, talented or well connected. Tough for everyone else. I suppose you could say if you are tired of Lagos, you are tired of life. Mind you, you could also say if you are tired of Lagos you are tired of living in a rather ugly, oppressively hot city ruled by an undemocratic government.

There was more to discuss with Makin in the car as we drove off to see some of the delights he had spoken about, but they had to be postponed to another night as the rain was coming down again. Perhaps we should not have come in the rainy season.

• Day 11: Crosses, Chains and Slavery •

This was the day we were to film in Badagry, the place which had caused the trouble even before I got to Nigeria. Badagry is 40 miles or so west along the coast road from Lagos, which takes you practically to the border with Benin. Probably this was the reason for the authorities being so sensitive about my colleagues going there without prior discussion, although quite what threat the tiny country of Benin could offer Nigeria, a giant in West Africa, is not obvious.

Badagry was once an important place which has also long been eclipsed by Lagos. Once upon a time it was a major port for the export of slaves to the New World, and later the site of the introduction of Christianity into West Africa. It sits on a stretch of classic West African mangrove-swampy coast. I took the chance to go out in a little fishing boat to pretend I was arriving like some intrepid explorer or missionary, instead of driving up the trunk road from town. In these days of mosquito repellent and malaria prophylaxes, Badagry is a charming relief from the hustle and bustle of Lagos.

The first mission house and, they claim, the first two-storey building in West Africa, was built in Badagry in the 1840s. It is still there, kept up, just about, as a museum. To take you round there is a guide who, before he retired, worked for the railways. Now he has a very firm line in patter, which no one would dare to interrupt.

In truth, there is not a great deal to see any more. Wooden shelves where the missionaries used to store their books; pegs for their cassocks; a safe, made in West Bromwich, where they kept their money; a cupboard for Bibles; that sort of thing. The guide, despite being hampered by his arthritis, walked me around, enthusing over these relics of the 'olden days'. There is a plan which shows you the layout of the place 150 years ago when it had a number of outbuildings and garden areas all long gone.

In short, it is a gem of a place at exactly the right level of tourist development. The Church Missionary Society, or the Church of Nigeria, or whoever owns it, could do a little more basic maintenance, but it would be ruined if there were queues to get in, colour brochures or a tea room. I urge you to visit it if you are in Badagry, and do remember to tip the guide.

Badagry's other tourist attraction is even less organized and much less happy. The Mobee Family Slave Relics House is a single room containing a memorial to an ancient member of the Mobee family and a sorry collection of articles – chains, mainly – connected with the slave trade. I could not quite establish who this member of the family was exactly, except that he had been a very powerful man thereabouts. This raised the suspicion that he had been involved in the selling of slaves himself, but perhaps I was being unfair.

A delightful girl call Dada Mobee showed me round the Relics House. In fact, she had accompanied us all the way around Badagry and despite her very diffident demeanour with us, she was a force to be reckoned with when dealing with local boys hanging around threatening mischief.

Her demonstration of slave relics is simple but ghastly. On display are neck chains, chains to tie two slaves together, locks to put over slaves' lips (together with a piercing bolt) to prevent the slave eating the crops being worked, drinking troughs for slaves to refresh themselves like beasts. All the impedimenta of cruelty.

Of course, every schoolboy knows the British abolished slavery in Africa. This is true, up to a point. In 1807, after twenty years of pressure from the anti-slavery society led by William Wilberforce, it was made illegal for British ships to carry slaves. Later in the nineteenth century, David Livingstone and other missionaries worked to suppress the slavery which still existed in the interior of the African continent.

But, before then, the bulk of the transatlantic slave trade was carried out by Britain, bringing prosperity to Bristol and Liverpool, and the bulk of the slaves were exported from the slave coast of Nigeria. Christian missionaries probably did something to restore the West Africans' view of British and other white people, but in Nigerian histories Britain does not emerge well at any time. The back of a street map of Lagos summarizes events in the nineteenth century in this way:

'Self-government was denied Lagos in December 1851 when British forces invaded the territory, claiming to eradicate slavery and to teach the tenets of Christianity. The truth, however, was that the result of technological improvement in Britain had rendered slaves redundant. Hence they wanted these slaves to return in order that they might till the land to serve British imperialism.'

After a look at the tree under which the first sermon in West Africa was preached, and round the landing stage from which slaves were shipped, we set off to drive back to Lagos. Since it is the main road from the border, we were stopped and inspected at a customs checkpoint by police and by some other officials whose exact position we never quite understood.

• Day 12: Delay, Cut and Match •

We were getting used to days beginning with delays, but this one threatened not to begin at all. Olu was not scheduled to be with us, so our right to film depended on Florence accompanying us. Unfortunately, it was on this day that she did not turn up for work. For several hours all we could do was pace up and down on the front steps of the hotel where we seemed to spend so much time. There, forlornly waiting with our tin boxes and cameras, we struck up a rapport with a French film crew who were also attempting to make a television programme and who, by a strange coincidence, were staying in rooms on the same floor of our hotel. They too found conditions difficult and also ran into trouble with the authorities for filming on a beach without permission. (Manifestly assisting Cameroon with the state of the tide for a seaborne invasion.)

In the afternoon we went to the Oneika football stadium to film a Premier League match between Julius Berger and Bendel Insurance. The secretary of the club, Richard Ofou, helped us to position our cameras and was generally one of the most friendly and agreeable people we dealt with in the whole of our stay in Lagos. The players are professional even though the clubs are named after the commercial or industrial companies which own them. Julius Berger is a German construction firm. I was disappointed that Berger were not playing another top club, Stationery Stores. I would have liked to hear the fans yelling 'Keep moving, Stationery!'

The stadium is quite well appointed, with something more than the capacity of the Queens Park Rangers' ground at Loftus Road. The pitch is not perfect but is perfectly playable. The crowd was smaller than I had been led to expect – not quite half-full, but then it was a midweek game played in the afternoon (there are no floodlights). The crowd was less excitable than at a comparable game in Britain, but what do you expect from those crazy British? There is a VIP area, where the VIPs, chiefs and directors sit on yet more comfy armchairs.

I sat on the regular seats with a former manager and journalist, and now agent, called Sogun Adenusa, who was happy to discuss the various players as the game proceeded, possibly because he had gained the impression that I might have a worthwhile connection with football clubs in Britain.

We agreed that Bendel seemed to be playing the better football, although in the end Julius Berger won the match 2 – 0. The ways of football matches are much the same the world over. I do not want to be rude but, as a general observation, the Nigerian players seem to play the game in a British rather than a Continental style. It confirmed my impression of the national side in the World Cup that their players could fit very easily into the FA Premiership. Nigerian clubs are worried that too many of their best players will be enticed not only to Britain but to the rest of the footballing world, but for the moment there was this match to play.

The pitch is surrounded by a wire fence, topped by barbed wire. The spectators are supposed to remain seated or, at any rate, well back from the fence, but as the game went on people drifted forward and stood with their faces pressed close to the fence. This was not dangerous or anything, the crowd was too small for a crush. But every ten minutes or so one of a group of policemen strolled along and whipped the fans back from the fence. It was slightly brutal (he seemed to give them no warning) and completely pointless as they drifted back to the fence the moment he had gone. It was always the same policeman who did it, the others were not interested. Perhaps it is just his hobby. A fight did break out in front of me towards the end of the game, but it was pretty small beer and just added to the feeling that football matches are the same the world over.

In the evening we were supposed to be filming at the club room of the Pyrates. The Pyrates is a somewhat self-conscious intellectual club. I was taken there by Makin, whose father Wole was one of the club founder members forty years ago. Before we got to Ankor Point (the Pyrates go in for misspellings in a big way) I had formed conflicting impressions of what the club would be like. A Nigerian version of a London gentleman's club (membership is restricted to male graduates); a revolutionary group dedicated to the restoration of political freedoms (they are dedicated to the betterment of man and his society); Freemasons (they have an attachment to philanthropy and funny titles).

On my first visit I did not get a much clearer picture. Ankor Point is at the end of a cul-de-sac alongside a railway line. But when we got there it was in darkness owing to a power cut. We were beginning to realize that Lagos is subject to many power cuts. Either that or our presence in the city was causing them wherever we went. The club did not possess a generator, but fortunately we had hired one to allow us to light the place sufficiently to film. Unfortunately the generator came with a very short lead which meant that the sound of the generator made it too noisy for our sound. We could have got by using candlelight but the Pyrates felt it would make them look too spooky and sinister. (They have obviously had dealings with television people before.)

Clive Maltby was close to tearing his hair out with yet another delay. I greeted another evening with my customary forbearance, a tolerance of inactivity which can be confused with laziness. We had a few beers and I tucked into a piece of cow leather with a very peppery sauce which the ladies in the kitchen brought round in the dark. I had seen quantities of bits of leather being sold in street markets, and it had not occurred to me to eat them. The effect is like chewing the bottom of your shoe dipped into your favourite chilli sauce. Real sole food, in fact.

Once filming for the evening was abandoned, we made our way back to our vehicles which were parked just round the corner. A large private house had a sign which claimed it had a private zoo or menagerie in its grounds. Naturally, I walked towards the house to have a look over the wall to see what type of animals they could keep in the centre of Lagos.

And naturally I failed to notice the storm drain lurking in the dark and plunged straight in up to my knees in an intriguing mixture of water, mud, oil and pond life. (Obviously my near miss outside Fela Kuti's house had been a dry run.) Strangely, none of my companions noticed my pathetic, soggy fall, although the pungent smell of my trousers drew it to their attention on the journey home. Despite the zoo sign, there were no animals to see apart from one or two nasty-looking bugs I eventually found making a new home in my sock.

• Day 13: Spiritual and Temporal •

For once, it was a reasonably good day for getting work done. We obtained permission to film me walking around ordinary streets meeting people, stopping at shops and stalls. Lagos is a very commercially-minded city and there is frantic activity going on the whole time. If you like city life it is the sort of thing you really miss when you are in the countryside, however beautiful. If you do not like city life, it is pretty much a nightmare.

Official permission apart, filming on the streets was much easier than we had once feared. When first planning to go to Lagos we had been advised that we might need armed guards with us the whole time to prevent the theft of our equipment or attack from local people. Others had suggested we should use a Nigerian camera crew to avoid animosity.

In fact, these fears were completely groundless. In the main, ordinary people displayed only ordinary reactions to our presence. On a crowded street one or two were keen to ask what we were up to, one or two shied away from being seen on camera. At one or two locations people going about picturesque activities demanded payment before they allowed themselves to be shown. But in the main, the man and woman on the street was either pleased to see us or, more often, ignored us altogether.

We could not afford to show pavement hair-braiders (they demanded money), but we did show little workshops and stalls; signs above more stagnant storm drains reading 'ice sold here'; a man trying to sell me an attractive vase for a few hundred dollars. What we were not allowed to show was the amazing amount of stuff sold to people sitting in traffic jams. I have already noted that Lagos's traffic jams are not as horrific as they once were, but there are plenty of places where inevitably you grind to a halt and might have to wait five or ten minutes before getting on to a bridge or a flyover or whatever. At these points car-to-car salesmen approach you with all the obvious items: newspapers and magazines, cartons of fruit juice, ice cold water, that sort of thing. But they also bring every other kind of thing: biscuits, cakes, brooms, brushes, lavatory paper, underpants. Anything you might expect to buy in well equipped ironmongers, clothing or food stores.

Since showing this would have portrayed Lagos as it is experienced by each and every motorist, and we imagined it would be quite fun for me to negotiate my way through this perfection of drive-in shopping, we started to experiment with ways of rigging cameras on the car to capture it on film. But our minders were having none of it. The activity of these salesmen is strictly illegal. Yet, since thousands of people do it every day, we could not quite see why we could not show it happening. It is not as though we thought it reflected badly on the city. All right, it is a fairly desperate and occasionally dangerous way to earn your living. There are a few beggars who go from car to car as well, which is always sad to see. But once you get used to it you can see what a boon it would be to the working man or woman to be able to do the household shopping without having to leave your car. No, it is strictly illegal, we were reminded. If you made a documentary on Paris you might well show people parking illegally, we said ...

According to Olu, the full reason for forbidding filming was this: selling on the street is against the law of the State of Lagos. The Ministry of Information which was supervising the filming is a federal institution, and so to sanction this sort of filming on the street would give the impression that the federal government was encouraging the breaking of the laws of the State of Lagos. We did not think that a little bit of colourful streetlife was worth risking another trip to the SSS so we left it at that. A pity, though, as it would have been fun.

Some of the official paranoia about filming in Nigeria can be traced to a *60 Minutes* documentary made in December 1994 by the American TV company CBS. It started with the assertion that Nigeria was the most corrupt country the producer had ever visited, continued with undercover filming to show the petty corruption of customs officials and then went on to the million-dollar scams I have already mentioned.

Undoubtedly Olu, along with other patriotic Nigerians, was personally affronted to see his country portrayed in such an unattractive light. But whatever the accuracy of the CBS film – and it was a very powerful piece of work which seemed to provide good evidence of the sort of corruption one experiences and hears about the whole time – it struck me that Nigerians were upsetting themselves unnecessarily about it.

In my experience, Americans are not very interested in foreign countries and television viewers there only watch documentaries if they absolutely have to. In America, the *60 Minutes* exposé will have passed almost without notice and by now will have long been forgotten unless it happened to be mentioned in the O.J. Simpson trial. And yet here in Nigeria it was still weighing on the mind. Come to that, if you do not like your country being revealed as a haven for crimes of dishonesty, the best reaction is to take steps to rid yourself of them, not try to keep them concealed. Anyway, we were not allowed to show Nigerians going about their honest business of selling useful stuff, car door to door.

Then, in the hot afternoon, we went to see His Grace Archbishop Theophilus Oluwasanu Olabayo (JP), Primate and Founder of the Evangelical Church of Yahweh (Worldwide). Apart from founding his own church – a good way to become a primate – Archbishop Olabayo brings out an annual publication called the *Book of Revelation for Today and Tomorrow*. This is a sort of up-market *Old Moore's Almanac* in which he predicts events in Nigeria and all round the world.

We thought an interview with him might be a useful way of discussing the future of Nigeria, and would also bring an insight into the role of fortune-telling in the country. According to one account, the Biafran War was won and lost on the turn of a soothsayer. But it turned out the Archbishop is quite careful not to get too caught out with his predictions in the uncertain politics of Nigeria. Glancing at his predictions for Britain you find a strange mixture of racing certainties – 'John Major's government will be rocked by sex scandals'; 'The Queen's children will continue to be under strain from marital problems' – and quite specific predictions about business, for all the world sounding as though his revelations come to him while reading in-flight magazines – 'BT and Lufthansa will sign skyphone contract.'

As much as possible, I like to be filmed doing things for real, largely because I find acting being surprised to see something harder work than just being surprised to see it. In this case, perhaps we pushed this principle too far. Although the cameras had been set up ahead of my arrival, I had no idea what to expect as I entered the Archbishop's house, a comfortable villa in a residential district of Lagos. Opening the door I came into a large sitting room with the smiling Archbishop surrounded by a group of twelve or so acolytes. His wife, the pastor of the local church, some elders of the church and a man who had converted from Islam were all sitting on the now familiar Nigerian armchairs. He began by introducing some of the acolytes to me in the manner of Jesus Christ presenting his apostles and a few examples of his miracle work. After that came a friendly chat with the Archbishop, whose walls are decorated with pictures of occasions when he has met various world leaders.

What to make of him depends on faith. If he is, or even if he genuinely believes he is, possessed of special powers and is on a mission from God he is a force to be reckoned with. If he is making it all up he is just another con man. Great leader or great fraud, the Archbishop was very hospitable and his group laid on a homely meal of salad and fruits and non-fermented grape juice which had the authentic feel of a vicar's tea party.

We also filmed at a church loyal to the Archbishop in an almost rural piece of Lagos. The picturesque building is reached by a long wooden walkway over marshy ground. As it happens, he would not let us film inside the church because it was empty of people. (We had given up trying to follow filming restrictions by now. We had intended to be there on the previous Sunday when the SSS intervened.) In the end we were not able to include the Archbishop in the film, but I suppose he must have foreseen that all along.

• Day 14: Why Don't You Stay, Just a Little Bit Longer •

By now it was clear that we would have to remain in Lagos longer than we had planned. There had been hold-ups caused by power cuts, the weather and officials, and we had yet to secure an interview with a government spokesman. So we changed our travel and hotel reservations and had another day achieving not very much. We went to an architect's office in order to interview a lawyer about the crime situation in Lagos. Someone had thought the lawyer's office would not look sufficiently like a lawyer's office on film. The trouble was the architect's office was even less suitable. We agreed to do the interview in a couple of days' time, at the lawyer's office.

In the evening we went back to the Pyrates. On the first visit there I had formed the impression that the Pyrates' clubroom was in a quiet cul-de-sac, which in a sense it was. But if you climb on to the roof of the two-storey club building you can see that just over the wall is a vast area of frantic urban activity. You have a panoramic view of railway tracks right through a vast expanse of land filled with people buying, selling and exchanging goods, queuing for buses, pausing for something to eat on the way home from work. Downstairs, earnest intellectuals gather for a twice-weekly brains trust; over the wall the proletarian masses get on with living life in all its mess, in all its glory.

Actually, downstairs they were not that earnest. I had a long chat without quite getting to grips with what the Pyrates' philosophy really is. They do charitable work, they exchange ideas, but any notion of them as a subversive organization drifted away with the beer and the conversation. There are Pyrates working for the government as well as the professions. All highly educated, they dismiss any suggestion that Nigeria is riven by tribal divisions. What they cannot really explain is why a country with so many intelligent and well educated people finds itself with a President who has an undistinguished academic record even within the military. They do not know why military governments have been in power for so many of the thirty-five years since independence.

It was clearly time for me to speak to the government. Fortunately, the next morning I was to interview the Minister of Information.

• Day 15: More Messing About •

Unfortunately, the interview with the Minister of Information was cancelled half an hour before it was due to take place. He had been called away to Abuja on urgent government business. Was this just an excuse? A Nigerian version of the diplomatic cold?

For a variety of reasons, Nigeria has built itself a brand new capital city at Abuja. Especially in the boom years, Lagos was too crowded and there was money available for a grand new Brasilia. Whatever its drawbacks, it does provide a marvellous alibi for officials, who can make sure they are in Abuja when anyone wants them in Lagos, and vice versa.

We contented ourselves with filming me arriving at the hotel, waiting for lifts and so forth, on the off-chance that we would need such sequences for the final film. At lunchtime we went to the Lagos Yacht Club where we had intended to film the week before. Broadly speaking, we detected a pattern developing – things would only happen the second or third time we attempted them. The Yacht Club is not open only to British and other European expats, but it might just as well be. Nigerians are, they told me at the club, not interested in sailing.

Nobody was interested in sailing when we got there, because – surprise surprise – it was raining buckets again, and blowing a gale. The regatta was cancelled so I settled down in the bar to get the views of club members. The club occupies a prime site on the waterfront of the centre of Lagos but, in atmosphere, it could be on the Isle of Wight. The premises are held on a lease, dependent in some way on government approval, so nobody was interested in speaking too critically in case they jeopardized their position. Nobody, as it were, wanted to rock the boat.

There is a substantial British expat community in Lagos; Britain is still Nigeria's largest trading partner. The Yacht Club is a godsend, somewhere expats can meet and relax, away from the strains of living in a strange city. Of course, it is no good getting too wrapped up in club life or you risk failing to make contact with the city where you have come to work. And in the end there was no real point in our film getting too bogged down in expat life either.

• Day 16: From Church to Shrine •

Taken all round, this day (on which I should have been flying back to England) was probably the best of our stay in Lagos. Even Florence was enthusiastic about our filming as we were going to her church to do it. Well, it is not her church exactly, it is Chris Okotie's church.

Chris Okotie was once one of Nigeria's top singers, but he has now found a religious vocation and given up singing. Well, not quite, because in his role as the pastor of his own church he does quite a lot of singing, and he still pulls in the crowds. His church is in the Oregun area. It is said to hold 4000 people and there must have been 3000 in attendance when we arrived for the 9 a.m. service.

I do not know if you would characterize the service as evangelical or charismatic. Certainly, Chris has charisma, and he does evangelize. He answers a string of questions on biblical study, explaining along the way why the church has no cross on display nor any other symbols. (He made the point that if Christ had been executed today the Christian symbol would probably be an electric chair, a concept which I think featured in Lenny Bruce's stand up act.) He coped with the intricacies of Bible scholarship to the satisfaction of his adoring congregation but eventually had to move on to the hymns..

They are not hymns ancient and modern, but performances virtuoso and impressive, with the congregation joining in the choruses and clapping and dancing. There is one song whose refrain is 'This is a dreadful place' – I think a reference to earth compared to heaven – and another which largely consists of the line 'Jesus is the sweetest name I know'. And they are both rather good. My notion of a church service is of dreary nineteenth-century (or earlier) hymns intoned by an unenthusiastic crowd to slow organ music. I thought it daring when chaps from the Christian Society introduced 'Lord of the Dance' into assembly at school. But Chris Okotie's service is compelling. It might not convert me to his church, but it could convert me to his church music.

Or possibly I was just carried away by the emotion. After the service we retired to Chris's white-painted study to record an interview. Happiness and certainty radiate from his face, which has that well-scrubbed look of the religious enthusiast. He was content to be interviewed although they were already waiting for him to begin the next service.

The style of the service has all the trappings of a cult of personality (his) but you could scarcely accuse him, as you might some American TV evangelists, of being in it just for the money. He was making plenty of money before he turned preacher. But, strangely, he is quite content to appeal almost exclusively to the young and well educated, a spiritual leader of yuppies. He feels that is where his ministry lies, rather than with the poor and needy.

He was prepared to say that he had given financial support to the President Elect, Chief Abiola. Although a Muslim, Chief Abiola had been to his church before being imprisoned. He did not think that a church service like his represented an escape from the troubles of the world. He was able in his preaching to comment and advise on the political questions of the day.

The next service was even more intense. People in the congregation leaped to their feet, speaking in tongues. Others got out of their seats to dedicate themselves to Christ. I somewhat lost track of what manner of man was Chris Okotie – Billy Fury, Billy Idol or Billy Graham? – but there is no doubting the intensity of religious feeling which grips this section of the Nigerian people.

Spiritually invigorated, we were able to go back to the Shrine to film Femi Kuti in performance. The scene at the Shrine had been pretty intense in the middle of the afternoon when we had been there for the rehearsal. After dark, and with a paying public, the Shrine and the street outside had an even heavier atmosphere. Before going on stage Femi was relaxed, laid-back and really friendly. Once the concert got going, the fans were also friendly although there was a characteristic

Lagosian element of people with tales of woe or propositions for business which after a while was beginning to get enervating.

For the purposes of the film, I sat in one of the rows of seats near the front but I think this was a bad choice. The lively fun-seekers danced around towards the middle of the hall, the talkative drinkers hung around the bar at the back, the head-bangers got as close to the speakers as possible, and the stalkers and the perverts were close to the stage where they could admire the girls' costumes. In my area were the intense experts on the music, the train-spotter element, and I did not feel I had the technical knowledge of the modern Nigerian music scene to be able to communicate at a sufficiently high level. Where is Andy Kershaw when you need him most?

• Day 17: Law and Order •

The day started in what for me was a very relaxed way: interviewing a lawyer about the 419 con tricks made famous by a thousand travellers' and businessmen's tales.

Section 419 of the Nigerian criminal code, using the same language as an English legal statute, creates a general offence of obtaining by deception. Segun Debayo Doherty, the lawyer I was visiting, was educated and called to the Bar in England, but on his return to Nigeria he has found many and various the deceptions practised on the unwary in Lagos. As I have explained already, many of these depend upon luring the greedy victim into breaking the law himself, which effectively rules out legal redress once he has been stung. But other frauds involve printing fake government documents, licences, letters of credit and so forth. And they do put some work the way of deserving lawyers.

We chuckled over old stories of victims being duped by being shown letters printed at local print shops or even by being taken to the Central Bank and shown a man passing by in a suit who, the criminal claims, is the Mr Big in charge of releasing funds. Nigerians, in their lighter moments, like to see themselves as the Italian's Africa. Corrupt but lively and fun.

While I conceded that there is a long tradition of big cities ripping off new arrivals, I really wanted to know why Lagos has such a poor reputation for offences like this. Counsel Mr Doherty could only offer in mitigation the effect of the oil wealth of the 1970s: gold fever. Who was it who said that the only thing worse for a country than not having oil, is having oil?

At long last that afternoon I got some information, or at any rate an interview with the Minister of Information. He is Dr Walter Ofonagoro, a famously formidable member of the government who, it turned out, was not avoiding me. He really had been called away on government business. Sometimes diplomats do get colds.

Not only was he prepared to be interviewed, he laid on a studio audience. Well, not quite a studio audience but he invited along a couple of under-ministers and civil servants to sit in on our conversation – a favourite trick of his, apparently, calculated to intimidate the visiting interviewer. In addition, he had his own camera crew to film the interview. Tony Benn always tape-records interviews with the media: once he gets wind of the fact that there are politicians filming them as well I am sure he will be pitching up to press conferences with a palm-corder.

Before we started, the air-conditioning in the room was switched off. There is nothing more humid than a room that has just lost its air-conditioning, and I began to liquidize as a result. But a sweaty presenter, apparently, is better for a documentary than the slight hum of an air-conditioning unit.

I asked Dr Ofonagoro about the reputation Lagos has for international fraud. In reply he made the point that all big cities have their share of miscreants and, additionally, that the victims of the fraud are usually behaving dishonestly themselves.

'What we have is a situation where certain businessmen come to this country with the intention of defrauding the Nigerian government, or the Nigerian Central Bank, or the Nigerian oil industry, or the Nigerian people,' he told me. 'And because they came with the intention of defrauding they get into contact with dubious and fraudulent elements. And when crooks meet and hatch their plans, if the European crook outsmarts the Nigerian crook, nothing is heard of it. When the Nigerian crook outsmarts the European crook, a great deal is heard of it.'

'Well,' I said, 'I've had people approach me and virtually the first thing they're telling me is that they have millions of naira, or millions of dollars, they want to get to England.'

'So when somebody's stupid enough to go for such fraudulent ideas and gets burnt he cannot then turn round and give the city a bad name. There are 8 million hard-working Nigerians here in Lagos.... Lagos is a sophisticated, complex, thriving and throbbing modern urban metropolis.'

'Is it thriving at the moment?' I asked.

'Well, times are hard all round the world for everyone.... Not only that, in 1980 a barrel of Nigerian crude was selling for forty dollars. Today it is about eighteen dollars.'

'Would you say that the oil revenues have been well spent? It has been suggested that a lot of it has been wasted on projects which didn't deserve it, and money's been siphoned off into private hands.'

'There are people who make a profession belly-aching about where money should be spent.... We have expanded the number of universities in this country from one in 1960 to about forty-six today.... Our power infrastructure – that is, dams and electricity – has been expanded to about a thousandfold.... We have a network of expressways that would be the envy of Britain, France or the United States....'

I was more concerned about money misappropriated by corrupt individuals, but Dr Ofonagoro was not going to accept that anything like that went on. He was insistent that there was free expression of opinion in Nigeria, and suggested that I would have noticed a free expression of opinion in Nigeria's papers. Up to a point this is true, although oddly enough one of the things the press complained about was the fact that newspaper editors had been harassed and publishers closed down. Conveniently, a paper called the *News* had that day summarized those journalists in custody, but the Minister dismissed this complaint.

'The *News* is an unimportant paper. A baby which belly-aches about things that are unreal.... When you pick up newspaper editors it's for writing incendiary articles and instigating public unrest. Social stability is fragile and we have a larger responsibility to the public.'

The Minister seemed to think that Britain did not have an irresponsible press or that, if we did, Brixton Prison was used to lock up turbulent editors. His other justification for arrests was that some papers were published without addresses. I tried to make the point that once you start arresting the people who run newspapers, you cannot be surprised if they do not want to tell you where they are. And I did mention the trouble our little team had run into.

'No, no, your little team ran into no trouble at all,' he corrected me. 'What happened was this. The security agencies thought you didn't have proper clearance to operate because they had not yet notified their boss in Abuja. But we had got clearance from the agencies locally for you to operate, but for some reason there was a breakdown in communication between their office in Lagos and their office in Abuja, so the Abuja team ordered your arrest. And I ordered your release, and you are properly released, so what's your problem?'

'Well, I am grateful to you personally, but we lost a couple of days' filming.'

'So come on, don't tell the international audience that you are harassed. In fact, you were not even restrained in any way.'

We moved on to the more serious matter of the government of the country. From 1985 onwards, Nigeria was ruled by a government headed by Major-General Ibraham Babangida – military governments have ruled Nigeria for twenty-five years of the thirty-five years since independence. A return to civilian rule was in prospect in June 1993, but the election which would have made Chief Abiola President was rejected by President Babangida, who instead ceded power to an interim military council.

General Abacha seized power in November 1993. Like almost all military leaders the world over, he claimed he was preparing to return the country to civilian rule as soon as possible, but as usual the return to democracy has taken longer than that. (By coincidence, I am writing this on Nigeria's national day. General Abacha has announced he now plans to introduce democratic rule in Nigeria in October 1998.)

On the anniversary of his election victory, Chief Abiola returned to Nigeria and declared himself President. That merely led to strikes and disorder and Abiola's arrest for treason. At the time of my interview with the Minister, Abiola was in custody and seriously ill. How could this state of affairs be justified?

'Let me explain,' the Minister said. 'An election was held on 12 June 1993. That election was illegal, because two days before the election the High Court in Abuja had given a decision and they challenged Chief Abiola's nomination as the candidate of his party [because] corruption was involved in his selection as candidate.'

'It's a real disaster for that to happen just two days before an election,' I said.

'Precisely, but you see the court can give an injunction asking the Electoral Commission to suspend the election.... You have to respect the laws.... No individual, no matter how rich, can hold himself above the law.'

'So you're saying in effect that Chief Abiola held himself above the law by being a rich man trying to distort the election, trying to win by some corrupt means?' I asked.

'I'm not saying that. I'm saying a Democrat should have respected the rulings of the court.'

This is the government line. The view of everyone else I spoke to in Nigeria, and the view expressed internationally, is that Abiola was cheated of his victory. Why was another election not held to replace the one declared void? The answer to that is that a whole new constitution is being worked out. And in due course a system of power-sharing for the various ethnic groups will emerge. General Abacha is unlikely to stand for elective office.

The Minister blamed previous British policy for the difficulties in establishing democracy during the thirty-five years since independence.

'When we inherited democracy from you we inherited it from a background of dictatorship because colonial rule was autocratic. So the first experiment in democratic government was bound to fail because we didn't have any experience of it…. Three years before you left you hurriedly put up democratic institutions. Universally it failed in Nigeria … it failed in Ghana, it failed in Uganda, it failed in Kenya. It failed virtually everywhere. Wherever the British Empire tried to introduce democratic institutions in a hurry before going home they crumbled.'

And so our conversation proceeded. The Minister was not going to accept that his government lacked legitimacy.

The interview over, I bumped into a businessman in the corridor outside the Minister's office who said he wanted to praise the efforts of the government. He had sought me out to tell me so. He was not there to seek any favours from the government. He was simply a concerned citizen who, bizarrely enough, knew when and where to find us.

We were going home the next day, so this evening was to be our last chance to show some of the vibrant street scenes in Lagos. Makin Soyinka was to take me to grab a meal at the side of the road.

All over Lagos there are stalls at the side of roads selling everything and anything. But at night, lit by flickering lamps and candles, they are at their best. At many of them, women sell food and drink. Makin wanted to take me to one of his favourite stalls but it looked like the rain was going to come on again, so we stopped at more or less the first one we came to on a main road in Victoria Island.

The food, heated in large pots on stoves set up on trestle tables, consisted of rice and beans and pepper soup and a variety of stews. I tried to ingratiate myself with the stall holders by trying out the few words of Yoruba I had learned. It did not get me very far. My Yoruba was not that great, but neither was theirs. The women were from the South East and spoke Ibo.

Just as we were ordering our food, a couple of plain clothes policemen came and took us away. Oh no, not again.

'Hold the rice and beans,' I had the foresight to say to the stall holder, 'I might be some time.'

This time we were taken to a real police station. The cameraman left his camera running as we walked over the road and the few hundred yards to the station. Somebody noticed this as we reached the door to the police station. There were cries of 'They are still filming!' and the discomforting sound of rifles being cocked. Where is Kate Adie when you need her most?

In the station we passed by a corridor leading to the cells. Behind bars was a noisy group of prisoners, singing and acting drunk. Was that the way we were heading? Not quite. We were taken into the Inspector's office while he grumpily went about establishing who we were. Apparently the road we had been filming in was next to a barracks and we should not have been filming there. Or maybe it was a post office. He demanded to see our press accreditation cards and set about checking up on us. It should not be forgotten that we had Olu, our minder from the Ministry of Information, with us, but that was not good enough for the Inspector.

The Inspector spoke to Olu's colleague, Irene, on the telephone. It was evident that she vouched for us in very forceful terms. We knew what she sounded like when she was cross and it seemed to aggravate the situation further. The Inspector resented being spoken down to and muttered to himself that he did not have to sort this out tonight, he could leave it to the morning.

Eventually, the Minister of Information, the very man I had interviewed that afternoon, was contacted. Indeed, I was able to talk to him on the phone. This was ludicrous. Imagine Sir David Frost having interviewed a politician or head of state and then, on being thrown in the clink, having to use his one phone call to speak to the very same VIP to negotiate his release. You can't imagine it, but it was happening to me.

The Minister was his usual affable self. He greeted me with 'Ah, you've got into another scrape, Mr Anderson,' and assured me everything would be all right because he had ordered the Inspector to release us. And so he did, although only after some more calls. To the SSS? To some other competing agency? Who knows? Whoever it was, coupled with a cabinet minister's say so, it was enough to spring us. We were even allowed to resume my meal and a very welcome couple of drinks back at the roadside.

• Day 18: The End •

We were flying home in the evening, but we were still trying to film some more sequences. In fact, we had just enough time for two more failures on the filming front. To balance the official line given by the government minister, we felt we ought to hear from some dissident or, at any rate, an opposition point of view. We found a journalist who was prepared to discuss the political situation, but at the last minute he decided it would be too dodgy to speak on camera. A replacement was found and we went to his house to await his return from some official procedure: getting a work permit or a licence or something. In the event, he never came home. There was nothing particularly sinister in this. His staff said he was usually late for appointments, and in our experience official business could take longer than expected, but this was our last day so there was no second chance for this sequence.

Our other failure was an attempt to film some graduates. Life is tough in Lagos, even for those with good educational qualifications, and the best way of showing that, we felt, would be to interview some educated people in their home surroundings. So we arranged to visit the crowded, shabby rooms occupied by a number of young people. When we arrived, we found there were two young men, a young couple and some children.

Olu was dubious about letting us film and, while Maltby was working out where to position the camera, Florence took me to one side and insisted in a very loud voice that these people were not graduates, they were idlers and I was to make the point that they should be out looking for work during the day, not lounging around at home.

Unfortunately, she did not take me enough to one side, or spoke in too loud a voice. A graduate (or idler) objected to being insulted in his own home. There followed a short, acrimonious discussion on this point, at the end of which we were all invited, rather forcibly, to leave. That may have been exactly what Florence intended, or simply another example of the rough surfaces of Nigerians rubbing each other up the wrong way.

The only thing we did achieve on this last day was to round up my visit to Lagos as I stood in Oshodi Market, a vast collection of stalls selling everything from raw meat to dressed tripe, clothes, shoes, stationery ... Well, everything, really.

The camera crew had me in long shot from their position on a road bridge and they were all but wiped out by a careering lorry swerving to avoid a car accident. So we very nearly did not film even this bit, which would have spoiled my day, obviously.

In conclusion, despite the guide books' warnings, Lagos is not the worst city in the world. Perhaps we were lucky but we weren't robbed or attacked, the offers made by perfect strangers to take part in million-dollar frauds were easy enough to resist, and in the main the people on the streets were really quite friendly.

Our Lagos film degenerated somewhat into a documentary about how difficult it was to make a documentary there at all, repeatedly interrupted as we were by officials. Oddly enough, Lagos would almost certainly have emerged as a much better place but for the interventions of those determined not to allow anything which would show Nigeria in a bad light. Perhaps a picture of the country emerged anyway – under military rule Nigerians can never exploit their great natural and human resources. As it is, some of them are just exploiting each other.

For the visitor, the abiding impression is that getting anything done in Lagos takes a tremendous struggle – to overcome the hot weather, the power cuts, the bureaucracy and the dangers of the city. How much more of a struggle must it be for the citizens of the city every day?

We had a trouble-free passage through the airport, but the last official to inspect my suitcase, the last person I was to speak to in Lagos, enquired if I had anything for her.

Oh no, would a refusal cause yet another delay? Was she going to insist upon a full search? Would I need to call upon my friend the Minister of Information again? Feebly, I gave in and offered her the only piece of Nigerian money that came to hand, a twenty naira note.

'Here,' I said, 'this is all I have. It is of no use to me.'

It was enough to buy her goodwill and get me straight on to the plane. Twenty naira is worth less than twenty pence.

OUR MAN IN... THE BRONX

'... the Bronx was like the Arctic. It was
somewhere to the north, and people didn't go there.'

TOM WOLFE, *The Bonfire of the Vanities*

I n Tom Wolfe's excellent novel, published in 1987 and
later turned into a somewhat less than excellent film, the
life of a successful Wall Street trader, Sherman McCoy, is
utterly destroyed as a direct result of accidentally going to the Bronx.

The Bonfire of the Vanities is, of course, a work of fiction, describing a
fantastic combination of events: McCoy and his mistress, driving in an
open-top Mercedes, take a wrong turning and become the subject of an
attempted robbery; their escape involves a fatal collision which sparks a
variety of press, political and racial campaigns which compel McCoy
towards a charge of manslaughter and utter ruin. The unfolding tragedy,
if not completely impossible, is clearly contrived by the author for maximum effect, but the underlying assumption of the book – that to the
comfortable inhabitants of Manhattan, the Bronx is alien territory to be
entered only at your peril – is real enough.

And it still is. On the first day of filming we went to Wall Street to do
what are known rather pretentiously in Britain as *vox pops* but which
are described more straightforwardly in America as street interviews.
The phrase *vox pops* is taken from the Latin: *vox populi, vox dei*. See,
for example, the writings of Alcuin (AD 735–804), Charlemagne's
adviser (born and raised in York, England). '*Nec audiendi sunt qui salent
docere, "Vox populi, vox dei" cum tumultuositas vulgi semper insaniae
proximae est*' – 'Nor should we listen to those who say "The voice of the
people is the voice of God", for the turbulence of the mob is always
close to insanity.'

Together with my camera crew, I advanced on office workers as they
hurried to work along the sidewalks below the skyscrapers of New
York's financial district and asked them if they ever went to the Bronx.
Or had anything to say about the Bronx. Or had any advice to give me
on my way there.

The exercise was not an overwhelming success. I found the occasional

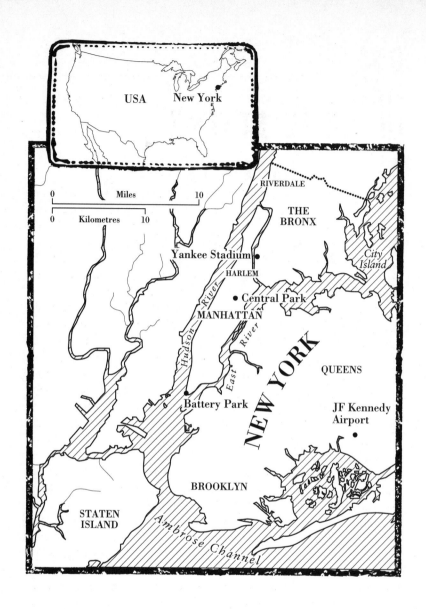

person who had been born in the Bronx or who had been to school there (a number of famous universities and academic institutions are within its borders), but the overwhelming majority had no reason to go to the Bronx at all, or had only ever been there on a handful of occasions. Many of them could only remember going there once in their entire life. Suggesting a visit is like asking a London taxi driver, late at night, to take you south of the river. Almost to a man (and a woman) they could recommend the Bronx only as the home of the New York Yankees baseball team, the Bronx Zoo and the Bronx Botanical Garden. What they knew of the horrors of life in the Bronx – crime, drugs, urban decay – came, in the main, not from personal experience but from news reports, magazines, urban myths and, I suppose, Tom Wolfe's novel.

As an opening to the film I emerged from the Wall Street subway station reciting the words, as best as I remembered, to the song 'New York, New York' (words by Betty Comden and Adolf Green; music by Leonard Bernstein).

New York, New York – a helluva town
The Bronx is up but the Battery's down
The people ride in a hole in the ground;
New York, New York – it's a helluva town.

I would have sung the words but I have had unhappy experiences singing on camera in these documentaries. (See, or worse still listen to, *Our Man In… The Maasai Mara.*) Besides, I did not want to disturb my fellow travellers walking up the stairs of the subway. On this account I should not have worried. New Yorkers do not pay attention to an idiot in a pale suit mangling the words to an old musical standard at 8.30 in the morning. They see that many nutters …

Eventually I did grab a few words with a man near Central Park who had a Bronx tale to tell. Not strictly a *vox pop* because he had been discovered in advance by a researcher. And not strictly a story about the Bronx because the action all happened in Manhattan, but a scary story, nonetheless.

The man concerned had been car-jacked. He and his girlfriend were held at gunpoint and ordered to drive to the Bronx. Before getting there, he was ordered to go to his bank to extract money from the 24-hour banking machine, the mugger holding his girlfriend hostage in the car while he went into the bank. What made it particularly worrying, he thought, was that it would be standard practice to kill the victims of a robbery like this. The detection rate is lower if the witnesses are not alive to testify. This particular victim managed to punch in an emergency number which was there to summon the police in just this situation. Turning round, he found that both the robber and his girlfriend had disappeared. Finally, it turned out the girlfriend had got away and hidden, and the robber had run away. But what the story established was the notion that for some people the only way they would go to the Bronx would be at gunpoint.

I had to admit I had not been to the Bronx myself. On previous visits to New York I had more or less confined myself to Manhattan. Visitors to foreign cities tend to stay in the show-piece centre of town, often forming a much more favourable impression of the place than its own residents. To the tourist, London is a charming city of parks and pageantry, of the Houses of Parliament, Buckingham Palace and St Paul's Cathedral. But to Londoners themselves, London is also 400 square miles of suburbia, car parks and traffic jams. The tourist discovers Kensington but not Kennington; Westminster but not West Ham; the Edgware Road but not Edgware. So I suppose it should come as no surprise that the Bronx impinges so little on the metropolitan consciousness and the visitor's itinerary.

New York City is not just Manhattan. Together with the other outer boroughs of Brooklyn, Queen's and Staten Island, the Bronx was incorporated into New York City in 1898. The area gets its name from a Swede, Jonas Bronck, who owned land there in the seventeenth century. (Bronck's farm or the Broncks' place was eventually contracted to Bronx.) It has an area of 42 square miles and a population of 1¼ million. (Thus there are more people living in the Bronx than in any city in Britain outside London.)

The Bronx's beginnings have not established themselves in the American mind as firmly as the story of the acquisition of Manhattan – one of the best known stories in American history. In 1626, Dutchman Peter Minuit bought the whole island from local Indians for a collection of tools and trinkets which were worth, legend has it, twenty-four dollars. The settlement was administered by the Dutch West India Company and named New Amsterdam, but was renamed New York, in honour of the Duke of York (later James II), when the British took over in a bloodless (and, as it happens, popular) invasion in 1664.

A further twist in the tale has it that the particular Indians who sold all this soon-to-be-expensive real estate for only twenty-four dollars did not do all that badly as they were from a tribe which did not live on Manhattan Island anyway, and did not own it. They thus started the tradition of New Yorkers ripping off newcomers.

The city limits are somewhat arbitrary. Going north from the Bronx you do not hit open countryside. The built-up area continues in the form of the separate city of Yonkers. On the other hand, Staten Island is part of New York City but it is largely rural. Across the Hudson River, west of Manhattan, are the cities of Jersey and Newark. Not only are they not part of New York City, they are in a different state: New Jersey. The boundary between the states of New York and New Jersey is based on the distribution of land made by Charles II between the Duke of York and Britain's allies in 1664, but American boundaries and institutions seem more fixed than those of the supposedly traditionally-minded British, whose counties and districts can be merged and abolished at the whim of Whitehall bureaucrats. Last year you were in the East Riding of Yorkshire, this year it is called Humberside. Next year it will be Avon.

In America, the boundaries of the State of New York stay where they have always been, and its capital remains the small town of Albany: population 100 000, not the city of New York: population 7 million.

But as a result of the redrawing of the boundaries which they did allow themselves at the turn of the century, the Bronx is included within New York, the only part of the city which is actually on the mainland of America, separated from the island of Manhattan by the narrow stretch of the Harlem River.

In the early part of this century, the Bronx was a fashionable place to live. Its Grand Concourse was developed with fabulous Art Deco apartment blocks. It was a place to escape from the urban problems to be found on the lower east side of Manhattan, or in Harlem. It was not yet a byword for urban decay itself.

By the 1970s, the rot had truly set in. The middle classes were inclined to leave the inner cities to find more comfortable lives in the suburbs. In particular, ethnic groups such as the Irish and the Jews, who had dominated Bronx politics and society, no longer saw the Bronx as a place in which to remain. Poorer blacks and newly arriving Puerto Ricans had nowhere else to go but found employment opportunities declining as factories were closed or relocated in cheaper parts of America and the world. The Bronx's elevated roadways and flyovers crossed a landscape of run down tenement blocks. And not just run down – often they were burnt down. Landlords who could claim on the insurance torched their own property; tenants set fire to their own homes to get rehoused. Rubbish and drug dealers gathered on the empty lots. Here was poverty and despair practically at the heart of the richest nation on earth.

Naturally, this came to the attention of the American public through television. Covering the 1977 World Series (baseball) from Yankee Stadium, the camera panned across a sky alive with fires while Howard Cosell, a famous and opinionated sports commentator, announced: 'The Bronx is burning.' It was as though the voice of God had spoken. Or, at any rate, Jimmy Hill. The Bronx's image was fixed forever in the public's mind, giving us the New York proverb: Red sky at night, the Bronx is alight.

The image was reinforced when Jimmy Carter used the ravaged Bronx cityscape as a backdrop to his election campaign. And again by Ronald Reagan when it was his turn.

• The Westchester Guardian •

Before venturing into this feared corner of Gotham City we thought it wise to take the advice of the Guardian Angels. Guardian Angels dress up in red uniforms – beret, jacket, etc. – and patrol areas of the city in an attempt to prevent trouble.

I remembered the Guardian Angels for the modest impact they made in Britain when they attempted to extend their operation to London five or six years ago. The police in England were highly dubious about this unaccountable organization going around unaccountably doing their job for them, but I knew, or thought I knew, that they had had more success on their native soil.

The Guardian Angels started in the Bronx but, like successful Wall Street traders, they moved to Manhattan. The Guardian Angels' head-quarters, on 8th and 46th Street, are housed in a disused shop donated by a well wisher (but only until the end of 1995). It consists of a single room divided by a couple of fairly basic partitions, a lavatory, a two-way radio communications system, a few hand-drawn notices and pho-tographs of applicants seeking admission.

The founder and president of the Guardian Angels – I suppose he is the Guardian Archangel – is Curtis Sliwa. He is more impressive than his surroundings and much more loquacious than the selection of Angels who were with him on the day we met. Curtis was not always a Guardian Angel. He used to be the manager of a McDonald's restau-rant in the Bronx.

'Imagine you're running a night McDonald's,' he explained to me. 'All the other merchants, come 5 o'clock, are slamming down the shutters, packing their bags and running to the suburbs. They can't get out fast enough. And the only things open late at night is Ronald McDonald land, and the all-night liquor store with the bullet-proof glass and the guard who looked like he had steroids that morning with breakfast … Junkies wanted to come and shoot up in the bathroom, hookers would try to pull tricks right there in the lobby while people were on line.'

Instead of just keeping his head down and biding his time and putting in for a transfer, he started the Guardian Angels. There are now about 250 Guardian Angels in New York. When they started, the street gangs were prevalent in the Bronx and so the Angels are modelled on a gang structure. Just like a gang, they have fierce group loyalty and wear funny clothes, but with the important difference that they are on the streets to do good and fight crime. Looked at in a good light, they are a cross between Boy Scouts and Batman. In a bad light, they are 'haemorrhoids in red berets,' as Curtis cheerily put it.

And it is not just a bit of fun. A wall in the office is decorated with memorials to young men who were killed while out on duty as Guardian Angels.

Curtis is a good talker. In fact, he has his own talk show on the radio. Mind you, everybody seems to have their own radio talk show in America these days. The former Governor Mario Cuomo has one, so does ex-Mayor Koch and one of the Watergate conspirators, and Oliver North. It is probably guaranteed in the Constitution, up there with the Right to Silence: the Right to Make Noise; a Duty to Sound Off. Or perhaps it is just the politicians' revenge on the media for all those entertainers going into politics: President Reagan in America; Giles Brandreth, MP, in Britain.

Curtis believes the Guardian Angels have improved the Bronx in a number of ways, as he explained to me.

'First off, we've proved that a group of predominantly black and Hispanic youngsters should not be feared. And secondly, we showed people how to improve and not to move ... Draw the Maginot Line and say: "Let's dig in. We love the Bronx, we want our children and children's children to grow up here." And thirdly, because I'm a broadcaster and I speak of the glory of the Bronx ... I can have an impact in swaying public opinion ... Potential risktakers say, "Well, Sliwa paints such a good, good picture of the Bronx, I haven't been there in twenty years, maybe I should go back there and check it out."'

Forgetting the unhappy precedent of the real Maginot Line, Curtis's claims for the Angels are impressive but not unique. Virtually everyone I interviewed in New York seemed to claim credit for the recent improvements. Curtis maintains that the police approve of the Angels' activities, and do not resent their job being done for them; nor do they regard the Angels as a problematic vigilante group.

He claims that the area around his present headquarters on 46th Street has been improved by the Angels' presence. It has to be said that passers-by did call out cheery greetings to Curtis as we stood on the pavement. And at lunchtime we happily left our vanload of camera equipment to be guarded by a Guardian Angel.

For the Angels themselves, it is worthwhile voluntary work, as long as they are not gunned down. If it does not keep them off the streets exactly, it keeps them *on* the streets with the best of intentions. But can they have any real impact on crime in America? I was puzzled that they no longer operated in the Bronx. Was coming to Manhattan taking the easy option? Curtis insisted that it is on the subways that they are needed, crime having been driven off the streets of the Bronx by more aggressive policing.

So was I asking for trouble intending to travel on the subway to the Bronx?

'Well, looking like Casper Milktoast there, with a sort of Poindexter look ...' Curtis scrutinized me. 'We could use you as a set up, put you in the last car which is the muggers' delight ... You would be like walking into a hungry cage of Dobermann pinschers, with pork chop pants on.'

Hmm. I was going off this assignment.

But perhaps I was wrong to doubt the Guardian Angels. A couple of days after my interview, an off-duty Guardian Angel hit the headlines for detaining a murderer who had gunned down another man in a Manhattan diner. Perhaps I should go home and start the Guardian Angel Islingtons.

On the other hand, it may have proved another point that Curtis made to me:

'The best kept secret in the world is how the Bronx is in fact better than many other parts of New York City.'

Not much of a rallying cry, but it is a start.

• Pardon Me, Boy •

Next stop was Grand Central Station, the beginning of my subway ride to the Bronx. It is an appropriately grand (and, indeed, central) place from which to leave Manhattan. It is a magnificent railway terminal built between 1903 and 1913 in what is called the Beaux Arts style. Its main concourse is more like a giant hotel foyer, across which commuters scurry en route from the street to the trains. The ceiling is decorated with delicate images of distant planets, while one high wall is made of glassed-in corridors and staircases. Inside this elegant space are shops and a cocktail bar where you can while away your time before going home to the suburbs. At a lower level there is another famous bar with one of the best selections of oysters to be had in this or any other city. In short, it is the epitome of New York metropolitan chic. Very Manhattan. Very Woody Allen.

From here I set off for the Bronx, taking the 4 Train. (There are no fancy names like the Bakerloo Line that you get on the London Tube.) The last thing I noticed before getting on board was the station's knife shop selling all shapes and sizes of knives at 30 per cent off – cut price.

The New York Subway's notorious reputation for crime is partially-based on the fact that it runs through the night. After midnight the lonely traveller can become an easy target for the subway equivalent of highwaymen – low-way-men, perhaps. During the day it is no more disagreeable to use than the London Underground or the Paris Metro. It is cheaper than London – you can go anywhere for not much more than a dollar – but rather less crowded. Certainly, there are fewer Scandinavian travellers knocking into you with their rucksacks as they adjust their cagoules.

Characteristic of the New York system, however, is the frequency with which you are approached by beggars. British beggars in the main prefer to slouch on the street to invite pity, attracting the passer-by with a simple chant of 'Spare any change?' Their more dynamic American counterparts approach the task of panhandling with much more gusto and more dynamic, upbeat tales of woe.

So through the train compartments come the poor beggars, desperately selling themselves to the passengers. 'I have walked all the way from Shucksville, Nebraska, looking for work. I am a Vietnam veteran, and I have five sick children, two wives and five parents to support. I have cancer, Aids and athlete's foot. But if you good folks could just spare some change …'

Most Manhattanites ignore these energetic cries for help. Only visitors to the city think these enterprising indigents have earned some reward and hand over the coins they have no use for anyway. More successful with the locals are imaginative carriage-to-carriage vendors of chewing gum and sweets. The ultimate travelling salesmen.

Subway stations are generally not like Grand Central, which is a proper overground railway terminal. (Even there, though, the trains are merely commuter lines now. Long-distance trains no longer go west, having gone west years ago.) Most subway stations are rather functional places, constructed from girders and other bits of industrial metal.

Until recently, the trains were covered in graffiti. Graffiti artists smothered the trains inside and out with drawings, symbols, initials and names. They took delight in seeing trains cross the city, from the Bronx, say, to Brooklyn, with their markings and signatures embossed upon them. Then they would photograph their handiwork to prove how pervasive their art had become. Some found a strange beauty in this ugly manifestation of urban life, but in truth it lent a threatening air to subway travel: an all too public manifestation of a public service being overcome by vandalism and social breakdown.

The subway trains now have no graffiti on them at all. This remarkable transformation has been achieved not by draconian punishments, nor by mounting armed guards, nor by cutting off the artists' spray cans. The transit authorities simply decided to take out of service any train with graffiti on it until it could be cleaned up. Presumably the graffiti artists could have kept going until there were no trains left and the authority was bankrupt. But they have more or less given up, robbed of their chance to see their work travel the length and breadth of the city.

We had anticipated that, as the subway train made its way north, the change in the racial composition of the passengers would become evident. The white areas of midtown Manhattan would give way to the black and Hispanic districts of Harlem and the Bronx.

Actually, the main thing we learned was that the trains are not that full during the middle of the day with either blacks or whites. Another discovery was that you can film on the subway without anybody batting an eyelid, ignoring each other and filming each other being the two things that New Yorkers do best, apparently.

Once it gets to the Bronx, the subway emerges from the ground and turns itself into an elevated railway. The elevated railway has itself starred in many a New York film and TV series. It is held aloft by concrete and metal pillars – more features to lend the cityscape a brutal air.

• Don't Dump on the Bronx •

We called first on Doris Quinones, of the Bronx Tourism Council. She occupies a basement room in the offices of the Bronx Overall Development Council and her job is to encourage people to see the Bronx as a tourist destination. There is a visitor's *Fun Guide* and a number of catchy bumper stickers, my favourite being 'Don't dump on the Bronx' – part of a campaign against littering and, I suppose, bad-mouthing. I suggested another – 'Three cheers for the Bronx' – but I do not know if it is going to get official backing. 'Bronx cheer' is an American term for what in cockney rhyming slang is called a raspberry.

I did know what to ask Doris. On BBC Radio 4's *Today* programme, about every six months or so, the wretched tourist development officer for a town which is a byword for urban deprivation, ugliness or dullness is stuffed into a radio car and given a light-hearted grilling by one of the presenters, surprised that they have run out of proper political stories that morning.

'Well, Mr Shufflebottom, are holiday-makers really going to spend their two weeks in Slagheapville, just because it's got an exhibition of nineteenth-century slum life? ... Yes, but are foreign visitors going to forsake the delights of London, Edinburgh and Stratford for a trip round your Municipal Museum?'

So I asked Doris this sort of stuff and she was able to point out all the fine attractions – the Bronx Zoo, the Botanical Garden, Yankee Stadium … And very charming she was about it. She laughed heartily throughout the interview, especially when the camera crew crashed noisily into the enormous collection of empty bottles she had stashed beside her desk. (She is the official recycling officer.) It occurred to me that people visiting the Bronx might be *expecting* urban deprivation, crime and violence. And might be disappointed if they did not get it. I thought that a theme park where Disney employees came up and pretended to mug you might be the answer. Doris, I suspect, thought I was mad.

Somewhat unconvinced that the many visitors to New York would necessarily wish to make the trip to the Bronx at all, I was persuaded to go on a special trip around the Bronx on a sight-seeing tour with a guy called Joseph and a minibus full of girls.

The girls were all staying at the YMCA. One was German with impossibly blue eyes, another Dutch with impossibly red hair. Another a very sparky Argentinian with a dreadful cough induced by the changes in temperature between air-conditioned cold and more natural sticky heat. Another was Swiss … Quite how Joseph, the driver and guide, hit upon the idea of taking these little United Nations groups of au pairs, actresses and tourists around the Bronx I never quite understood. But it is, I suppose, nice work if you can get it.

Joseph comes from the Bronx himself and took us off to see the sites and the sights. Starting in the South Bronx, first there are the sites. Here a boarded-up club, there an empty lot which was once a tenement block; along here the site of a new housing project. Moderately deprived inner city areas, but nothing to write home about.

And then off to the sights. With Joseph keeping up a commentary we drove past the zoo, the Botanical Garden, the Yankee Stadium. The Bronx Zoo is, apparently, officially the New York Zoological Park. According to Joseph there is a plot to remove the name 'Bronx' from anything of real worth. But everyone calls it the Bronx Zoo anyway.

There was no time actually to visit the zoo (then or throughout the rest of our stay, as it turned out) but we admired the parkland in which it is set and the tree-lined avenues leading to Fordham and other universities in the area.

If it comes as a slight surprise to see so much open space, and so many fine institutions in the Bronx, the next part of the tour was a real eye-opener. Riverdale is in the north-eastern part of the borough although, thanks to the geography of New York, just a hop over the Harlem River from Manhattan Island.

Riverdale is luxury housing in the full American style: expensive villas built in a variety of architectural styles from neo-classical grand through to elaborate folksy; suburban Palladian alongside National Lottery Hänsel and Gretel. All set amid winding roads and manicured lawns. Here a basketball hoop, there a clapboard outbuilding. But no people. In the middle of the day there were no children playing in the yard, no housewives pegging out clothes, nobody enjoying the luxury of enjoying the luxury at all. It was so empty it had the spooky air of a film set for *Hallowe'en* or any of those other horror movies set in suburbia.

My companions in the bus were contemptuous of Riverdale. They dismissed it as a ghastly, lifeless area, with all the intensity of twentysomethings possibly as much as ten years away from their own bourgeois dream-homes in the suburbs of Hamburg or Zurich.

But they were right. Riverdale is lifeless. You cannot even film there. The winding lanes of Riverdale are private property, as we were informed by security guards who appeared from nowhere the second we stopped to film our van driving past. A permit from the city and the borough will not do. Riverdale ain't big enough for the vanload of us.

For lunch we went to the other side of the borough, to City Island. This is the Bronx in its seaside, holiday mood. Crammed on to a small island, now joined to the mainland by a roadway, is a collection of desirable waterfront properties, boatyards, souvenir shops and marinas. At the end of the road are two restaurants where you can eat to your heart's content any amount of fish, shellfish and fast foods. It is an incongruous spot. City Island sticks out into Long Island Sound, and it is an extremely pleasant location if you come with preconceived notions of the Bronx. But the restaurants themselves are not attractive. They are single-storey structures designed to accommodate as many people as possible but with no discernible attempt at beauty.

It was the end of the school year and children of a variety of ages had graduated from a variety of schools. Straight from the graduation ceremonies, fifteen-year-olds and eight-year-olds and other-year-olds, dressed in colourful versions of academic dress, joined the queues for clams and hamburgers. And in among all this excitement we ate our lunch too. A good time was had by all, although the food, I have to say, was awful.

This was all very well. We had established that there is more to the Bronx than the bad bits, but really it was the bad bits we had come to find out about. And hanging around beach-front restaurants with young European women was not getting to the heart of the matter. Our next call was likely to be more to the point – Captain Silks of the 41st Precinct.

• Fort Apache •

The 41st Precinct is another piece of Americana to have starred on film. It had the title role in *Fort Apache, the Bronx*. You may or may not recall this 1980 movie. Leslie Halliwell, in his usual forthright way in the 9th edition of *Halliwell's Film Guide*, dismissed it as 'instantly forgettable'. He went on to describe the film as 'an ultra-violent *Dixon of Dock Green*', but reckoned that Paul Newman 'is no Jack Warner'. A denunciation from which Mr Newman must have worked very hard to recover.

As I recall the film, the police officers led by Paul Newman find themselves under attack in a police station, the 41st Precinct. This is about to be closed down and is already cut off from the support of the rest of the force. They are manning an outpost of American civilization in hostile territory, just as the soldiers did in the original Fort Apache in Indian country, depicted in the 1948 film starring Henry Fonda. (Halliwell decribed this as a rather stiff and unsatisfactory epic.)

In real life, the 41st Precinct building was indeed closed down and it has now been rehoused in a new twenty million dollar facility just off Bruckner Boulevard. So it does not look like Fort Apache any more. What it does look like is a scene from *Hill Street Blues* or *Cagney and Lacey*. In the area around the busy front desk, New York policemen come and go, suspects are brought past to go to the lavatory, prostitutes are taken to task, relatives wait in line for news of those under arrest. It is a swirl of activity which seems so open, free and easy compared to the sterile area in the front office of a British police station.

Captain Silks is the man in charge of the station. His office is just off the busy entrance hall. He has a souvenir tomahawk but allows himself no other mementoes of the bad old days. He sat ramrod straight in his chair, a personification of the American eagle, to talk to me. Times were hard when he joined, and they had been even harder. An old sergeant had told him a story of his first day on the beat. Discovered walking on his own, he had been told off by his superiors. He was told he was just asking for trouble patrolling around the Bronx alone and was driven to a cinema and told to watch films until his tour of duty was over. But now the crime rate is dramatically down in the 41st Precinct, although Captain Silks modestly declines to take any special credit for it.

Curtis Sliwa of the Guardian Angels blamed the increase in crime ultimately on the white-collar crime of burning down buildings for insurance money. Broadly, Captain Silks agreed. In fact, he agreed with pretty well everything Curtis Sliwa said, except he remembered the Guardian Angels making no contribution to the improvement of the Bronx whatsoever.

He reckoned it is all down to spending money, community action and firm policing. And he pointed to the malign influence of drugs which has corrupted and destroyed any other system of values. I wondered whether the criminalization of drugs caused more problems than it solved, making the obvious comparison with the Prohibition era. But Captain Silks was not inclined to agree with that.

He said that the Bronx, even the South Bronx, is a safe area to walk around in now, although you should take precautions. As you should anywhere. He gave the example that somebody going to the Alps in summertime might not realize it is possible to get frostbite.

'So the Bronx is a good place to visit?' I asked.

'Well, maybe not a top vacation destination, but then is Liverpool?'

I started to work on a couple more slogans for the Bronx: 'In the Bronx at least you won't get frostbite.' Or 'It rivals Liverpool as a holiday location.' But instead I thought it might be useful to compare the crime rates of Liverpool and the Bronx. In fact, I dug out the homicide rates. General crime rates are notoriously unreliable. Rates of reporting of property crimes vary with fashions for classification, faith in the police, demands of insurers. Statistics for serious crimes of rape and sexual assault are equally difficult to establish, as they vary with the approachability of the police. However, homicide figures are generally regarded as a good indicator of what is actually happening. Dead bodies have a way of getting counted eventually, and only the most sophisticated murderer can disguise a death as a suicide or accident.

So if we take Liverpool, Captain Silk's example of a notoriously hard British city in some way comparable to the Bronx, this is how the figures look. In 1992 in Liverpool, there were 10 homicides in a population of about 450 000. The Bronx has a population of about 1.2 million, so if homicides occurred at the Liverpool rate there would be no more than 30 a year. In fact, in 1992 there were 547. In another comparison, Northern Ireland has a population of 1.6 million. The year of 1992 was another in the many years of sectarian violence which had been spinning out of control for 25 years. In 1992 there were 112 homicides.

So, here in America, a stone's throw, almost literally, from the Empire State Building, people are killing each other at a rate twenty times that of a famously tough British city and nearly five times the rate of a province in the middle of something approaching a civil war.

• New Birth •

After those cheery thoughts we decided we would go to hospital. We went to the Bronx-Lebanon Hospital on the Grand Concourse, to see Dr William Caspe in the special care baby unit.

Bronx-Lebanon is an inspired name for a hospital. Imagine having an accident and waking up in casualty.

'Where am I?'

'Don't worry, you're going to be all right. You're in the Bronx-Lebanon.'

'Oh, fine … I thought for a moment I had been taken to the Sharpeville-Hiroshima Infirmary.'

'Your mind is wandering. The Sharpeville-Hiroshima changed its name years ago to the King Herod-Dracula.'

The Bronx-Lebanon is housed in a new building, no more than two or three years old. The baby unit has impressively high-tech equipment, containing depressingly underweight babies. In plastic incubators, barely-living dolls as much as twelve weeks premature are nursed, pumped and monitored back to sustainable life. To look on the bright side, these scraps of humanity enjoy very nearly a 100 per cent survival rate. But the outlook in general is not so good.

Dr Caspe is witty, warm and wise. A New York Jewish doctor who has chosen to work in this inner city hospital rather than follow the dollars in private practice in swankier parts of the city. It turns out that he was interviewed for British television ten years ago. Since then, he says, the fires in the Bronx have gone out. But other problems remain. For instance, 40 per cent of the children in the nursery continue to be born to mothers who either have a history of drug use or test positive for drugs. This is primarily cocaine which induces premature labour. Another problem is new. At the time of the first interview, Aids was non-existent in Dr Caspe's patients. Now Aids is the primary cause of death among children. The babies contract it from their mothers. It is not a great start in life.

Dr Caspe cheerily complained about the reduction in public funds for his hospital. He thinks the political mood is against the 1960s' liberal paternalistic tradition in which he operates:

'… white men in this country, white Protestant males, are very angry at this point and becoming very tribal in their orientation. Basically they're saying, "Hey, we've tried those social programmes of the 1960s. We've given in tax dollars for thirty years now, since the Kennedy years, and it ain't worked. It just hasn't made any difference to our lives. I'm paying more money and I still can't walk on the streets with a sense of safety. I have to get alarms for my house and my car battery's getting stolen. … I'm not giving any more. I want my money back."'

Even more depressing is that he thinks (and he is a liberal) there is a permanent group of people – not an underclass, they are below an underclass – who just cannot be reached by social programmes. They are stuck in a distinctly un-American state of permanent poverty. They have low aspirations, poor education and bad health.

Oh, dear. And yet you somehow know that if a British TV crew goes back to the Bronx-Lebanon in another ten years, Dr Caspe will still be there cracking darkly humorous gags about how things are still getting worse. And he's still there trying to get his patients better. It is being so cheerful that keeps him staying.

• In the Neighbourhoods •

If Doctor Caspe is a typical New Yorker, so is Billy Procida. Billy is a property developer; the first, he says, to see the potential of the rebuilding of the Bronx. Not the smart luxury bits, the South Bronx. The bits which twenty years ago were in flames.

He picked me up on the corner of 156th Street and St Ann's. Billy has not been in a film or on television, but he could have been. He is noisy, brash and short. What he lacks in inches he makes up for in length of cigar. And in all-conquering self-confidence. Even the way he walks is enthusiastic. Halfway between a bantam cock and a schoolboy who wants to go to the toilet but cannot bring himself to leave the scene of the action, he nervously pitches himself this way and that. Smiling as he grasps the end of his cigar between his teeth. He could be the next-door-neighbour in a sitcom, brought in to provide contrast with the lacklustre life of the main character.

Billy bundled me into an open-top car for another tour of the neighbourhood. This time there were no foreign girls, just Billy, the cameraman in the front seat, and me. Giving me no time to settle in the restricted space of the back seat, he set the car going and started his running commentary:

'You're now on 156th Street, which used to be a very dangerous area. And as you can now see it is not dangerous at all.'

'Except when you're driving,' I quipped as he took a corner with both hands on his Corona.

'What we're going to do today is take you to see a couple of new developments … I've been involved in about a quarter of a billion dollars of newly constructed or substantially renovated housing.'

From the car he waved to passers-by, to police officers, to young and old, black and white. An obviously successful and rich young man, he has never had any trouble going around in the Bronx. He is not afraid of being mugged by young criminals. Looking confident and unafraid is protection enough. The only thing we have to fear is the appearance of fear itself.

His tour of the area took me to housing units, low-rise blocks of flats, condominiums, houses, blocks and squares he has developed or helped to develop. These have been built where large tenement blocks stood before they were burnt down.

Billy agreed that this area has had its problems. The Bronx was burning, it did have its gangs and drugs, but the media coverage had made it seem even worse than it really was. As a result, banks were not interested in financing any rebuilding projects which, of course, tended to make the reality become as black as the media image. Somehow he, and then others, broke through the prejudice, and buildings instead of weeds sprang up on the empty lots.

Billy took me on a whirlwind tour. We strode through an award-winning courtyard, somehow securing an invitation from a resident family to have a look in their flat.

'Hi, I'm Billy Procida,' he breezed. 'I'm the guy that built the place … How's it going? … The place is nice?'

'We could do with a playground for the kids,' they told him.

'Yeah, well, we'll have to see … This was meant to be a playground, but then everybody decided to make it a private place … Look at the detail in that brickwork …'

We marched into a chemist's shop – part of a national chain risking establishing itself in the Bronx – and asked questions that were as intelligent as possible, given the circumstances. 'Is business good?', 'How long have you been established here?', that kind of thing. In the street we bumped into the leader of Mid Bronx Desperadoes, a housing and community building organization, and we all went in to see the plans for a large shopping centre.

We were an incongruous sight driving around. Billy with his cigar, me with my cameraman. The odd person called out to us.

'Hey, where you from?' asked a man in a car.

'England.'

'England, really? How is that guy?'

'Benny Hill?' I hazarded.

'Benny Hill, that's it. He's funny. What is he doing at the moment?'

'Not much. He died a couple of years ago.'

The guy in the other car looked … not sad, exactly. These stars come and go. He looked as though he had committed a *faux pas*. He might have offended me personally, as though he had mentioned the name of a dead relative.

'Oh, I'm sorry … I didn't know.' For a moment, the sensitivity in the middle of the Bronx was almost touching.

'Hey, when you go home, if you see the Queen of England, kiss her ass for me, will you?'

It is hard to say what I had learned by the end of this tour. Certainly Billy is a great salesman – after half an hour in his company he had half convinced me that I needed a two-bedroom duplex on Melrose Avenue. And he has had the enterprise to get the ball rolling and new housing built. It is unlikely that progress will be made in America on anything other than the profit motive.

He is, I suppose, an acceptable face of capitalism. Sure, he has made a fortune out of property development. But making money is the American way. And a proper way. He invited us to think about the great plutocrats who have done well in oil, or railways.

'… those guys that have made tons of money, all they are doing is servicing society,' he informed me.

Which is true enough. Depending on what meaning you give to the word 'servicing'.

• Community Leadership •

Someone else involved in the rebuilding of the Bronx is Genevieve Brooks. As a young woman she came to New York from the south expecting to find her fortune. Instead, she found herself living in the Bronx while it went into its steepest decline. For nights on end she would sleep, shoes at the ready, prepared to dash down the fire escape if it turned out that her block was the one to be torched that night.

She was disgusted with the state of her tenement block and found that her complaints were fobbed off by the landlord until she and the other tenants banded together. From being a member of a simple tenants' association, Genevieve has developed into a full-blown community leader. She has even, to her surprise, been appointed a deputy Borough President.

Her first efforts were directed at reclaiming the neighbourhood from drug dealers and gangsters. And then she went on to organizing the building of housing for the middle classes, encouraging them to stay in the Bronx as their income increased. She was prepared to face down threats from the more malign forces in her community. As Genevieve airily put it, she was widowed at an early age and had no dependants to worry about.

She took me to look at one of the developments. It is in the same area covered by Billy Procida. Charlotte Street is a noted example of the progress which has been made in the Bronx. It has also come in for criticism, because instead of the high-intensity high-rise blocks which used to be there, now there are a few rows of little houses. Small, detached villas with neat lawns surrounded by wire fences. Little homes on the prairies, but right here in the South Bronx. These are streets just waiting for shiny-faced schoolboys to come cycling along delivering papers.

The criticism is that this low-density housing can only be for a relatively wealthy few. Where are the homes for all the people who used to live here? Genevieve is impatient with that sort of criticism. The whole of the South Bronx is not going to be covered in these little houses. But they establish that it is no longer an embarrassment to live in the Bronx. And she points at other improvements: the streets are not piled with rubbish, the schools are re-opening.

I was getting the message. The Bronx is on the up, it is no longer burning. It is much better than it was. This was all good news. But you did have to keep in mind just how bad it had been ten years ago if you were to get really excited over some pleasant housing schemes and moderately well-cleaned streets.

And there was a further, nagging worry. Had the fundamental problems been addressed, or were we looking at cosmetic changes?

• The Battle for the Bronx •

The southern portion of the South Bronx is officially called Mott Haven. Running through it from west to east are the Bruckner Boulevard, the Major Deegan Expressway and East 138th Street. This, if you are looking for problems that still exist in the Bronx, is where to find them.

Our filming in the area took place on several days. And, to be honest, we did not take the subway to get there every day. Our usual route was to load a van full of camera equipment and go along the Franklin D. Roosevelt River Drive over the Willis Avenue Bridge and into Willis Avenue.

Willis Avenue Bridge is one of several bridges which cross the narrow Harlem River that separates Manhattan from the Bronx. I got to know it pretty well because, apart from driving over it several times, I was also filmed walking over it. I also spent quite some time standing on it while a helicopter pilot, carrying our camera, remembered where it was. It is a metal bridge. Not just the supports – the roadway itself is made of a metal grille.

Now there are plenty of bridges made of this kind of stuff – footbridges, pre-fabricated military structures, out of the way sections on industrial premises – but it came as quite a surprise to find something like this carrying a main road right in the centre of New York. The only London equivalent I can think of is a rather tacky structure which takes a line of traffic over the Hogarth Roundabout in West London. Anyway, once over Willis Avenue Bridge you are in the Bronx, although in fact we were looking for Cuba.

Cuba is another concerned individual doing his bit to clean up the Bronx. He is employed as a janitor at a block of flats in Mott Haven but has been inspired to expand his job to include providing security and social services in the area. 'Inspired' is perhaps not the word for it. Five years ago, Cuba's brother died of Aids contracted as a result of his addiction to drugs. In a death bedside promise, Cuba pledged himself to the fight against drugs.

Cuba explained all this to me in his tiny office which he almost filled with his giant frame. Cuba – I think he is of Hispanic origin – speaks in that special strained, husky voice you only hear in New Yorkers and *The Godfather* films. He goes out on the streets to scream at people from outside the area who come to buy or sell drugs. He reports illegal activity to the police. He organizes young people to be on patrol to deter drug activity. (These are not Guardian Angels but the Community on Patrol, the 'eyes and ears of the police'.)

All of this makes him popular with residents of the block. And unpopular with drug dealers. And round here, being unpopular with drug dealers is not a healthy state in which to be. Cuba has received death threats. How many? Maybe two or three. A week, that is. So how seriously does he take them?

'I take them very serious, but I pay them no mind because we have to make a change in some ways … If I'm going to die, I'm going to die for something that means something to me.'

Just to reduce the chances, he does employ a bodyguard to watch over him. Somebody who really does take care of the caretaker. But think of it: a block of flats with a chief of security who has to have his own bodyguard. Even so, there have been improvements here.

'Ten years ago, you couldn't walk up and down this neighbourhood,' Cuba told me. 'Every step you would take, there would be someone there to sell you drugs … People, a lady would come up and snatch your pocket book. These people are crazy, you know.'

I wanted to know if we could have filmed here, then, walking around with a camera?

'You wouldn't even be able to drive in this neighbourhood at that time, because they would have someone follow you and take your van … We made a big difference. When I started here, I was down here on a Friday … Some people called me to go up on top of the block which is Brown Place. About twelve people in a green van shooting up drugs. So I went up with my little nightstick and I chased them away. But I was shivering.'

Other people, too, have made a difference. In the next door block, Jose and Tamarez Ortega have been working with young kids off the street, attempting to offer them more positive values than drug dealing. Tamarez teaches dancing to little kids.

On the day we were there they had organized a street party. A simple affair: some food and soft drinks. Dancing displays by the kids. A basketball hoop for the older boys. A sound system for DJs to show off their skills. In a country village it would have been small, charming and unexceptional. On these mean streets it was small, charming and extraordinary.

Apart from the general fun, having a party on the streets necessitates blocking them to traffic, and the mere absence of cars for the afternoon made the area seem more friendly, more human for children and grown ups.

Of course, streets must have always been busy, dangerous places. Horses' hooves and carriage wheels are as deadly, in their own way, as cars and lorries. But by the time inner city areas are criss-crossed by flyovers, and every cross street turned into a death trap – and every country lane, come to that – you begin to wonder if, for all its convenience, we really get the best out of our Faustian pact with the infernal combustion engine.

At the party, the local policeman put in an appearance. It was one of those duties they have to perform these days, like cheery bobbies dancing for the cameras alongside floats in the early hours of the Notting Hill Carnival. In fact, the officer did have a little bit of police work to do as someone from another block attacked the DJ and a fight started. It was like a playground fight, all scuffling and grabbing, with a few punches thrown. But you never know round here. At any moment someone can go for a knife or a gun. In the end, nobody did get shot and the officer did not make an arrest.

So nothing much for him to do that day, but I did discover that the local cop is something of a local hero.

• Robocop •

Ed Ramirez has been patrolling this beat since 1990 and has earned everybody's respect. He tends to work on his own, he has got to know everybody on his beat and is utterly fearless despite, for him too, the threats from the drug gangs.

His time on duty has corresponded with an improvement in the crime rate. In an area of 1 square mile there used to be more than eighty homicides a year. This has been brought down to fewer than forty. This vast improvement, which has reduced the number of murders in a square mile to only four times the number in the whole of Liverpool (see above), has not been achieved by community policing alone. In fact, it has largely been achieved by aggressive policing.

Mayor Giuliani has set about attacking crime with a will. And, indeed, the Bill. Only the day before we were filming, there had been a 'sweep' along these streets. A clean sweep is a straightforward procedure involving as many police officers as are available arresting as many criminals as possible: anyone with any amount of drugs, hanging around in large groups on street corners, drinking alcohol in public, carrying weapons. This sweep had produced 242 arrests.

By this means, gangs hanging around on street corners have been broken up, the sale of drugs in public has been eliminated, and general drunkenness cut back. It is obviously a pretty blunt instrument. In fact, it is not so much a clean sweep as a sweep under the carpet. Drug dealers have to conduct their business in the back rooms of shops or on the flat roofs of apartment buildings. All sorts of minor miscreants are pulled in, while the big guys get away. The locals seemed reasonably in favour of their neighbourhood being cleaned out in this way (certainly Cuba and the other community leaders were all in favour). But a rough and ready method like this cannot help but be unfair.

A little liquor store had been caught selling alcohol to a minor – which is anyone under the age of twenty-one. In this case, it was a twenty-year-old, plain clothes policeman, *with a beard*, who had bought the drink. All this liquor store owner needed was just one of O.J. Simpson's lawyers to nip along to court on his behalf to get him off the charge by arguing that it was a case of entrapment, *agent provocateur*, or the police officer drinking on duty, and he would be all right. As it was, he would probably be put out of business.

Officer Ed Ramirez does not go in for this strong arm stuff. He is much more Dixon of Dock Green than Paul Newman ever was. We sat in his police car while he explained how he went about his work. And I tried to work out why he is so popular. I thought I would start with a tough question.

'You're a bit of a hero?' I suggested.

'No, I'm just doing my job, you know, what every other cop's supposed to do.'

And he seems to be doing better than most. Coming from the Bronx himself helps; speaking Spanish helps even more. He also came to policing relatively late in life, which might help as well. He was twenty-seven when he gave up a career in air-conditioning and breezed into law enforcement. This perhaps gave him the maturity to deal firmly and fairly with the public. Mind you, like every other NYPD cop, on duty he carries a gun and wears a bullet-proof vest. Always. There is even an organization called COPSHOT on whose free phoneline you can ring in with info about policemen being shot. Many of the police cars advertise it on their bumpers.

Even while we were chatting in the car, the work on his beat carried on. A man with a pit bull terrier dressed in a startling range of studded leatherware went by. Ed pointed out that pit bulls are the chosen breed of drug dealers. Actually, this is not news to me. For many years I have practised law in criminal courts in England. I am not a *complete* innocent abroad ...

'They cut the vocal cords off the dog,' Ed informed me.

'What? Why do they do that?' I asked, startled.

'So when we hit on a search warrant, you can't hear the dog. Until it's running towards you and at your throat.'

Cutting off the noise to spite the force?

Most of the Bronx pit bulls seemed to have had their ears cut off as well, but I did not get round to asking the Officer Ed about that. The only owner we spoke to just said it made the dog look better.

'My dog's got no ears.' 'Your dog's got no ears, how does he hear?' 'Not very well. Tyson, do stop biting that man's testicles. He just won't listen.'

A drunken woman approached the car and tried to give some information to Ed. A man with an amputation, she told him, is keeping drugs in his false leg. She tried to get her message across, half in English, half in Spanish; half-cut. A usually unreliable source.

The area was littered with half-crazies and crackheads. Everywhere we set up to film, our camera attracted them like moths round a magnet. Generally, we had the same conversation with all of them.

'Hey, you making a movie?'

'Television. We're making a tv documentary,' one of us would say.

'Television? Which channel are you on?'

'We're from the BBC in England.'

'No kidding. When's it going to be on?'

'Well, it is being made for British television,' we would repeat.

'Which channel is it going to be on in America?'

'That rather depends on whether the BBC manages to sell the programme to any of the American networks,' we would reply.

'What?'

'We're from the United Kingdom.'

'Do you know Benny Hill?'

Another man volunteered a full explanation for the troubles of the district, the city, America, the world. It all sounded plausible until he informed us that the entire human race was the product of an alien-conducted breeding experiment with cows.

To think that Officer Dibble was hard-pushed dealing with Top Cat and his gang. The gangs nowadays are just a little more challenging. Ramirez insisted that recent improvements in the crime figures have been achieved by laws being vigorously enforced. But even this has a darker side. A 25 per cent reduction in the homicide rate resulted from a Puerto Rican drug dealer being murdered by some rival gangsters. A notoriously violent man who controlled a substantial part of the drugs trade, he was gunned down on his way to see his probation officer. So we will never know if probation was going to make him see the error of his ways. Not that Ramirez is in favour of the death penalty.

'It's not going to solve anything. Let me give you my views.' He began what I imagined was going to be a liberal-minded analysis. 'It's not going to solve anything, because the District Attorneys are not going to order the death penalty in New York City.... I guess it's a moral thing with them.... Plus it costs too much money to kill somebody ... three or four million after the appeals.... Prison should be what it used to be.... You get your three square meals. You get visitation once every six months.... And I guarantee these people will never go back to prison.... You should make prison tough and harsh like in South American countries.'

The message from the police is 'crack down, not crack'. Actually, I made that up. It's surprising how quickly you start speaking in slogans in America. It's a soundbite society. To use another one.

But cracking down is what the police are certainly doing. Never can an area have had so many police cars driving up and down as you see all day in the Bronx. It is keeping crime, and drugs, off the streets, but where is it going? Everywhere else seems to be the answer.

We filmed a short chat with a guy called Manzanet. He has reclaimed an empty lot between two tenement buildings and re-created a Puerto Rican villa, a reminder of home for the many Puerto Ricans like him who have come from the Caribbean island to live in New York. (Puerto Rica was acquired by America in the Spanish America war in 1898, along with Cuba and the Philippines. It now occupies a constitutions position, but is not quite a state. It is something like a self-governing colony of the US where many of its people, who have US citizenship, have come to make a living.)

The villa has chickens and ducks scratching around to give it an authentic, rural Puerto Rican feel on the city streets of New York. But its main function is to provide a social centre for Puerto Ricans in the neighbourhood. In order to film me going into the villa, the camera went on to the roof of an apartment block just across the road. While I chatted to Manzanet about reclaiming the empty lot from drug dealers, the cameraman and director were on this rooftop crushing under-foot crack files. Looking like mini biro tubes, it is in these files that crack cocaine is sold. In fact, you come across them everywhere. And cocaine is not supposed to be the biggest problem round here. These days that is heroin.

• Another Fix •

Another, larger, lot which has been reclaimed from drug dealing and gangs is on the corner of 138th Street and St Ann's. It is now a commu-nity park next door to a drug rehabilitation centre. On a sunny after-noon we went there to film a barbecue or 'cook out' organized by Joseph Rowntree – appropriately named for someone philanthropically inclined – who is in charge of the centre.

It was one of the few really hot, sunny days of our unseasonably cool and grey stay in New York. In the sun, the little park looks good. Good for somewhere that used to be waste ground. It has a pond and a play area and seats for sitting out and taking the air.

A recovering alcoholic and drug addict, Anthony Stephenson, filled me in on the background. As an empty lot this had been run down, derelict and covered in rubbish. It was not hard to imagine. It is still like that across the street. The empty lot was a major site for the sale of drugs. So when Joseph Rowntree and others started to lay it out as a park, the drug dealers objected. Led by the big chief, the one who was eventually killed outside his probation office, the drug gangs beat up a workman employed to erect fences around the site. The park was finally only laid out when police were posted to guard the workmen. It took armed police guards to build a park.

Anthony has himself been to hell and, hopefully, back again on drugs. In the depth of his addiction he found himself on the point of using a brick to dash out the brains of an old man for his pension money. Fortu-nately for both of them he was interrupted before he could put into action what he can now wryly call his 'masterplan'.

As people gathered for the party it became clear this was a very ordi-nary tale. Everyone had a similar story to tell. A young mother clutched a pale-looking baby, a few days old. Her first child lives with her sister in New Jersey. This one is going to take its chance in the Bronx. The mother and her friend quizzed me about prices in England. I started by explaining that we do not use dollars, we have a different unit of cur-rency called the pound, and they lost interest.

The music started up. Actually, there was a slight cock up on the music front. The band failed to show. So from the gathering of recover-ing narcotics addicts was assembled a scratch trio. Piano accordion, guitar and bongos. Musicians anonymous who were, I regret to say, dreadful. Playing percussion without a sense of rhythm makes you miss the beat. It also kind of misses the point. The amplification was faulty, which troubled the band more than it did us. Not so much unplugged as unhinged. But in the end it did not matter. The weather was hot, the food was good, the drinks were soft. Most of the audience had endured enough horrors in their life not to care if the music was unbearable. Anything in an agreeable park like this must be music to their ears.

• Roxanne •

At the cook out I met Roxanne Artuz and we agreed to meet next day for another tour of the Bronx but, mainly, for a trip through her life. This was to be an insider's guide to twenty-one years of drug addiction, prostitution, violence and crime. Those of a nervous disposition might consider skipping the next few pages; they should definitely avoid a lifetime like Roxanne's.

In any discussion of the decriminalization of drugs, someone will maintain that even if a soft drug is not particularly harmful, you must keep it off limits because those addicted to hard drugs have always started on something relatively anodyne like cannabis. Perhaps Roxanne's story would prove the point, although in her case what got her going was egg nog, at the age of nine.

To be fair, what also got her going was coming from a family in which her mother was an acidhead and user of marijuana, and growing up in a district in which her cousins, school friends and mates (they are called her 'peer group' in this sort of story) were into cocaine and other drugs from an early age.

At fifteen she was into sniffing cocaine and selling it. Not only was it fun, she was making money and buying gold chains and sneakers and TV sets. After two years it was no longer fun: she was an addict and was selling gold chains and sneakers and TV sets and anything else of value she could get her hands on.

Cocaine made her paranoid. She could not stand talking to anyone in case they were after her money, she could not stand her baby because she couldn't tolerate her crying. Help was at hand, though, in the form of heroin.

'Heroin was the total opposite of cocaine,' Roxanne told me. 'Where cocaine got me paranoid, the heroin brang me down in the head and it did not allow me to feel very much. You know, I wouldn't think about the fact that I left my daughter with friends for about two months and never went back to make sure things were all right. I didn't care. The heroin medicated all those feelings, so it was easy, I loved it.'

But whereas she had had no withdrawal symptoms from cocaine, from heroin they were truly awful.

'You have no control over your bowel movement ... I couldn't walk down the street without taking a crap on myself. My bowels – I didn't have no muscles to hold it, so it would just come out ... I would literally take a number two in my pants ... I was deep into that addiction ... We have a certain acid in our stomach that chews up the food for us so we can digest it. That lining I was constantly throwing up, a yellow liquid, because I wouldn't be able to hold anything in my stomach until I got a hit. So when you're sick like that everything is gone. You can't walk, you can't eat, you can't function. That's dreadful.'

As we drove around the Hunt's Point Market area, Roxanne explained how the expense of all these drugs led to the inevitable – the disposal of all her worldly goods, stealing, mainly from her mother, and prostitution. The great stand-by for the desperate woman.

Hunt's Point has a desolate look. Wide streets, brick walls, warehouses and lock ups. A market area for women 'on the stroll', selling their bodies to truckers, lawyers and other low life.

'When you're desperate for money for heroin, you can't be too choosy, can you?' I asked her.

'Oh, that's another thing,' she nodded. 'When you are desperate for heroin and you're out on the stroll, no matter how sick you are, no matter how sick I was, I would wait for somebody I knew. Because if I knew you, then you would take me to get my drugs first, and then we would do what we had to do. It was better for me to do it that way because being heroin sick and trying to have sex or oral is no good at all. Because like I told you about your bowels, you're throwing up. It's not a pretty sight.'

It is not a pretty tale. And it gets worse. High on heroin, she wandered in front of a car and was knocked down and broke her leg. This being America she was not crippled for life, her leg was fixed and she was awarded more than twenty thousand dollars in compensation. And how long does twenty thousand dollars last in the hands of a heroin addict? In her case, two months.

Her brother, the one member of her family who was not sucked into drug addiction, was killed by a stray bullet in a gang fight. And then there were the killings she witnessed.

'I was working in a factory bagging cocaine in a house in the Bronx. And we had got word that we were about to be robbed.... Half an hour later three fellows came knocking on the door and robbed the place and they were brutally beat up. Beat up so bad that they died. Right in front of me.'

'So are we talking about fists or sticks?' I wondered.

'No, we're talking about an electric knife, a hammer that they were beaten up with. And they died, they literally died there in the apartment ... what I'd never seen was somebody trying to live ... I remember seeing this man laying there and jumping like a fish out of water for two days. It was like he was still alive but, I guess, he probably had to be dead because his head was so smashed in, you know.... He was still twitching.'

These stories are made even more disturbing by the fact that Roxanne is so, well, ordinary. That may sound like damning with faint praise, condescending even, but I mean it as something between a compliment and a tribute. She has been off drugs for just a year and now she could be a woman you would meet in the supermarket or in the bus queue or chat to over the garden fence. She is cheery, concerned and informed. And yet she has lived through what are almost on a par with twenty-one years of wartime atrocities. The war, I suppose, against drugs.

• Drug Warrior •

With everything and everyone pointing to the drugs trade as the cause of so much misery and destruction, you might imagine it would be difficult to find a drug dealer prepared to talk about it on camera. In fact, we had more than one volunteer.

Mike, as I was to call him, explained his life while we sat in a car parked alongside the East River. To preserve Mike's identity the camera was positioned outside the car and some distance from it. It was an overcast, but otherwise dry, night, apart from the twenty minutes it took to do the actual interview, during which the heavens opened. This created a wonderfully lachrymose atmosphere for the film, but somewhat obscured visibility through the windscreen. It also steamed up the car and played havoc with the sound. I also found it distracting. In the interview, which dealt with serious matters, from time to time I was on the point of giggling as I caught sight of my trusty film crew getting soaked to the skin.

Mike started selling crack cocaine in the Bronx when he was fifteen. From it he made between 500 and 600 dollars a day. Rather better money, it struck me, than you could get from a paper round. He has now moved on to heroin, which is where the money is nowadays. Crack cocaine had given him his start but he had to move on. In this business there is no room for sentimentality.

Having just been reminded of the horrors of heroin addiction I wanted to know if the moral side of it worried him at all. I asked him if he knows the problems heroin causes?

'If you can't get it you get sick.... Your whole body starts crapping up, you start throwing up. And it's bad.'

'But this is from the drug you're supplying them?' I asked.

'Right. They know right from wrong. I'm not putting a gun to their head.'

'If somebody supplied crack cocaine or heroin to your daughter, what would you think about it?'

'I'd go out and kill them.... Which I know is not going to happen, 'cos you know my daughter's wise enough. She's young but she's wise,' he said.

Mike told me he gets his supply of drugs from a lawyer in Queen's. (Is it always the case that lawyers are involved in dodgy trade? Or do people only mention it when talking to me?) Mike's customers are either Bronx locals or respectable people who come into the Bronx to buy. (Everybody from ambulance drivers to, er, lawyers.) The threat of arrest does not put him off. He is not particularly worried about going to prison. He has not been there yet, but he is about to. He is going to be pleading guilty (to something he tells me he did not do) and is anticipating two to four years, but some more plea bargaining might get it down to one-and-a-half to three years. The only thing he really worries about is dying in the streets.

'Two years ago I got shot on the corner ...' he said. 'Six times ... I got shot in my bladder, I had a collapsed lung. Got shot in my buttocks, my leg, my hip. I was in a coma for two weeks. I was in the hospital for two months. The guy was reloading to kill when the cops came. So he ran.'

'So there was a cop there when you needed him?'

'Yeah, and I thank God for that.'

'So you are grateful to the New York police?'

'Just that one ... I have shot people myself ... it's a jungle.'

'Pretty well everybody points to the fact that drugs are a big problem, causing misery, illness, crime and agony,' I said. 'How could it all be eliminated?'

'The only way to stop that is to take the dirty people out of politics ... they're the ones that are bringing in the drugs.'

'But you're bringing in the drugs ... You go to Queen's,' I said.

'Yeah, I go about my business and collect my money.'

'What other career could you have followed?' I asked. 'What do others in your class at school do now?'

'The majority of my friends from school are all drug dealers.'

'Does it not depress you that so many people in your neighbourhood are drug addicts?'

'I don't care what they do ... they could kill each other. Doesn't bother me none. As long as they don't mess with me and my family.'

Mike definitely wants his children to get an education and avoid the drugs trade, so I asked him if he had his time again whether he would go into drug dealing.

'If I was to go back in time I would go and get my education, get a job ... and do this on the side.'

'So you're kind of addicted to supplying drugs, not the drugs themselves, the excitement?'

'It's just like the Wild West,' he said. 'This is going to be worse than the Wild West.'

Drugs in the Bronx operate like a pyramid selling scheme. An addict needs to create other addicts in order to finance his own addiction. It is the perfect capitalist product. You sell something whose main effect is to create an insatiable desire in the purchaser to buy some more.

The libertarian in me says that if people want to buy something, they should be allowed to. The pragmatist in me observes that legal controls do not work anyway. Making the drug trade illegal in some respects aggravates the whole problem. Young people in particular are attracted to illicit activity because it is illicit, and instinctively reject things which are approved by authority – kids who will consume E but not E numbers.

But after meeting so many people whose lives have been destroyed by drugs I am not sure their misery is a price worth paying for the pleasure of the recreational drug user. Legalization would certainly create interesting new moral dilemmas. Already people blame the Establishment for promoting the importation of drugs into poor areas. How it would feed that paranoia if the government made it all legal and allowed big corporations to manufacture narcotics.

Still, they are making some progress in the control of drugs around here. You cannot smoke cigarettes in any restaurant in New York City.

• A Sheep in Wolfe's Clothing •

The next day we took time off from the troubles of the South Bronx to go to see Tom Wolfe. The author who so graphically captured the turmoil of the inner city does not actually live in the Bronx. He lives in Manhattan. In the summer months he also lives in his Long Island home in Southampton. Rather like the rich New York socialites and bankers he satirized in *The Bonfire of the Vanities*.

Long Island stretches east from New York City into the Atlantic Ocean. The boroughs of Brooklyn and Queens are at its western end but after that it is 100 miles or so of luxury beach-front properties and green and pleasant countryside. It is as though the citizens of New York ordered their own strap-on section of the Home Counties so they would have somewhere smart to go at the weekends.

They ordered Home Counties names or, at any rate, English names to go with it. Apart from Southampton, and the fictional-sounding East Hampton and Westhampton you find on either side of it, there is a Brentwood and a Huntington, plus Wainscott, a place name I always thought had been made up by Monty Python. Another community chooses to call itself Hicksville, but I imagine it consists entirely of hip advertising executives and record producers enjoying a post-modern joke.

It may be that we were lucky with the traffic, but it seemed much easier, and quicker, to get out of New York than to make the equivalent journey out of London. Just before you get to Southampton – which boasts the oldest English church on the American continent – there is a nod towards a non-English past. An up-market Indian reservation is represented by a roadside shop selling tax-free cigarettes. After all these years, they are still selling tobacco to palefaces.

But Southampton, Long Island, is not quite like Southampton, Old England. It is a sort of rich person's ghetto. Antique shops and smart restaurants. No littering, no excessive noise, no unpleasantness on show.

Tom Wolfe welcomed us to his elegant home from home. It had that not-quite-lived-in feel of a property kept for weekends and holidays, which seems to characterize the whole of this part of Long Island. At the time of our visit, however, Tom Wolfe was a writer in residence, finishing off his next book which is on real estate.

The house has an extensive lawn leading down to a freshwater lake which is just beside the Atlantic Ocean. The lawn seemed a perfect place on which we could film an interview. In the Bronx, all our outdoor recording was troubled by the sound of traffic, shouting, passing trains, police sirens. But here, way out east on Long Island, it was interrupted only by lawn mowers, gardeners chain-sawing tree branches, and pet dogs barking. Round here they might dock the tails but they do not cut the vocal cords.

Tom greeted us in his trademark white suit and high-collared shirt. Buttoned up though he was, he was happy to open up about the writing of *The Bonfire of the Vanities*. He had set out to write a *Vanity Fair* for 1980s New York. He had written it as a partwork, delivering a chapter at a time to *Rolling Stone* magazine. This was to adopt the methods of nineteenth-century novelists and also to force himself to get the whole thing finished by using the repeated pressures of journalistic deadlines. We chortled over the filming of the book. The demands of Hollywood had cast the supremely likeable Tom Hanks as the essentially unlikeable

Sherman McCoy, and had turned a ferocious Jewish judge working in the Bronx into a black man, which deliberately missed the point about racial politics to accommodate political correctness. Mr Wolfe reminisced about his research for the book, sitting in on the working practices of Judge Burton Roberts (the inspiration for Judge Myron Kovitsky in the novel).

All in all, the whole visit was most agreeable, except that what he had to say about the Bronx and the condition of New York generally was quite unlike the thrust of the message of his book. Early on in *The Bonfire of the Vanities*, an admittedly outrageous character lets rip about what is happening to the city:

'It's the Third World down there! Puerto Ricans, West Indians, Haitians, Dominicans, Cubans, Colombians, Hondurans, Koreans, Chinese, Thais, Vietnamese, Ecuadorians, Panamanians, Filipinos, Albanians, Senegalese, and Afro-Americans! Go visit the frontiers, you gutless wonders! Morningside Heights, St Nicholas Park, Washington Heights, Fort Tryon – *por qué pagar más*! The Bronx is finished for you! Riverdale is just a little freeport up there! Pelham Parkway – keep the corridor open to Westchester! Brooklyn – your Brooklyn is no more! ... And do you Saturday do-it-yourselfers really think you're snug in your little rug? You don't think the future knows how to cross a *bridge*? And you, you Wasp charity-ballers sitting on your mounds of inherited money ... do you really think you are impregnable?'

Anyone writing like that in the 1980s must have had some apocalyptic views about New York. Gore Vidal in chat show mode is, if anything, more condemnatory of America and all things American than he is in his writings. But no, Tom Wolfe himself reckons the various racial groups will learn to get along. People in similar income groups or similar professions have more to bring them together than racial differences to keep them apart.

But surely, I asked him, there is little in common between a comfortable author sitting on his manicured Long Island lawn, and the black, Puerto Rican or Korean man on the streets of the Bronx? Oh yes, he replied, the racial mixture of the Bronx changed between the time of his research for *The Bonfire of the Vanities* and its publication. And it had changed again by the time it had been filmed. This was evidence that people of all types do move onward and upward.

He was sounding not so much like a Thackeray or a Dickens as a Patience Strong. Less a social satirist, more a Social Democrat. And more WASP than waspish. It was good to hear an optimistic view from such an an unlikely source. But we headed back to town for another opinion.

• The Disunited Nation •

A radically different view comes from the Nation of Islam.

The Nation of Islam – originally the Lost-Found Nation of Islam – developed in 1930 among black Americans as a radical, religious and political movement which was firmly against integration of the races. Instead, it advocated black self-reliance and separation from white society. Famously, Malcolm X was a convert to the cause in 1947 but broke from it in 1964, shortly after which he was assassinated.

After several name and other changes, the main organization moved away from its more controversial policies and its membership was encouraged to associate more closely with the wider world of Islam. But an offshoot continued the name and ideals of the Nation of Islam under the leadership of Louis Farrakhan.

We had hoped to film a meeting of the Nation of Islam in the Bronx, but that proved impossible. Instead, I spoke to Conrad Mohammed, a leading figure in the movement, on a sidewalk in Harlem, surrounded by what I took to be a group of bodyguards, but which he assured me were merely 'Brothers in the service of Islam'. They were all dressed in dark suits, crisp white shirts and bow ties, the Nation's regular uniform. Conrad Mohammed did all the talking:

'On the ground level, the Honourable Louis F., who is our leader, teacher and guide, has established a mosque in every major and minor city in this country. We go into the worse neighbourhoods and we establish an example of pride and cleanliness and dignity so that our people see that they don't have to live in squalor and poverty and want.'

The Nation of Islam are against the use of tobacco, alcohol and all drugs, and preach a wholesome, moral message. They are disgusted that black people so often get the worst housing and worst conditions. And that one in four black men is in gaol, in prison or on parole.

'Who is to say that a black baby, born in a hospital on the same day as a white baby, is born with a biological inclination towards crime? How is it that eighteen years later the white baby is at Penn State and the black baby is in the State pen?'

It is a good quip and a good point. By any standards, black people get a raw deal from the American dream, but Conrad Mohammed insists that the worsening state of inner cities and crime is deliberately contrived. On his analysis, the crime, the drugs, the degradation are the intended result of government policy, not a product of its incompetence.

'We believe that there are several industries that benefit from the ignorance and the frivolous and riotous lifestyle that black people have been forced to live.... If you clean the black man up, then that means the lawyers don't make money, the bail bondsmen don't make money. The judges are out of a job.'

This is very much the conspiracy rather than the cock up theory of policy. In the face of such overwhelming paranoia, my earnest suggestions that everyone should pull together seemed rather feeble. The Nation of Islam is impatient with the idea that black people should join in with the whole idea of a melting pot America. Black people were brought to America as slaves and have waited too long to overcome white racism. When I pointed out that black people are now succeeding as Supreme Court judges, big businessmen, entertainers, sports stars, Conrad Mohammed was having none of that. He said the black man has to be appointed by a panel of whites, or is employed by a corporation owned by whites. However successful he is, he is still a slave on a plantation.

The solution, apparently, is for there to be a complete separation between the races. The Nation of Islam has now got its own farms from which it wishes to supply black people right across America. It wishes black people to refuse financial assistance from the government and live their own lives with their own institutions, courts, etc. Strangely, many of the policies they advocate sound eerily like those popular with Republicans; right wing, not to say the apartheid, policies which were pursued in South Africa.

Conrad Mohammed pointed to Orthodox Jewish areas of Brooklyn as an example of racial groups existing culturally and economically on their own (a rather unrepresentative example of Jewish life in America) and went on to cite Israel and Pakistan as examples of states set up to accommodate one racial or religious group. Neither, perhaps, holds out the hope of immediate peace and harmony. In fact, leaders of the Nation of Islam have gained notoriety with their anti-Semitic sentiments and anti-Jewish remarks in speeches; which perhaps make it surprising that they so turn to Jewish examples as ideals to aim at. Or perhaps not.

Anyway, there should be black farms, black corporations, black laws, black judges. A separate black nation. Oh, and what about the Hispanic nation? The Asian nation, the Italian, the Filipino, the Chinese? And laws about mixed marriage and miscegenation? It all sounds like the disintegrating, disunited states of America – what I would call the Balkanization of America, unless someone has done so already.

But in any event, Conrad Mohammed said that the white man is finished, brought down by his own evil nature expressed in imperialism, slavery, racism and greed.

'America is becoming a black and brown nation ... All the social scientists see that the white birth rate is down. But black people just look at each other and our women get pregnant. So we see in a few years a more powerful and empowered position for black people.'

The Nation of Islam finds it difficult to get a hearing, he said, on the American media, because their message is too challenging and does not fit into the stereotypes of black culture.

'They won't put our message out, but if a young black rapper comes up with a rap – "kill the niggers" or "the black woman is a bitch" – they'll print him, they'll make CDs and records, they'll promote him.'

This puts the Nation of Islam full square behind Newt Gingrich's campaign against Time Warner and others for promoting immoral rap music.

'Well, the difference is, Newt Gingrich and his mindset created the problem. And they don't really want to solve it.'

'But he is saying to the corporations that you shouldn't be making money out of that,' I pointed out.

'And we make no apologies for agreeing with Mr Gingrich on that.'

• It's a Rap •

Anything that can unite the Nation of Islam and Newt Gingrich in opposition cannot be all bad. Rap music, and its close relation hip hop, are both authentic products of the American inner cities, so off I went to meet some young and, they hope, up and coming rap artists called Hoodz uv Misbehaviour. (I may have spelled that wrongly. Rap artists go in for a form of aggressive phonetic misspelling which befits a form popular in a borough which turned 'Bronck's' into 'Bronx'.)

These particular rappers hang out in the Williamsbridge/Baychester area. It is not the South Bronx, but it is not one of the show-piece smart districts either. Outside a block of flats of rather a brooding aspect, the Hoodz and their chumz waited to meet us. They are called Devon, Bubz, Nasty Noah and Rob B. Rob. Plus there is a manager called Shawn. They were dressed in the black street style which is popular among dis-affected youth and affected fashion victims the world over. Multiple layers of underpanting were on display at the waistband, above ludi-crously baggy shorts. They were wearing the last word in trainers, track-suits, baseball caps and bandannas. I could tell they were impressed with my lightweight suit and blue poplin shirt.

They seemed happy enough to see me, generally. Mind you, I do not know how I had been described in advance. A certain amount of poetic licence is employed by the production team in setting up these inter-views. For thoughtful discussions with slightly older interviewees, they claim I am the Phil Donahoe of the UK; for younger, more upbeat occasions I am described as Britain's answer to David Letterman; for the Hoodz they probably said I was the English Arsenio Hall and they were therefore sympathetic because they thought my talk show had been cancelled.

We hung around, discussing life, art and police harassment. They said the police campaign to keep crime off the streets largely consists of keeping *them* off street corners. Everybody round here, they said, hates the police and assumes the police hate them. It is an ex-officio hatred, like the way the soldiers of opposing armies have to feel in a war. A patrol car checked us out while we were filming and the officers were roundly abused as they drove away. A couple of other blue-uniformed men got even less respect. They are employed as security guards and are regarded as copper's narks, too cowardly to become police officers themselves, authority figures without any authority.

I wondered if it would be better if local people, people like the rappers or people they actually knew, were to become police officers. They entertained the idea for a moment or two before dismissing it as totally impractical. Why? Because anyone round here joining the police would be rubbed out immediately.

While we were chatting they seemed unconcerned by police action against them and sent off younger kids to get cannabis for them to smoke. But the main thing they are addicted to is their music. In particular, the improvised mixture of verse-making, singing and ranting called rapping. Naturally, they did some for me and my cameras. At which point I hoped they had not seen *Whose Line Is It Anyway?* (which is shown in America on an all-comedy channel, Comedy Central). On this show I introduce improvised games and, in what was once a regular round, I would get the performers, who were usually white and British, to improvise what we called a 'rap'. Although rap is what we called it, it was not much like what these black American guys were doing. I hoped they had not seen the programme as they might not have seen the joke.

For this authentic rapping, Rob B. Rob created a backing drum beat with his mouth, while the others took it in turns to lead the rest through the rhymes and rhythms of the improvisation. If you know anything about rapping you will know what to expect. Tales of violence and aggression give way only to graphic boasts of sexual prowess. Delicate rhymes are deployed to point up indelicate subjects. On the street they were singing a cappella. 'A cappella' literally means in the style of the early church, but church was never like this. Hatred, anger, lust ... It is all very impressive, but *It's a Wonderful World* it ain't.

As I was being filmed while all these merry roundelays about cop killing, bitch slapping and body pumping were being performed along-side me, I found I had to play another *Whose Line* game, Fixed Expression, so-called because in the course of the game each player has to maintain a fixed expression on his or her face. Throughout the rap, I maintained a look on my face which suggested I admired the skill of the verse construction and the exuberance of language expressing a powerful range of emotions but did not endorse the celebrations of violent, homicidal and misogynistic attitudes. I kept this up throughout, except when I laughed.

Actually, we had quite a few laughs afterwards and wished them luck with their record deal. Perhaps they will tone down the language for Newt Gingrich and the Nation of Islam. After we bid a fond farewell I heard one of them mutter that I was not *that* much like Oprah Winfrey.

• Take Me to Your Mother •

Leaving the others to go on a trip to the beach, we went to Rob B. Rob's home in Morris Heights on the other side of the Bronx. Here he introduced me to the art of being a DJ. Being a disc jockey in this case does not involve playing the top ten and taking phone calls from the crazy people who work in Allied Carpets in Basildon. Rob is into scratching and sampling – he has being doing it for years, even though he is only twenty. You take little sections of music, lyrics, drum breaks from records (vinyl – CDs are no good for this) and put them together to make your own sound. It is like taking bits from lots of different jigsaws and making a whole new picture. It all seemed a lot harder than just learning to play a musical instrument, but my job was to try my hand at doing it in front of the camera and being completely hopeless at it.

Needless to say, Rob B. Rob comes from as pleasant a family as you could hope to imagine. (Mother, father and sister in a comfortably furnished apartment.) I chatted to his mum about her work in a bank and the need to provide a moral basis for her children's upbringing, and to his dad about the baseball he was watching on television. I will not say any more for fear of harming Rob's future career as a gangsta rapper. Look out for him and the Hoodz uv Misbehaviour on North Pole Records. (They referred to the Bronx as the North Pole, as in the quote from Tom Wolfe at the beginning of this chapter.)

• Damn Yankees •

Baseball at the Yankee Stadium was the only one of the big Bronx attractions that I managed to visit. (My producer/director flatly refused to film inside the zoo or Botanical Garden. I don't know why. I am sure we could have made some point about how well the animals are cared for compared to the humans. For the animals it is a zoo, but out on the streets, it is a jungle … Something subtle like that, but it was not to be.)

I had never been to a baseball match before, but the Yankee Stadium was a good place to start. It is occasionally referred to as 'the house that Babe built' because the stadium was built in 1923 in the wake of the success of the Yankee's great hero, Babe Ruth. It is one of the great baseball venues. In fact, according to the *Bronx Visitor's Fun Guide*, it is the most famous athletic arena in the United States. It is, however, a little long in the tooth and, horror of horrors, the owner of the Yankees, George Steinbrenner, is threatening to take the team to play in a new location with better access for cars, more modern facilities and, above all, one which *will not be in the Bronx*.

Well, stranger things have happened. In the 1950s the Boston Braves moved to Milwaukee, the Brooklyn Dodgers to Los Angeles and the New York Giants to San Francisco. But the removal of the Yankees would be a body blow to the borough, especially as the main reason why George Steinbrenner wants to make the move is the fear that fans from other boroughs are too frightened to go to the Bronx to attend the games.

There was no sign of the threatened move on the evening I visited the stadium. Arriving early for an evening game I, and all the other unfrightened-looking fans, were welcomed by a pre-recorded announcement practically bursting its tannoy with pride in the location.

'This is Yankee Stadium … Welcome to Yankee Stadium … Home of the New York Yankees …'

After the pride there were the restrictions. As a British football fan, it came as no surprise to be told there was no question of taking bottles, cans or anything else into the ground. No surprise either, I suppose, to discover inside the stadium that beer is on sale in huge amounts at even huger prices ($9.50 for two plastic cups of beer: *What made Milwaukee famous made a loser out of me*). Apart from that, the stadium seemed all right to me. Mind you, where I come from, Wembley Stadium is supposed to be the best there is.

I do not want to be racist, but Americans are very fat. Not all of them, obviously. There are skeletally thin fitness freaks who exercise away every last ounce from their skin and bones, and showbiz celebrities who have enough bits removed by plastic surgery to keep several Third World villagers in body mass for a year. But, on average, the availability of huge amounts of cheap, fattening food has turned Americans into a nation of porkers.

You certainly get that impression looking at baseball fans. Middle-aged Michelin men threatening to burst their replica baseball shirts accompany their pudgy young sons, threatening to burst into tears if they do not get another hot dog. Throughout the game, the ground echoes to the sound of the eating of giant buckets of popcorn along with oil tankers of Coca Cola. Never can consumption have been so conspicuous or continuous.

Fortunately, my companion for the game was not a middle-aged man with an over-fed son. She was Elizabeth, a sassy lady from the Bronx, accompanied by her teenage daughter, Chastity. Elizabeth has always been a Yankees fan and she talked me through the game which, in actual fact, is not difficult to understand. I entertained the idea that she liked coming to the game because she thought the players looked cute in their outfits but no, she is really into the game; she even played to quite a high standard herself when she was young. Chastity looked less impressed. But with a name like Chastity, I suppose you have got to do something.

Traditionally in Britain we put baseball down as merely our children's game of rounders with knobs on. This is true as far as it goes. But all sports are for overgrown children, apart from fox hunting which is for overgrown fox cubs.

Before the game, the national anthem was played on what sounded like a cinema organ. A display board flashed a representation of the Stars and Stripes, the whole stadium rose to its feet and the players stood with their hats held over their hearts as though they were in military rather than baseball uniforms. (My special baseball history correspondent, Greg Proops, tells me this custom started in the Second World War and never went away.)

Anyway, 90 per cent of the game consists of the pitcher hurling the ball as hard as possible at the batter, and the batter not hitting it, which makes it 90 per cent the same as cricket. Managing to hit the ball is hard enough, but if you do hit it hard enough a couple of times a match you can more or less win the game for your team. Batting requires great strength and brilliant hand and eye co-ordination, unless it comes down to just hitting and hoping. The pitching and throwing, though, are very obviously highly skilled. Few Test Match fielders could be so consistent in their throwing as the players on these two league sides.

Baseball is the all-American sport, and America is the land of commercialism. But, bizarrely, the teams take to the field in outfits completely unadorned by advertising logos. Just think, all you football, cricket, tennis and motor racing aficionados. All those wasted square inches of cloth rapped round expensive, televised sporting bodies, and nobody is getting any advertising. How quaint.

Another oddity, to the British visitor, is that although there are two major league teams based in New York, they never play each other. The New York Yankees play in the American League while the New York Mets play in the National League. They would meet only if they won their respective leagues and thus got to play each other in the World Series. Given the amount of excitement and money generated by local derbies in Britain, and indeed the rest the world, this American arrangement is rather curious.

There is an even greater curiosity. The whole basis for this film was that the Bronx is a borough torn apart by social problems and violence. I have already drawn attention to its homicide rate compared to those recorded in the United Kingdom. And yet at the Yankee Stadium they sell baseball bats to the fans – toy ones and full size ones. Sometimes they give them away as a promotional gesture to the kids. Can you imagine the mayhem at a British football match if fans were even allowed to bring baseball bats to the ground, let alone were supplied with them once they got there?

But the important thing is that the New York Yankees, with me as their new fan, won the game, beating the Detroit Tigers. I think the final score was 5 – 2. To tell you the truth, though, we had to leave before the end of the game. Even so, if you are in New York I would recommend a visit to the Bronx to see the Yankees play at the Yankee Stadium, while you still can.

• Mr President •

We could not finish a visit to the Bronx without meeting the Borough President. It is sometimes said that the third most difficult political job in America, after the President and the Mayor of New York, is to be the President of the Bronx.

Fernando Ferrer, generally known by his nickname Freddy, was elected to the job in 1987 when he was only thirty-six. It was a better time than most to get the job. Things have been getting steadily better in the Bronx since he came to power, and whether or not this has anything to do with his actions, by the ordinary rules of politics he is bound to reap the benefit. He is also bound to be favourably compared with his predecessor, Stanley Simon, who was imprisoned for corruption. Certainly he has done well enough to be considered as a possible contender for the election to Mayor in 1997.

The Borough President's office is the Bronx County Courthouse building. This is a monumental edifice built in the 1930s in a mixture of neo-classical and Art Deco styles. It dominates the southern end of the Grand Concourse. It is confidently decorated with classical figures and uplifting texts about government and justice, supplemented, until Mr

Ferrer's dynamic administration tackled the problem, with liberal amounts of graffiti. Now the building is as graffiti-clean as a New York subway train.

Freddy Ferrer was born in the South Bronx of Puerto Rican parents. He is an amiable person to interview, comfortable with TV cameras as you have to be in America to hold any sort of political office. We met in a boardroom, the walls of which are completely obliterated by shields and memorial plaques presented to Mr Ferrer at civic and community functions. You would think these would be in the President's own office but that, instead, is full of memorial hard hats and spades presented to him at ceremonial starts to building projects. If he is ever voted out of office he would be able to earn a living as an ironmonger.

For the moment that is unlikely. New York is growing more and more Hispanic. Hispanics are likely soon to outnumber blacks in the Bronx, and in the next century it is anticipated that in New York as a whole there will be roughly 40 per cent Hispanics to 25 per cent each of blacks and whites. Freddy Ferrer does not wish to be seen as a Hispanic politician, but the demographics will not hurt him if that is how he is perceived.

On the day I saw him he was reasonably upbeat about the prospect of the Yankees leaving the borough. He seemed to think that George Steinbrenner is bluffing, seeking to gain as much as possible from the threat to leave. He rattled off a number of statistics which indicated, he claimed, that virtually all crime in the immediate area of the Stadium is baseball-related – ticket touting, drunkenness, etc. – so there can be nothing in the fans' alleged fears of coming to the ground. At a recent meeting he had said, rhetorically:

'If you have a better deal in New Jersey, George, go to New Jersey. Go to Tampa. Or go to hell.'

It was time for me to go to London.

• In Memoriam •

First, I had to leave my mark on the Bronx. Or, at least, have somebody make my mark for me. All over the Bronx, spray-painted on walls, are memorials to local kids – home boys, they are called in America – who have died on the streets: victims of shootings and other everyday features of life and death round here. As a somewhat macabre end to the documentary, betraying goodness knows what subconscious wish fulfilment, the director arranged for a memorial to me to be painted on a wall by a top spray team called Tat Cru.

The Tat Cru (Bio, Nicer and Beegee) started as graffiti artists covering the trains and public buildings in favourite motifs and designs. Those canvases are now denied them but they have developed into more commercial artists. They paint a portrait here, a cityscape there, on walls set aside, even sponsored, for the purpose. They even have a colour brochure of the works they have done. They were asked to do a spray painting, to illustrate a part of the documentary, on a wall in the Bronx. The mural of the story, if you like.

While they put their finishing touches to the picture, I worked out something to say to the cameras. Compared to people in many parts of the world, the people of the Bronx are materially well enough off. They are not hungry or condemned to walk miles to collect water or to live in shanty towns. They do not live in the lap of luxury but, tantalizingly, are within sight of it.

Many of their specific problems have been addressed in the Bronx: drugs, crimes and violence. Things have got better, possibly because they could not have got worse. But these problems in America as a whole, and in the world generally, are not improving. For how long will the Bronx manage to maintain its progress?

Of course, people in abject poverty anywhere else in the world can always dream of solving their problems by going to America. But the people in the Bronx are in America already. What are they to dream of?

To end on a positive note, I fell back on the lyrics to another song. Of the city as a whole they say, *If you can make it in New York, you can make it anywhere.* (To be more accurate, the words are *If I can make it there, I'd make it anywhere, It's up to you, New York, New York,* from the song 'New York, New York'; words by Fred Ebb, music by John Kander.) But of this borough, I suppose you could say that if you can survive in the Bronx you can probably survive anywhere. It is not very positive, but it is another slogan I could suggest to the Bronx tourist board. Failing that, all I can recommend is that they put directions in their *Fun Guide* to see a picture of a pasty-faced creature in a New York Yankees cap expertly sprayed on a crumbling wall at 148th Street and Morris. It is one New York Yankee who is not leaving the Bronx.

OUR
MAN
IN... CALCUTTA

CALCUTTA needs no introduction as a disaster area. It has enjoyed a dreadful reputation since it was founded, 300 years ago, as a trading post of the British East India Company. Calcutta was not built in a day but its Romulus was Mr Job Charnock. He cannot have realized he was founding a great city, but everyone seems to agree that he chose a very bad spot to start anything.

In 1690, Job Charnock had risen to become the East India Company's Governor of the Bay of Bengal. In that year he sailed along the Hooghly River looking for a site on which to establish a new settlement to replace the Company's base at Hooghly town, further upstream, where the river was silting up.

The East India Company had been trading in Bengal, on and off, for about one hundred years. Trading was on when a British surgeon successfully treated the daughter of the Mogul Emperor of India and was rewarded with privileges for the British company; it was off when disputes over profiteering degenerated into expulsions and warfare.

Charnock sounds rather a romantic figure. In 1663, when he was a young factory manager, he had decided to take a look at the spectacle of a Brahmin's funeral which was going to feature the distressing custom of suttee: the widow being put to death in the flames of her dead husband's funeral pyre. At the last minute Charnock intervened on the widow's behalf – apparently, she was extremely beautiful – and undertook to marry her himself. And thereafter they enjoyed a happy and fruitful married life together.

It was a chancy way to select a spouse, but the founding of what eventually became a vast metropolis was almost as haphazard. Charnock's search for a suitable site took him to a stretch of the east bank of the Hooghly River where there were three villages quite close together: Sutanati, Govindpur and Kalikata, from the last of which Calcutta probably derives its name. If that sounds a bit prosaic, there are plenty more imaginative derivations: from *khal* (ditch) and *kata* (dug), a reference to early canal works; from *kal-kuta* (cut yesterday), which assumes a conversation in which there was a mutual misunderstanding between an Englishman asking for the name of the place and a local workman think-

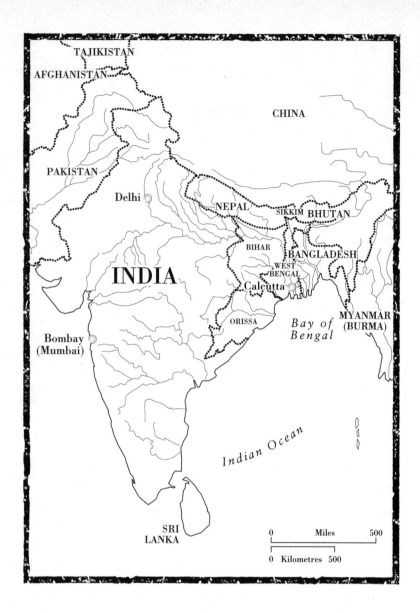

ing he was being asked when the grass was last cut; from a distortion of Golgotha, the place of skulls, a name earned by the unhealthy conditions and high death rate; from *Kali kota* (the house of Kali) – Kali is a Hindu goddess who has strong associations with the city. She is discussed later in this chapter when I describe my visit to the Kalighat Temple.

Under a tree, to provide shelter from the midday sun and the rain (it was in the monsoon season), Charnock pitched his tent and fixed the spot for the East India Company's centre of operations. And the rest is history, geography and economics.

The geography was never very encouraging. Located around the site of Charnock's tent pole, Calcutta is built on marshy ground, prone to flooding during the monsoon. It suffers from stifling heat in the summer months and malaria all year round.

As far as history is concerned, Calcutta first became famous because of its Black Hole. In 1756 the Nawab of Bengal attacked Calcutta, which by then had grown into a substantial, and partially fortified, town. Most of its British population (including the Governor) went into a panic and ran away, frightened of being seized by the Nawab. According to John Zephaniah Holwell, who came through the whole incident and may have exaggerated some of the details, the 146 Britons who remained on 20 June were rounded up by the Nawab's men and confined for the hottest night of the year in a small cell in the town's Fort William, a cramped prison already known as the Black Hole. By the next morning, according to Holwell, no more than twenty-three were still alive, the others having died an awful death in the suffocating conditions. Holwell's graphic account is reproduced in John Carey's *Faber Book of Reportage*, an excellent collection of first-hand accounts of great events in history:

Figure to yourself, my friend, if possible, the situation of 146 wretches, exhausted by continual fatigue and action, crammed together in a cube of eighteen feet, in a close sultry night, in Bengal, shut up to the eastward and southward (the only quarters from whence air could reach us) by dead walls, and by a wall and door to the north, open only to the westward by two windows, strongly barred with iron, from which we could receive scarce any the least circulation of air ... Before nine o'clock every man's thirst grew intolerable, and respiration difficult. Efforts were made again to force the door, but in vain. Many insults were used to the guard to provoke them to fire in upon us.... By keeping my face between two of the bars, I obtained air enough to give my lungs easy play, though my perspiration was excessive and thirsts commencing. At this period, so strong a urinous volatile effluvia came from the prison, that I was not able to turn my head that way, for more than a few seconds at a time....

My friend Baillie ... and several others, for whom I had a real esteem and affection, had for some time been dead at my feet: and were now trampled by every corporal or common soldier, who, by help of more robust constitutions, had forced their way to the window, and held fast by the bars over me, till at last I become so pressed and wedged up, I was deprived of all motion....

My poor friend Mr Edward Eyre came staggering over the dead to me, and with his usual coolness and good nature, asked me how I did? but fell and expired before I had time to make a reply....

I was observed by one of my miserable companions on the right of me, in the expedient of allaying my thirst by sucking my shirt sleeve. He took the hint, and robbed me from time to time of a considerable part of my store.... This plunderer, Mr Lushington,... I found afterwards was one of the few who escaped from death, and since paid me the compliment of assuring me, he owed his life to the many comfortable draughts he had from my sleeves. Before I hit upon this happy expedient I had in an ungovernable fit of thirst, attempted drinking my urine; but it was so intensely bitter, there was no enduring a second taste, whereas no Bristol water could be more soft or pleasant than that what arose from perspiration....

The Black Hole story begins as a tale of British incompetence, cowardice and even cruelty. In the days leading up to its fall, in a desperate attempt to maintain order, the British defenders of Calcutta beheaded Indians daring to loot from damaged properties. But from the jaws of this defeat was snatched not only victory but effectively the beginnings of Britain's Indian Empire.

Britain was angered by the treatment of the prisoners in their confinement, and took pride in revenge on the Nawab which was in due course exacted. This came in the form of Robert Clive, another man who had risen in the ranks of the East India Company. Clive retook Calcutta in early 1757 and went on to defeat the Nawab and his French allies at Plassey later in the year. For the horrors of the Black Hole of Calcutta he was able to extract compensation many times over from the Nawab and the people of Bengal, while establishing British rule over the whole area.

Clive is undoubtedly one of the most extraordinary characters in the history of the Empire. As a young man he had tried to kill himself but, having failed to do that (a cock up on the firearm front), went on to become an outstanding soldier and administrator. In due course he was elected as a Member of Parliament, and later ennobled as Clive of

Plassey (although he is remembered even more grandly as Clive of India). Having spectacularly enriched himself when Governor of Bengal, he later returned to India to reform the administration and suppress corruption. This provoked a parliamentary inquiry into his own early career, an investigation which lasted six years, culminating with a just-about-successful clearing of his name in an all-night sitting of the House of Lords. An opium addict, he died, mentally disturbed, by his own hand in 1774. I am named after him.

But more than anything it is economics which accounts for Calcutta's growth. For it was the riches to be made from Bengal which sustained a city planted in such an unfavourable location. Or, as Geoffrey Moorhouse puts it in *Calcutta, A City Revealed:* 'On this bog the British created their capital in India. Nothing but commercial greed could possibly have led to such an idiotic decision.'

Rudyard Kipling, the poet laureate of the Indian Empire, had no kinder words for Calcutta either. He called it 'the City of Dreadful Night'. This verse is taken from his poem *A Tale of Two Cities:*

Once, two hundred years ago, the trader came
Meek and tame.
Where his timid foot first halted, there he stayed
Till mere trade
Grew to Empire, and he sent his armies forth
South and North,
Till the country from Peshawar to Ceylon
Was his own
Thus the midday halt of Charnock – more's the pity!
Grew a city.
As the fungus sprouts chaotic from its bead,
So it spread –
Chance-directed, chance-erected, laid and built
On the silt –
Palace, byre, hovel – poverty and pride –
Side by side;
And, above the packed and pestilential town,
Death looked down.

And all he was doing was comparing Calcutta to Simla. Mind you, Kipling was born in Bombay, and there is no love lost between the various cities of India, so he may have been prejudiced.

Yet precious little love of Calcutta has ever been recorded. As early as 1779 William Macintosh described it as: 'An undistinguished mass of filth and corruption equally offensive to human sense and health ...' In 1863,

Sir George Trevelyan said that it united 'every condition of a perfectly unhealthy situation ... The place is so bad by nature that human efforts could do little to make it worse; but that little has been done faithfully and assiduously.'

However, as Geoffrey Moorhouse notes, William Hunter, a new recruit to the Indian Civil Service, did once write: 'Imagine everything that is glorious in nature combined with all that is beautiful in architecture, and you can faintly picture to yourself what Calcutta is.' But he had just arrived from Peckham.

The twentieth century has dealt Calcutta further blows. Its Bengali population prospered under the British Raj but with that prosperity went strong intellectual development and political awareness. This posed a threat to British rule which could only partially be contained by the fostering of divisions between West and East Bengal, and Hindu and Muslim Bengalis.

To avoid the immediate threat of Bengali activism, the British capital of India was moved from Calcutta to Delhi in 1912. And when independence finally came to the subcontinent in 1947, East Bengal was detached from India to form East Pakistan. The division of Bengal along religious lines separated Calcutta's jute factories from the jute-growing areas of East Bengal and the turmoil forced thousands of families on to the streets and slums of Calcutta to try to scratch a life. They were followed in 1971 by further waves of refugees from the fighting associated with East Pakistan breaking away from West Pakistan to become Bangladesh. Thereafter, economic migrants have arrived in Calcutta from Bihar, India's poorest state, and elsewhere to seek their fortune in the big city.

So, nowadays Calcutta is famous for its slums. Oh, and Mother Teresa who is famous for working in Calcutta's slums. Other cities around the world have poverty and destitution to cope with, but they are generally famous for other things as well. Poor old Calcutta has only its deprivation and the slightly controversial figure of its benefactress. Before I set off to film in Calcutta, the first question asked by everybody I mentioned it to was 'Are you going to meet Mother Teresa?' It's as if London were known abroad only for the Child Poverty Action Group.

And, lo and behold, on the aeroplane to Calcutta I found myself sitting next to Mother Teresa. Well, not quite. But a small, demure Indian lady was my companion for the flight via Delhi. We had passed over most of the countries of the European Union before we started talking. But by about Eastern Turkey we were exchanging personal details. Her son (who was also on the plane) was a barrister appearing in a high-profile case reported in that day's papers. In due course I discovered the son's professional address in England was in a set of chambers in Lincoln's Inn where I had once done a pupillage.

With this reminder of the close links between Britain and India, and the words 'it's a small world' ready to form on our lips, we found we were just the length of an in-flight movie, plus an in-flight meal, from entering Indian air space.

Here I found a more Indian approach to life. My Indian neighbour stuck firmly to the vegetarian option, and insisted on taking away in a bag any food she could not manage to eat. 'It is such a waste,' she sighed, gazing around at our fellow passengers picking at their food, and politely not noticing the scraps of dinner I was leaving on the side of my plastic plate.

But, as I say, nowadays India is just a few hours from London Heathrow. On a good day, somewhere as exotic as Calcutta takes no longer to get to than Inverness or Penzance might on a bad day. We tried to capture on film the confusion of emerging into the reality of Calcutta from the some-what unreal world of an airline flight. But, in truth, Calcutta does not hit you until you get away from the airport and into the city.

Calcutta has a pleasant and recently redeveloped airport. The only thing really disconcerting about it is its name, Dum Dum – as in the nasty bullets which were developed at the nearby munitions factory. The calm of the airport gives it a distinctly provincial air, clean and tidy but sur-prisingly quiet considering the city's size.

Not far down the road from the airport you soon get an idea of what Calcutta is really like, which is choked. It is choked with traffic, choked with people, choked with pollution. Choked with poverty.

• Shocking City •

It is difficult to convey quite how overcrowded and shabby are Calcutta's streets. If you start to explain to people in Britain that there are people living on the streets in Calcutta, inevitably they picture the homeless people you can stumble across in the Strand, or the cardboard city at Waterloo. 'Everywhere has these problems,' they mumble. 'London and New York are like Third World cities now.' Well, it is a disgrace that there is destitution on the streets of rich cities of the West, but the Third World they are not.

Calcutta is what the Third World is really like. The homeless here are not a few hundred teenage runaways and other unfortunates left to lack of care in the community. The homeless in Calcutta are numbered in tens of thousands – millions, if you include those who live in the worst of the slums. And what you first see, on your first day, are whole families living on pavements; cooking on roadsides, washing at stand-pipes and doing everything else in the gutters. Mile after mile of what are in effect urban campsites, where all the rituals of rural villages are performed on a few square yards of inner city pavement. Here and there are pigs, goats, sheep and even horses. Sacred cows roam free in all except the very centre of town. Stand-pipes gush water at regular intervals where, inches away from the passing traffic, people wash away the dirt and grime of the day. Bathing in so public a place is done with all the delicacy of a 1950s holiday-maker on the beach. Always a loin cloth or a pair of shorts to preserve the dignity of men and boys; women generally washing only under cover of darkness.

The children play in the gutter, or in the mess of a thousand not-quite-finished road repairs, often inches away from the rush of traffic or the stride of those on their way to work. The children are astonishingly well behaved. Perhaps the disobedient ones do not survive the dangers long enough to be a nuisance. But, having little, they seem to demand less. Not for them temper tantrums if the yoghurt with the right Disney character on the pot is not available for tea. With no nappies, the children empty their bowels wherever they happen to be. There is nowhere else for them to go, nor is there for the grown-ups.

The pissing and shitting are decorously ignored by more prosperous passers-by and fellow street-dwellers alike. Rather like a crowded train where each person manages to arrange himself to avoid too intimate a contact with his neighbour, so here no one looks on as others go about their business.

The foxes have holes, and the birds of the air have nests; but the son of man hath not anywhere to lay his head. And in Calcutta he hath scarcely any air to breathe either. The roads are clogged with fleets of India's old-fashioned-style cars and polluting lorries, plus fumes from the many stoves set up to cook at the side of the road. And, as if they were worried that the air might not be quite polluted enough (Calcutta has lost a lot of smokestack industries in recent years), every morning litter is swept into piles which are set alight everywhere. Bonfires to the great god Smog.

• Don't Mention the Empire •

My first stop in Calcutta was the Fairlawn Hotel, a famous piece of British eccentricity. In Suddar Street, right in the middle of one of Calcutta's busiest districts, the Fairlawn is an island of something approaching calm. There is a tree-shaded terrace where you can drink tea, coffee or beer. There is an airy dining room where set meals are served at set times of day. Travellers from all round the world seem to make their way here, but the cuisine is not exactly international. It is not very Indian, either. For example, for lunch on a steaming hot day we had a fish and chips starter, followed by Irish stew – mutton and dumplings in what tasted like mushroom soup – topped up by rice pudding with a blob of jam in it. This may well be redolent of life in the Raj, but it certainly recaptures the authentic flavour of Blighty in the 1950s.

The hotel is owned and run by a Mr and Mrs Smith. Mr Smith is British but a long-term resident of Calcutta, retired from a career in the army and other jobs. He is quietly spoken and seems to take a back seat in the organization of the hotel. Mrs Smith is much more upfront and warmed to the task of being filmed as I checked into the hotel. The hotel has been in her family for several generations.

She pointed out that Patrick Swayze was filmed there in *City of Joy* and told me of the various other celebrities who have stayed over the years. These may have included Her Majesty the Queen and the Duke of Edinburgh, or it may just be that their portraits were on the wall.

In our film, the booking-in sequence introduced us to the physical layout of the hotel, Mr Smith relaxing on their private balcony, their pet poodle and the souvenirs of decades in the hotel trade. Actually, although everyone says the place is rather eccentric – an overseas branch of Fawlty Towers – it seemed to be doing good business. Mrs Smith did manage to forget to bring the key when showing me to my room, but you cannot have everything. (The rooms are adequate rather than luxurious. If you have stayed in one of the poorer Oxbridge colleges you would feel perfectly at home.)

In conversation Mr and Mrs Smith are, as you might expect, nostalgic for the lost days of Calcutta's high life, when there were parties and balls at every turn, and they were young. They hinted at the problems of running a hotel within the rules and regulations of the city as it now is, but were careful not to criticize anything or anyone too strongly. Lashing out at red tape can sometimes entangle you in greater knots.

However, my visit to the Fairlawn was not entirely to wallow in a corner of a foreign field which is forever England. It was a convenient base from which to explore the city centre.

• Unfair Lawns •

Just off the busy city streets are the busy city slums. *Bustees*, they are called in Calcutta: houses, huts and hovels linked by alleys and lanes which serve as farmyards for animals and playgrounds for children.

This is the stereotypical image of Calcutta familiar to anyone who has read a book, skimmed through a magazine article or watched a documentary about the city. Nevertheless, it is the reality for over five million people. Some estimates claim that half the population lives in *bustees*.

Bustees vary enormously. Some are almost – *almost* – pleasant rows of brick-built structures. Overcrowded but supplied with electricity and more or less convenient access to running water. Perhaps only the over-privileged Western visitor would call them slums at all. At the other end of the scale there are ticky-tacky shanty houses propped up along muddy alleyways. You assume the inhabitants of these desperate structures are dying to get out, but others are queuing to get in. On the side of the busiest roads are families who have yet to find a place in the slum and are having to make do with a stretch of pavement.

I was filmed walking along just such a section of road. What had once been a wide pavement and perhaps a grassy verge had long since been taken over by the homeless. The ground around the homes of the home-less was covered in a dark grey silt made of ashes from cooking fires, engine oil and dust. As I strolled past a family group, a small pig they were holding keeled over and died. I could not work out whether this was a sickly piglet they had been attempting to revive with veterinary care, or a beast raised for the pot achieving its destiny.

Either way, had I happened upon an event like this in a rural area I suppose it would have seemed a charming example of the simple life: man involved with life and death in the raw. A few feet from passing urban traffic, it is merely grim.

In the nature of filming, I had to walk up and down a few times before the director was content with the shot of me striding past the squalor. By my third pass, a fire was alight and the piglet was being cooked or at any rate having the hair singed off its back. It was no death for a piglet. It is no life for people.

Back at the Fairlawn, over a beer, I chatted to Sanjay, a more prosper-ous resident of the city. I wondered how he coped with life in Calcutta when he was driving past, if not walking past, scenes like this every day.

Sanjay cheerily accepted that conditions in Calcutta are a total sham-bles. The city, he said, obviously comes as a shock to the visitor from Europe, but so it is to anyone coming from Bombay, Delhi or Madras. But he claimed that things are much better than they were ten or fifteen years ago. Then there had been power cuts every day, the telephones did not work and labour disputes had driven factories and whole industries out of the city. The economy was now in better shape and services were much more efficient. Even the slums were now being improved with electricity and water supplies.

But that still left the thousands living on the streets. Sanjay airily sug-gested that living in the street is not such a bad thing in a hot city like Calcutta as it would be (or as it is) in a cold place like London. Mind you, he has not tried it himself.

More convincing was his description of Calcutta as a safe city. I had already noticed this. Rich tourists and comfortable members of the middle class stride past the desperately poor with no fear of attack. There is little or no prospect, so it would appear, of mugging, let alone violent revolution. Sanjay put this down to a karmic approach, a Hindu acceptance of what fate happens to offer. Faith is put in anticipation for better times in the next life. Perhaps that accounts for the placid atmosphere in the face of adversity. Of course, it may also account for some of the adversity in the first place.

• In the Club •

Some have to wait for the next life; for others there is already the high life, which is where I headed next. In the days of the Raj, Calcutta was famous for its clubs and some have survived. The Tollygunge is not the snootiest but in some ways it is the most typical. These Indian clubs used to exclude Indians, but now they are open to all, of the right sort.

The Tollygunge occupies a vast area in the south of the city. Well, they have lost some of their grounds recently with the building of the new underground railway, so they only have about 100 acres now, but there is still room for a golf course, horse-riding ground, two swimming pools, tennis courts and a view of grass and trees as far, more or less, as the eye can see. And as far as the untutored eye can see it resembles a piece of English parkland, which I suppose was always the intention.

You do not have to be British to run the place, but it helps. The man in charge is Bob Wright, who if he were not here would have to be in a Somerset Maugham short story or a Merchant Ivory film. He has a couple of faithful golden retrievers which he chatted to between barking orders at the staff and taking me on a tour of the club.

He has to keep a close eye on things, he told me, because nobody does any work when he is not looking. Nothing gets done when he is away on leave. He keeps in touch with England through the *Daily Telegraph* – 'frightfully right wing, of course' – and the steady stream of visitors who make this their home from home. Calcutta, he thinks, is much worse than it used to be, more crowded and much dirtier. They used to keep the streets clean and pick up the garbage, but that was before everyone was overwhelmed by the increase in population. I asked if the people living on the street troubled him at all.

'Well, the thing is,' he said, '50 per cent of the population are not Calcuttans, they're not Bengalis. They come from the adjoining states of Bihar, Orissa and UP to work here. They've heard the streets of Calcutta are paved with gold, they come here …'

'And they find the streets are paved with themselves. I suppose you get used to it?' I asked.

'One has to harden oneself. One has to harden oneself.'

The day of our visit was a special one in the history of the club: its 100th anniversary. The club house is even older. It was built in 1781 by a Scots family, the Johnsons, who grew indigo on the 400-acre estate until they all died of cholera. They are buried under the trees beside what is now the golf course.

The club is named after a Colonel Tolly who owned the right from the East India Company to charge a levy on the boats going up the small river which runs through the property. But one hundred years ago, the British being what they are, they turned the house into a club. Surrounded by a lot of foreigners they had a place where they could club together.

During daylight hours there were to be a number of special events, including a none-too-serious pageant recounting the history of a volunteer regiment nicknamed the Bengal Boxwallahs, followed by a display of tent-pegging. For those who do not know, which until then included me, tent-pegging consists of riding straight at a peg in the ground and skewering it on the end of your lance. A sort of vegetarian pig-sticking. I did not participate beyond taking tea and biscuits with the small crowd of onlookers lending their support.

In the evening was the Centenary Ball. Men in formal black tie, women in beautiful saris, me in an ill-fitting white shirt which had suffered collar damage on the journey from England. Although we were in India and most of the guests at the ball were Indian, it was all very British. It even started to rain just as night was falling. Indians who are more British than the British are or were, were once derided as being brown sahibs but I am not sure the world would be a better place if all the sahibs were white.

Documentaries are almost duty bound to poke fun at this sort of thing but it all seemed quite agreeable – perhaps I was just helping myself too liberally to the chota pegs (the ball was sponsored by Seagrams) as I waited for the cameras to be ready to film. It struck me these might be the best days of the Tollygunge. How frightful a joint it must have been when it was for the ruling race only; how miserable when independence came and an era looked as if it was over. But now Europeans and Asians can meet on equal terms inside this sort of institution, and its Britishness, although quaint, is just another element in a whole clutch of traditions and influences absorbed over the centuries into the Indian subcontinent.

In this benign mood I even entered into small talk with perfect strangers. Well, not so strange as it turned out. I was approached by a distinguished-looking gentleman, Brigadier Chopra who, I discovered, had been the first Indian to be President of the Tollygunge. I have no military experience but I reckoned I should ask which regiment he had served with. 'The 4th Gurkha Rifles,' he replied.

What a stroke of luck. The 4th Gurkha Rifles is the one military unit in the world with which I can claim any connection. I wondered if he happened to have heard of my late father-in-law, Brigadier F.E.C. Hughes ...

'Ted, do you mean? Of course, I do. We used to see him every time we went to England.' And it turns out they were the greatest of friends.

Such are the echoes of Empire that, thousands of miles from home, practically the first person I speak to in Calcutta who has not been pre-selected by television research is an old friend of my father-in-law. I was just trying to remember the logic behind John Guare's play *Six Degrees of Separation* (it is the idea that anyone in the world can be connected to anyone else by six steps) when I found myself in the company of a young lady in a sari. She wanted to say hello because she has a cousin who lives in England, and she knows that I am her cousin's son's godfather. This was getting ridiculous. I had to get on with discovering how exotic Calcutta is.

Apart from showing the members of the Tollygunge at play (good food and drink, rather less good music and dancing), my task was to take to task the rich, well-bred and successful and ask how they can enjoy themselves with so many of their fellow citizens enduring such hardship so close by.

Of course, it is an unfair question. The poor are always with us, whether they live at the end of our road or at the other end of the Earth. It is not obviously better to enjoy your wealth with the poor always in your sight or always put out of your mind. I was also coming to realize that it does not take a lifetime to get used to seeing roadsides crowded with the homeless and impoverished. In just a few days in Calcutta, it was already seeming absolutely normal.

Yet virtually everyone I spoke to seemed to be involved in good works of some sort. Even the Tollygunge Club itself, with its acres of golf course in a city of pavement-dwellers, does charitable work among Anglo-Indians and others. Bob Wright's wife is a campaigner on behalf of the endangered Bengal tigers; at the ball I chatted to Nina Karluka, a famous Calcuttan beauty and socialite. She has cast off most of the high-life ways of her earlier years to run and work in a trust for destitute and orphaned children.

My other tasks at the ball were to meet two women, Moon Moon Sen and Sudeshna Roy. Moon Moon Sen is a glamorous film actress. Her mother was a huge star who discouraged Moon Moon from going into show business. However, unusually for an Indian actress, she took to making films after getting married and having children.

So that I could look at the Calcuttan film and television industry, Moon Moon was supposed to suggest that I act in a Bengali TV programme which was always desperate for British-looking performers. This was something of a staged sequence but reflected the fact that both the researcher and the director of my documentary had been pressed into action in just that way when they had been investigating what we should cover in our film. Moon Moon played her part well and teased her many admirers at the ball by waltzing off on to the dance floor with me, camera crew in tow.

Sudeshna Roy, my other date for the evening, was to be a central figure in the documentary and the all-purpose guide to my stay in Calcutta. At the ball she modestly introduced herself as a journalist who could speak Bengali and could get by in Hindi. In fact, she is a great expert on all things Calcuttan. She is not too bad in English, either.

• Queen Victoria and King Rat •

I arranged to meet Sudeshna the next morning at Rat Park, but before that we thought we would round off our section on the Raj and the British in India with a look at the Queen Victoria Memorial.

So far, I have given the impression that Calcutta is a dreadfully run-down place, choked with traffic and people sleeping rough and, if so, that is because that is the impression one gets for most of the time one is there. But it does have a whole range of attractive buildings. It is even occasionally known as the city of palaces. It has a huge central park, the Maidan, centred around Fort William. The fort was rebuilt by the British at vast expense in 1781 to ward off any further attack and prevent any more Black Holes. To give the fort's cannons a clear line of fire, the ground was cleared all around it, which accounts for the Maidan's existence today in an otherwise overcrowded city. At the southern end of the Maidan is the Victoria Memorial. This is a huge museum built in white marble in a mixture of European and Mogul styles – the Taj Mahal meets Greenwich Naval College. It was built between 1906 and 1921 with money voluntarily given by the princes and people of India. The whole thing sounds as though it ought to be ghastly, a memorial to the fag end of Empire, but actually it is rather beautiful and impressive.

Inside there is a collection of paintings at present under restoration, but we were not permitted to film the interior. Indeed, we were not really supposed to film the exterior either. The memorial is surrounded by signs prohibiting every activity you can think of, from walking on the grass to bathing in the ponds and taking pictures of the building. Perhaps these signs are Victoria's true memorial.

Queen Victoria is present herself as a large statue set up in front of the memorial building. The Queen Empress never managed to visit her Indian Empire, and she does not look that happy to be here in monumental form either, but perhaps that was just the permanent set of her face. She gazes out at the largest area of green – or, out of the monsoon season, the largest area of dusty brown – very much still the monarch of all she surveys. Although chiefly what she surveys now are courting couples using the park as a place to meet and giggle and amuse each other.

Victoria, we decided, looked magnificent but was pretty irrelevant to the modern city, so off I went to find Sudeshna who was feeding the rats. At Rat Corner, rats come out of their burrows to be fed. This is in the centre of the city and these are ordinary rats (*Rattus norvegicus*, the brown rat, I would say, rather than *Rattus rattus*, the black rat – at last my Alevel in Zoology has come in useful), the rats which around the world are pursued and attacked by all mankind. The rats which throughout history have been blamed for spreading the Black Death, bubonic plague, Weil's disease and all manner of other ailments. The rats which have ruined crops, spoiled food stores, attacked babies in their cots. The rats nobody loves, but here you can buy some nuts and feed them. Now, I know it makes no real sense to feed the pigeons in Trafalgar Square, but rats which must have quite enough food to get on with in the rubbish dumps and sewers of Calcutta, surely nobody wants to encourage them?

Well, Sudeshna laughed, here in Calcutta they welcome everything and everybody. Even visiting British documentary-makers, and rats.

Let's Have Another Cup of Coffee, Let's Have Another Piece of Your Mind

Sudeshna then launched me on a whistle-stop tour of some of the delights of the city. We started in the College Street area. Bengalis, with some justification, like to think of Calcutta as the intellectual heart of India, and College Street is the intellectual heart of Calcutta. Sudeshna and I walked up and down the street lined with bookshops and bookstalls. Textbooks seem to predominate; the student who is reading for civil service or academic examinations has a huge range of new and second-hand guides and instruction manuals to choose from.

We were not actually buying. We were on our way to a vast coffee house which goes by the name of the India Coffee Workers' Co-operative Society Ltd, once known as the Albert Hall. This is a magnificently decayed building. At the street door you pass a 'roadside Ronson' – a burning piece of rope put there for smokers to light their cigarettes. The walls of the staircase are covered in posters advertising events of interest to students, intellectuals and pleasure-seekers. The first floor is a cavernous room with a 40-foot-high ceiling, once a political hall, now given over to a vast café/restaurant/meeting room. It has green limed walls which might have been redecorated at the time of independence, but certainly not since. At each of the hundred or so tables a group of people – mostly, if not quite exclusively, men – sit over their coffee engaged in voluble conversation. Above them whirl precariously suspended fans which stir the heavy atmosphere like giant teaspoons.

A spirited conversation, political discussion or dispute in Calcutta is known as an *adda*, very much a Bengali tradition. Sudeshna had arranged to meet three or four friends of hers used to arguing at length about the issues of the day. Since I was a newcomer to the city I decided to mention Calcutta's best-known aid worker, Mother Teresa.

Not long before my trip to Calcutta, Mother Teresa had been savaged in a Channel 4 TV programme presented by Christopher Hitchens (since followed up with magazine articles and a whole book). This had subjected her saint-like reputation to rigorous and highly critical analysis. Apart from suggesting that Mother Teresa had only become famous because Malcolm Muggeridge on another television programme years ago had mistaken some filming technicality for a glow of godliness – hailing an improved type of film as a modern miracle – the Hitchens' film had denounced her as the friend of right-wing politicians who provided limited benefit to those she purported to help. In particular, it had been suggested that she had not spent the millions she had raised wisely: that her homes for the destitute were places in which the sick were cared for while they died, rather than true hospitals where they could be treated properly. She was also condemned for opposing abortion and contraception which, since she is evidently inspired by her Roman Catholic faith, seemed to be an odd charge levelled against her.

Against that, she has devoted her life to caring for the destitute and dying of Calcutta, and was awarded the Nobel Peace Prize in 1979. (This must have something to do with Calcutta: India has won four Nobel Prizes – the others were for medicine, physics and literature – and all the recipients lived or worked in Calcutta.)

The participants in our televised *adda* were happy to accept that Mother Teresa was doing good in her own way but were annoyed that Western media attention always focuses on her when they look at Calcutta. She may or may not have the best approach to assisting the destitute, but there are plenty of other people and institutions who are doing good work as well – local people, not outsiders like Mother Teresa (she comes originally from Yugoslavia, although she has been an Indian citizen since 1948), who put their efforts into providing education and foundations for the future.

So off Sudeshna and I went to look at some of these other projects.

We were not going to make the mistake of looking at the already over-exposed figure of Mother Teresa: a tribute to our imagination and originality. And pragmatism: my director had already contacted Mother Teresa and, perhaps not surprisingly, she felt she did not want to appear on another television programme, just for the moment, thank you very much. (Saying that I appear regularly on Channel 4 was probably a mistake.)

• Street Life 1 •

Early in the morning, Sudeshna took me to Maidan Street, just over the road from the newspaper office where she works when not shepherding me around the city. Here, on a section of pavement, a group of fifty or so young children ranging in age from about five to ten were being taught by an animated young teacher. During his ordinary working day he teaches dance, but in the early morning he is one of the many volunteers to be found on pavements around and about Calcutta giving a primary education to the children who would otherwise get nothing.

Classes have to take place in the early morning, because for the rest of the day these young children have to earn their way in the world. Small children rummage through waste dumps to find articles of some small value, and they do menial jobs to earn vital rupees to keep themselves and their families from starving.

In the class, the children were learning songs. One was in English: 'Jack and Jill', taught to give a very basic grounding in the language of government and commerce. Another was in Bengali. This was a song about the importance of girl children, the mothers of the future, how they should not have to pay a dowry to get married and should be educated along with the boys.

I had a number of points I wanted to raise with the teacher. He assured me that although attendance at the classes was entirely voluntary, there was no shortage of volunteers. He also told me that it was not just the presence of our camera which made the children behave so well, attending to his every word with a minimum of fooling around by the mischievous ones at the back, near the lamp posts. He also claimed that nobody complained about liberal notions such as female emancipation being introduced along with literacy and sums.

As the class proceeded, one or two parents turned up to watch – the concerned ones who took part in the organization of this sort of effort to improve the prospects for the next generation. They had brought smaller children and babies along to watch. Little kids born to a life on the street whose best hope was a kerb-side classroom in which they could learn English nursery rhymes and the rudiments of their own language.

I wanted it all to succeed because the teacher had infectious enthusiasm, but I still had my doubts. Surely this was just scratching the surface? Sudeshna remained enthusiastic: it is only a drop in the ocean, but a lot of drops make up an ocean.

One girl, an eight-year-old perhaps, was clearly the star pupil. She knew all the songs, knew all the answers to the questions. She had the confidence to develop an understanding of the world. So what would happen to her? Well, there would be a way of finding a proper schooling for the brightest children. A place in a charity school could be found and if she was in a position to take it up she might get somewhere from this start in life, literally in the gutter. I hope so. But for the others?

As the class was coming to an end and the pupils had to go back to their garbage-sorting and car-washing businesses, other children who had had the good sense to be born to wealthier parents were going past, pulled along in rickshaws.

• Street Life 2 •

Rickshaws. I have managed to come this far without mentioning rickshaws. They are only to be found in the centre of the city, and their numbers are supposed to be in decline, but they remain a distinctive feature of the Calcuttan street scene. The authorities have been trying to get rid of them for years. In 1981 an amendment to the 1919 Hackney Carriage Act was going to put them off the road, but somehow they survive. So Calcutta is the only city in the world where, to get around, you can climb into a giant wheelbarrow and pay some poor blighter to pull you along to save you the trouble of walking, while you sit back and contemplate the world as it passes by and also the notion of using a fellow human as a draught animal.

The rickshaw wallahs vary in condition from young and thin to old and skinny. Their work involves a bodybuilder's level of exertion without the bodybuilder's intake of protein. And since they trot around streets choked with traffic and traffic fumes, they are permanently involved in aerobic exercise without any air.

Officially, there are 6000 authorized rickshaws although many more are not. The wallah does not own the rickshaw himself but rents it from an owner or middle-man. (The sums of money involved are very small.) I was told rickshaws come into their own during the monsoon when the streets often flood. So to the delights of pulling a cart around is added the joy of wading through water backing up from blocked drains.

The rickshaw wallahs, the owners and those who use them all oppose the abolition of this mode of transport on the grounds that the rickshaw wallahs would starve without this work. This is plausible enough, although the same argument could have been made about boys who were sent up the chimneys in Victorian Britain.

Anyway, I resisted the temptation to be filmed riding around grinning from the back of a rickshaw, but instead we found a rickshaw-puller prepared to talk about his trade. He was from Bihar, a thoughtful-looking Muslim man with a grey beard. You could mistake him for a university professor if he was not standing in the shaft of a one-man-operated cart.

Through Sudeshna's translation he told me he had been pulling. rickshaws for thirty-five years. It is harder nowadays because of the crowded state of the roads. And, he added, he sweats a lot in the summer. He says he prefers the rickshaw to the bicycle-rickshaw (which has replaced it elsewhere) because the cycle-rickshaw is harder work. In the cycle-rickshaw it's the chest which gets hurt instead of the arms.

I asked if he was happy being a rickshaw driver. He said because there are no jobs he has to do it – at least it gives him a living, but he's not very happy about doing it. He does not like one brother pulling the other. He thinks it is something to be ashamed of but there's no alternative. However, he thinks the government has no interest in keeping rickshaws. He noted wryly that they have already removed the cows and buffaloes from the centre of the city and implied the rickshaw wallahs were to be treated no better. He feels that it is primarily because they are migrant labourers.

I am not sure I quite agree with him on that last point. I think it is because they are all migrant labourers that Calcuttans have tolerated this demeaning work being done for so long. Time and again, Calcuttans dismiss serious social problems as affecting only those who are new to the city. Since something like 50 per cent of the residents of Calcutta are not Bengali, there are a lot of social problems not to get worried about.

• Temple Fortune •

Sudeshna said I could not come to Calcutta without visiting the famous Kalighat Temple. As it happened, our driver, Saroj, goes there regularly (twice a week) to worship or perform *puja*, as it is called.

Hinduism is the oldest of the world's great religions. It has a bewildering array of gods, goddesses, texts and precepts which make its understanding difficult to achieve for someone born outside that tradition. I am not sure I even came close during my visit to the Kalighat Temple.

Hinduism varies from place to place and there is no founder and no central authority like a Pope to lay down canon law, so many and various are the aspects of Hinduism to be found in different parts of India. In Calcutta especially, a cocktail of influences has given a strong local flavour to the form of Hinduism practised.

The Aryan people brought Hinduism to India in the sixteenth century BC but did not get to Bengal until the fourth century AD. (The roads must have been bad even then.) But the main Hindu cult followed in Calcutta is Shaktism, which has apparently absorbed elements of the mother goddess beliefs which existed in India before the arrival of the Aryans. Followers of this cult worship Shaktis, wives of the male gods.

Kali is a form of the goddess Durga, the consort of the Lord Shiva. (She is also known as Parviti.) She is an exciting-looking creature. She has four arms, wears a necklace of skulls, and is the symbol of female energy, destruction, creation and preservation, generally shown smeared with the blood of Raktaviya, a demon she was obliged to kill with her sword. Traditionally, she is pictured standing on her husband, Shiva, who threw himself at her feet to wake her from a trance. She is sticking out her tongue to show the shame she felt when woken up in this way from a dance which threatened the whole world. (This is the story in outline.)

The Kalighat Temple is supposed to be built on the site where the little toe of Kali's right foot (or it could be her finger) fell when Vishnu (the god of preservation) sliced her in pieces to bring Shiva to his senses after he fell into a rage following Kali's death.

A market has flourished in the Kalighat area to serve the pilgrims, worshippers and tourists who crowd the place. There were plenty crowding the area on the day Sudeshna and Saroj took me there. We had to queue up to make our obeisance to the goddess. First, we had to remove our shoes and socks. Saroj felt confident in suggesting we left our shoes at a little stall and we shuffled off on the damp and muddy pavement. I wondered if there is a deity called Verruca.

At one end of the temple area was a small enclosure where a couple of goats were tethered. As we were paddling by, after a few words were said over it, one of the goats was held down and its head was chopped off. It was dragged, bleeding from the neck, just past me.

Pure ignorance, of course, but I had no idea that Hindus went in for meat, let alone animal sacrifice. But animal sacrifice, I came to understand, is somewhat of a local indelicacy. Time was when they slaughtered buffaloes here as well. But nowadays you come to Kali with a wish or a prayer (to get pregnant, find a wife, come through an illness, that kind of thing) and you offer the goat in payment. Afterwards you can eat some of the goat. Goats, if cooked without garlic, onion or ginger, are regarded as vegetarian meat: honorary vegetables, if you like. Tough luck on the goat, but a convenient fiction for the hungry worshipper.

As we approached the shrine we were kept in line by Brahmins and I think I was sold a garland of flowers. (To tell the truth, it all got a bit confusing.) Eventually you get chivvied up the steps to the altar of the goddess where there is a tremendous press of people pushing themselves forward to make offerings. Such was the shouting and shoving, it felt more like fans at a football match or a pop concert than a place of spiritual worship. While I was trying to work out what to do next, the Brahmin attendants demanded a monetary contribution. I had been warned they would seek huge sums from someone so obviously a tourist and parted with something like one-tenth of what had been demanded, which seemed fair enough, especially as I had a camera waiting for me outside, but Saroj still berated me afterwards for letting myself get ripped off. But I emerged from the other side of the temple, my forehead decorated with a blob of vermilion dye to indicate I had performed *puja*. It was all quite strong stuff for me; I was brought up as a Presbyterian. They will have me whistling on the Sabbath next.

Sudeshna tried to explain some of the tenets of belief of the Hindu faith to me as we sat drinking tea from a pavement stall. There is a lot to understand. Each god and goddess seems to come in a variety of forms and is known by a variety of names. They seem like a very lively bunch with heroic and human qualities and failings. I put Hinduism on my list of things I really must read more about.

Sudeshna assured me that the caste system no longer means much in the cities. Only in rural villages would much importance be placed on your caste when it came to marry. 'Untouchables' have been abolished by law, replaced by the more politically correct 'scheduled class'. I thought that jobs were reserved for members of the scheduled class, but Sudeshna cut short discussion about such matters by pointing out that if untouchability had not been abolished, she would not be able to sit and talk to me as she is married to a Brahmin, the highest, priestly class.

• Street Life 3 •

After that spiritual interlude at the temple, it was back to matters temporal just along the road. To show another example of social work being carried out for the people on the streets, Sudeshna took me to see some work being done among prostitutes.

There is a red-light district in an old, busy part of the city just by the Kalighat Temple. Red-light is perhaps not quite the term – it is a couple of streets of intensely occupied houses where the prostitutes live with their children and their men, usually immigrant workers who have a wife and family in their home village and might live with a prostitute on a temporary or occasional basis while they are in Calcutta.

The girls stand on a bridge or hang around the entrance to their street, offering themselves for hire. By Western standards they are not provocatively dressed. All are fully covered in saris but it is obvious to passers-by what they are there for.

There is a great deal of stigma attached to growing up in this area. Boys find it difficult to get jobs if anyone discovers where they come from and girls are often sucked into the trade themselves. To avoid that happening to their own children, prostitutes are in the habit of buying young girls from elsewhere so they do not have to force their own daughters to take up prostitution to keep them in their old age.

We filmed in the area in the afternoon, as business was beginning for the day. Ashamed as they are of their station in life, the prostitutes covered their faces if there was any chance of being caught on camera.

Actually, we had a more constructive intention than showing women walking the streets; we were there to film another social programme in action. Sudeshna took me down one of the rows of houses to a sort of community hall by the side of a muddy creek. The water in the creek looked filthy from the mess of city rubbish tipped into it, but even so it was being used by a couple of hardy souls as somewhere in which to bathe. On the creek bank a few pigs rooted through the rubbish and a dog pulled lackadaisically at the body of a dead lamb.

But in the hall, things were more hygienic. A dozen prostitutes, dressed in special issue green jackets, were to be taught the dangers of HIV and other infections associated with their profession. Actually, they were not referred to as 'prostitutes' but as 'sex workers'. This is considered a more politically correct, less judgmental term, although it does take any romance out of it. A sex worker sounds like somebody sitting down to work at a lathe.

The object of the programme is not to persuade the women to give up their trade. Nobody imagines that sort of campaign would work. The idea is to introduce the use of condoms and other healthier practices to cut down the spread of infection. In general, to turn them into safe sex workers. This is done with flip charts and detailed diagrams. The further idea is that, thus educated, they will spread the message among their peers.

Hopefully it will do some good in restricting the spread of Aids but it was a very unglamorous glimpse of the world of prostitution. I made the point that it is tough to be a woman in Calcutta. Sudeshna thinks it is tough to be a woman anywhere.

• They Want to Put Me in the Movies •

The next day was definitely more glamorous as it was time for me to make my acting debut in Bengali.

Bombay is famous for its movie industry. Its prodigious output of all-singing, all-dancing, all-action movies means that its film industry is wittily and endlessly referred to as 'Bollywood'. But India is a large country with many languages and there is a market for Bengali films and television, production of which is focused on Calcutta.

The idea of my making a cameo appearance in a Bengali TV production had spun somewhat out of control. We arrived before lunch at the studios to discover the filming of *Des Ray* in action. *Des Ray* is, I discovered, a highly popular comedy programme featuring a team of two comedians called Robi Ghosh and Tapas Pal. It is a soap opera except it is played for laughs; a situation comedy except there is no studio audience. I was happy to play a British businessman, except I had not seen a script. The director of *Des Ray* assured me there was plenty of time for that, as we would not be starting my scenes until after lunch. He asked me to excuse him while he went into the studio to film other bits of the programme.

We sat in the grounds of the studios, which consist of a series of buildings and warehouses – film studios rather than a television centre. Moon Moon Sen had not yet arrived and I seemed about to be humiliated in front of two sets of cameras.

The ubiquitous crows flew overhead and mocked me with their inharmonious cries. It was a standing joke that every day a crow would manage to target my shirt with a large dropping, but at least that did not happen in the grounds of the film studio. Instead, one of them dropped a dead rat at my feet. Was this a good sign?

Moon Moon turned up in a flurry of activity. The various people who were hanging around the grounds perked up at the arrival of a star. (The studios were an island of relative calm but nowhere in Calcutta is empty of people.)

When it arrived, the script was a document, hand-written in Bengali, which I was supposed to learn before the shooting. Once I had it explained to me (Sudeshna took on yet another role as an assistant director), I understood the story as a fairly standard sitcom plot which had been hastily adjusted to accommodate Moon Moon and me. We were to play husband and wife and the episode was to start with a fairly raunchy bed scene (well, as raunchy as Terry and June would have had). As we are about to rekindle the fire in our marriage we are interrupted by some travelling salesmen: the two comedy stars playing an old uncle and his nephew. They are desperately trying to shift some useless products and fearful of losing their jobs.

By the end of the programme it turns out that I am the generally incompetent and annoying British businessman who has taken over their company. I am supposed to be someone relatively new to the country who speaks in a mixture of Bengali and English. (Mostly English, as I interpreted the part.)

The final scene involved me saying nothing at all, and this was the first thing to be shot. (Some things are the same the whole world over.) It did, however, give me a chance to get used to the director, who I rather took to. Used to getting things done in a short time and quite often used to dealing with actors of my ability (i.e., low), he gave his directions very clearly. There was no nonsense about motivation or stuff like that. Instead, he kept it very clear.

'"Action" means stand up and start walking over to the door. When he says "Hello" you turn round and see him and look surprised,' I was instructed.

Once the last scene was shot we had several hours to wait while they reset for the first scenes. So my crew and Moon Moon and I went off to the Tollygunge Club, which was nearby, for a few drinks. Moon Moon probably needed them before doing the bed scene with me; I needed a few drinks to improve my Bengali accent. Moon Moon brought with her to the club an extraordinary, small man of some years who had worked as a dresser and general errand boy for her mother. He was now firmly attached to Moon Moon when she was engaged in film work. We had a fine old time and eventually got back to the studios for the rest of the shoot.

The bed scene was easy enough: Moon Moon had to look sexy and I had to look ridiculous. She was wearing an attractive silk negligée, I was in a Bri-Nylon smock and droopy pants. I think we got away with it. The big scene with the two comedians involved learning a bit of dialogue and we clustered around the script and read it over to each other, then tried to get on set as quickly as possible before we all forgot it.

There was no use my complaining I did not know what was going on: Indian actors are used to switching between Hindi, English, Bengali and a dozen other languages. Besides, I was in no mood to complain. A style of acting which involves doing everything at the last minute, improvising your way around lapses in memory, adapting to your fellow performers' mistakes – that is my style of acting. If they had given me the script weeks before I could not have learned it any better. I decided Bengali TV is my spiritual home.

And Robi Ghosh and Tapas Pal were very funny. You did not need to speak Bengali to appreciate that. I felt like one of those guest stars that used to appear with Morecambe and Wise. I had no idea what I was saying half the time, or why I was saying it, but it was providing good feed lines for them.

We concluded that, although we were filming late at night, it had all gone really well and we all loved each other and all that stuff that real actors say at the end of films (I think). So we had achieved two things at once. *Des Ray* had filmed an episode with a genuine British actor – well, genuinely British, anyway – and we had filmed what must be a funny sequence for our otherwise rather serious documentary.

But half of it was not to be. As far as I know, the episode of *Des Ray* was broadcast, but the sitcom sequence was not included in the documentary. It was all too long to fit in, or too silly for the rest of the programme, or something. Also, it turned out that Clive James had been recruited to act a part in a Bollywood film in a documentary about Bombay, so my raunchy bed scene with Moon Moon Sen never saw the light of day in Britain. Try to get a bootleg copy from a Bengali friend.

• Heads You Win •

There was an opportunity for me to look stupid which was included in the documentary. On the pretext of my finding the strain of life in Calcutta too much to cope with, I visited Raman Dutta to receive some instruction in yoga.

Raman Dutta lives in an airy, high-ceilinged apartment with his wife and daughter. For a time he lived in Canada but was happy to return to Calcutta where he finds life more agreeable. He is eighty-five or eighty-six years of age but could pass for fifty or sixty. How much of his good physical condition is the result of yoga is impossible to say, but it seemed worth trying.

Of course, you do not have to go all the way to Calcutta to learn about yoga, which represents another branch of Hindu teaching. There are plenty of yoga teachers in London. But the fact of the matter is I have never made any efforts in a yogic direction at home, so this seemed a good opportunity to try.

Mr Dutta had me clenching and unclenching muscles from top to bottom, twisting my spine, sitting on the floor with legs crossed and generally tying myself in knots. Most elaborately, he got me to stand on my head. I mentioned someone had once explained you could cure baldness by standing on your head every morning, and he wondered why it was not working for me. Apart from anything else, I said, I had never tried doing it. So perhaps learning yoga might give me some help in that direction.

Mr Dutta inverted himself next to me and we discussed life, art and the cosmos while blood rushed to our scalps. I have always said I can do interviews standing on my head.

• Politics •

But my visit to Calcutta could not be all standing on my head. I also had to get my head around the politics of the place. I have already mentioned that, despite the dreadful poverty, Calcutta feels a very safe place to be in. That was not always the case. Indeed, for most of its existence Calcutta has been a famously violent city.

This was particularly so at the time of independence. Muslims dominated the political scene in Calcutta because they were in the majority in the population of Bengal as a whole, although in the minority within the city itself. The Muslim League argued for an independent, Muslim, state of Bengal; Hindus wanted Calcutta to remain within Hindu India. In the year before the partition of India (which in the event divided Bengal in two), there was a frenzy of violence in Calcutta, thousands were killed and many left the city altogether.

In August 1947, Gandhi came to Calcutta to put an end to the violence. He and Mr H.S. Suhrawardy of the Muslim League spent the days leading up to Independence Day in a symbolic fast together. While this gesture did bring peace to Calcutta, this did not last forever. In the 1960s and 1970s, far-left activists kidnapped feudal landlords and led attacks upon the rich, businessmen and diplomats. There were even riots at the racecourse.

Strikes were common in industry, as was a peculiar Bengali form of intimidation called the *gherao*. In a *gherao*, an employer or manager is surrounded by a mob of workers. They do not attack him physically but neither do they let him go until he agrees to their demands. Hunger, thirst and other calls of nature are usually enough to make him give in or give up after a few hours, or days. Strikes, together with demonstrations and political violence, threatened to turn Calcutta into the centre for world revolution, or reduce it to complete chaos.

From 1967 onwards, Calcutta's Chief Minister has been a Communist, Jyoti Basu. He and a combination of People's, Marxist and Leftist parties have held power in Calcutta, often in conflict with India's federal government in Delhi which has almost always been formed by the Congress Party.

For many years Jyoti Basu has held a highly ambivalent attitude towards the violent or near-violent assertion of the rights of the masses over the land-owning and business classes, generally reluctant to send in the police to control the actions of what were, after all, his natural supporters. But nowadays, it is his attitude to capitalism which is ambivalent. India as a whole is opening up to the outside world economically, after decades of protectionism designed to promote indigenous industry, a policy that has largely meant that India has lagged behind other economies. Calcutta and West Bengal are now throwing themselves enthusiastically into the battle to attract foreign capitalists to invest in their city and state. It is quite a transformation in attitude.

I was able to interview both Chief Minister Jyoti Basu and the man tipped to succeed him, Somnath Chatterjee, an MP and head of the West Bengal Industrial Development Corporation.

Mr Basu received me in a conference room in the Writers' Building which stands on a square either known as Dalhousie Square to commemorate Governor General Lord Dalhousie or, officially nowadays as BBD Bagh to honour three revolutionaries who were hanged for trying to kill him.

The Writers' Building once provided office space for the clerks and employees – known as writers – of the British East India Company, but in the fullness of time these rooms full of weary British bureaucrats have become rooms full of weary Indian bureaucrats. Several guide books to the city make the point that there is no public tour of the building but recommend finding a reason to go there on some business or government matter in order to witness the long corridors dotted with tea wallahs, and room after room piled high with dusty files and fading clerks. Box wallahs, pen-pushers and clock-watchers going about their business like nobody's interested.

There is a smell in the corridors of some detergent or cleaner which I am sure I remember from the schools of my childhood. Also familiar are the lines of wiring and pipes for succeeding systems of power and telephone supply which cling high up on the walls, permanent memorials to decades, maybe centuries, of make do and mend. Everything is so British and so Indian. Nothing is malignant but you feel the life being crushed out of you by the stifling, suffocating growth of regulations, red tape, files and forms.

I was here to meet Jyoti Basu. A forceful factotum took us in hand before our discussion. Mr Basu is a busy man, he explained. He can only spare twenty minutes from the time he comes into the room. Speak clearly, he has a perfect command of English but he is in his eighties, so make allowances ... A short list of requirements. I can recommend this preparation to anyone approached to take part in a documentary.

As it turned out, Mr Basu did indeed have a perfect command of English and, indeed, of politics. He was another Calcuttan octogenarian who did not show his years. He happily stayed beyond his twenty minutes, and he was of course a lawyer and a member of my own Inn of Court in London, so I found yet another connection.

As to the politics of Calcutta's decline, Mr Basu was no more inclined to accept responsibility for the city's problems while he has been in power than a government spokesman in Britain thinks anything that has gone wrong with Britain since 1979 has anything to do with the Conservatives. It is especially difficult to pin responsibility in the Indian context.

One of the weaknesses of a federal system is that it is difficult to get the buck to stop here, there or anywhere.

Calcutta's industrial decline, Mr Basu claimed, is less to do with the policies he has pursued and more to do with the discriminatory policies of Delhi. Federal equalization measures have robbed Calcutta of its former pre-eminence in heavy industries. But had not union and labour practices made it a difficult environment for industry?, I wanted to know.

'Not qualitatively different from other parts of India,' he replied.

'Have you not concentrated on the rural areas at the expense of urban Calcutta?'

'We have, because that is where we had power under the Constitution.'

'Is it not odd,' I asked, 'that a Communist party should now be so keen on capitalist investment?'

That, apparently, is because West Bengal is not an independent state and has to fit in with the central government. I also gathered from Mr Basu that he has always been in favour of inward investment, it is simply that no one listened to him until it was suggested by the IMF. He agreed it was extraordinary for a Communist city still to have hand-pulled rickshaws but insisted they are going to be abolished as soon as possible. He dismissed the suggestion which is sometimes made that Calcutta is a dying city.

'I think the pulse of life beats here, whether in politics or economics or in social life, art, culture and so on. So I am very optimistic,' he said.

From Somnath Chatterjee I got much the same message. He has a well-appointed office in another building, from which he is charged with the task of attracting investors to Calcutta. He foresees a bright future for the Calcutta he is tipped to inherit. This led me to ask if he had converted from being a Communist to being an optimist. He maintained that Communists were optimists, and pragmatists, too, come to that.

However true that may be, he reckons the conditions are now right for Calcutta to expand and eventually be in a position to deal with its social problems. His message to the outside world is come to Calcutta to make money, legally and properly. Not quite a socialist rallying cry but one which Mr Chatterjee has no difficulty in promoting.

I mentioned a number of companies which in recent years have left the city to go elsewhere: Hindustan Motors, the Bengal Lamp Company, several jute mills, one of the old staple industries. These, he accepted, were lured away by other cities and by some of the policies of the government of India. He, too, had complaints against Delhi: he gave an example of a petrochemical complex in a nearby port which took twelve years to get clearance from central government. But now, with greater freedoms, things were getting better. He accepted that Calcutta has a bad image but insisted that those who come here love the city and are inclined to stay.

• Calcutta Mon Amour •

I cannot really say why, but when I came to sum up my feelings about the city at the end of the film I was inclined to reflect, if not Somnath Chatterjee's optimism, at least his affection for the city.

We filmed the end piece early in the morning in a flower and vegetable market just by the Calcutta end of the Howrah Bridge. This was built in 1943 when, at 2150 feet, it was the longest cantilever bridge in the world. No doubt that record has long since been broken, although it probably remains the busiest bridge in the world.

The Hooghly River has very few crossings so the crowded buses, carts, lorries and cars have to cram on to the ones that already exist. On the other side of the river is Howrah, home of a great deal of Calcutta's industry and millions of what an outsider would call Calcuttans. But, to Calcutta, Howrah is a separate city. To live on the wrong side of the river here is to be very much beyond the pale.

There is another bridge, Vivekananda Setu – known as the second Hooghly Bridge – which was finally built in 1992. It is less popular because of the inadequate roads leading to it and the fact that you have to pay a toll, but you would have thought it was a positive thing to show in our film. Unfortunately we were forbidden to film the bridge and, indeed, the new underground system. I suppose this was in case any future enemies of India, who cannot afford a guide book, are let in on the secret of where these huge structures are hidden.

I was able to admire both bridges on the day we spent drifting up and down the river in small rowing boats which you can hire by the hour. They appear to be sponsored by Castrol and allow you to enjoy the waters of the Hooghly while Calcuttans bathe and wash in the river and the sun beats down, filtered by Calcutta's Factor 20 atmosphere.

Anyway, early in the morning at the flower market I addressed the camera in the heady atmosphere of scented flowers and rotting vegetable matter: silage delivered by Interflora.

'So how does one say farewell to this extraordinary city? Centuries apart, writers such as William Macintosh, Rudyard Kipling and Geoffrey Moorhouse have catalogued its horrors, sometimes picking out beauty and charm amidst the chaos. But to summarize my feelings at the end of a short stay here, I'll turn to a different social commentator – the comedian, Dick Emery – to bid my goodbye to Calcutta: "Ooh, you are awful, but I like you."'

BIBLIOGRAPHY

Our Man in Goa

Crowther, G. and Finlay, H. *India* Lonely Planet Publications, 1993.

Fish, Curry and Rice, A Citizen's Report on the Goan Environment Ecoforum.

Hall, M. *A Window on Goa* Quiller Press, 1994.

Richards, J.M. *Goa* C. Hurst, 1981.

Shales, M. *The Footloose Guide to Southern India and Goa* Simon & Schuster, 1992.

Our Man in Havana

Calder, S. and Hatchwell, E. *Travellers' Survival Kit CUBA* Vacation Work, 1993.

Cameron, S. and Box, B. *Caribbean Islands Handbook* Trade & Travel, 1994.

Rius, *Cuba for Beginners* Pathfinder, 1986.

Greene, G. *Our Man in Havana* Penguin, 1971.

Horowitz, I. *The Conscience of Worms and the Cowardice of Lions* Transaction, U.S., 1993.

Murray, M. (interview with Ricardo Alarcón), *Cuba and the United States* Ocean Press, 1993.

Murray, M. *Cruel and Unusual Punishment* Ocean Press, 1993.

Fundacion Magazine, Summer 1993 Cuban American National Association.

Our Man in the Maasai Mara

Finlay, H. and Crowther, G. *Kenya* Lonely Planet Publications, 1994.

Beckwith, C. *Maasai* Harvill, 1991.

Trillo, R. *Kenya, the Rough Guide* Rough Guides, 1993.

Our Man in Dominica

Cameron, S. and Box, B. *Caribbean Islands Handbook* Trade and Travel, 1994.

Evans, P.C.H. *Dominica: Nature Island of the Caribbean* Hansib, 1989.

Higbie, J. *Eugenia* Macmillan, 1992

Honychurch, L. *Dominica Isle of Adventure* Macmillan, 1991.

Thomson, R. *Green Gold* Latin America Bureau, 1987.

Our Man in the Timberlands

Foreman, D. and Haywood, B. *Ecodefense* Abbzug Press, U.S., 1993.

Seidman, D. *Showdown at Opal Creek* Carroll & Graf, U.S., 1993.

Warren, S. and Long-Ishikawa, T. *Oregon Handbook* Moon Publications, U.S., 1994.

Our Man in Hawaii

Bendure, G. and Friary, N. *Hawaii, Travel Survival Kit* Lonely Planet Publications, 1993.

Hoffer, H.J. *Insight Guides: Hawaii* APA Publications, 1988.

Queen Liliuokalani, *Hawaii's Story by Hawaii's Queen,* C.E. Tuttle, U.S., 1976.

Our Man in Beirut

Fisk, R. *Pity the Nation* Oxford University Press, 1992.

Glass, C. *Tribes with Flags* Picador, 1992.

Randal, J. *The Tragedy of Lebanon* The Hogarth Press, 1990.

Sluglett, P. and Farouk-Sluglett, M. *The Times Guide to the Middle East* Times Books, 1993.

The Middle East Lonely Planet Publications, 1994.

Our Man in Lagos

Harden, B. *Africa, Despatches from a Fragile Continent* HarperCollins, 1992.

Hudgens, J. and Trillo, R. *West Africa: the Rough Guide* Rough Guides, 1992.

West Africa Lonely Planet Publications, 1995.

Our Man in The Bronx

Dunford, M. and Holland, J. *New York: the Rough Guide* Rough Guides, 1992.

Fitch, R. *The Assassination of New York* Verso, 1994.

Our Man in Calcutta

Crowther, G. and Finlay, H. *India* Lonely Planet Publications, 1993.

India: the Rough Guide Rough Guides, 1994.

Moorhouse, G. *Calcutta, the City Revealed* Penguin, 1994

Roy, S. *Calcutta Live* The Ananda Bazar Group.

Vatin, M. and others, *Insight City Guide to Calcutta* APA Publications, 1982.

INDEX